Training for Change Agents

Change Agents

A Guide to the Design of Training
Programs in Education and
Other Fields

Training for Change Agents

A Guide to the Design of Training Programs in Education and Other Fields

RONALD G. HAVELOCK
and
MARY C. HAVELOCK
with

The Staff and Participants of
The Michigan Conference on
Educational Change Agent
Training (CECAT)

Center for Research on Utilization of Scientific Knowledge

Institute for Social Research
The University of Michigan
Ann Arbor, Michigan
1973

ISR Code No. 3450

Library of Congress Catalog Card No. 72-86637
ISBN 0-87944-126-7

Published by the Institute for Social Research
The University of Michigan, Ann Arbor, Michigan 48106

First Published 1973
Third Printing 1975

Manufactured in the United States of America

PREFACE

Several persons deserve credit for contributing to this work at different stages. Charles Jung of the Northwest Regional Educational Laboratory participated in all phases of planning, contributed most of the ideas contained in Part One - Chapter III, and served as chairman of the Conference on Educational Change Agent Training (CECAT) on which this volume is largely based. Also contributing to the conference planning effort were Henry M. Brickel[1] of the Institute for Educational Development, Thomas D. Clemens of the U.S. Office of Education, and Ronald Lippitt of the Center for Research on Utilization of Scientific Knowledge.

All those who attended CECAT can truly be counted as contributors to this work also. Mention will be made of their individual contributions throughout the text.

Baker, Dr. Robert
Southwest Regional Laboratory
for Educational Research &
Development

Beaird, Dr. James
Oregon State System of
Higher Education

Benne, Dr. Kenneth D.
Human Relations Center
Boston University

Boyan, Dr. Norman J.
Graduate School of Education
University of California

Bushnell, Mr. David S.
Battelle Memorial Institute

Carey, Dr. Thomas F.
City College of New York

Chandler, Dr. Charles S.
South Carolina Vocational
Rehabilitation Department

Chesler, Dr. Mark
Educational Change Team
The University of Michigan

Chickering, Dr. Arthur
Project on Student Development
in Small Colleges

Clemens, Mr. Thomas D.
National Center for Educational
Communications
U.S. Office of Education

Crockett, Dr. Stanley
Western Behavioral Sciences
Institute

Dalin, Mr. Per
Organization for Economic
Cooperation and Development

Davis, Dr. Richard E.
Shool of Education
University of Wisconsin

Dershimer, Dr. Richard A.
American Educational Research
  Association

Dionne, Dr. Joseph L.
California Test Bureau

Dorros, Dr. Sidney
National Educational Association

Ellis, Dr. Betty
Department of Education
University of Florida-Gainesville

Engler, Mr. David
McGraw Hill, Inc.

Glatthorn, Dr. Allan A.
Abington (Pennsylvania)
  School District

Glaser, Dr. Edward
Human Interaction Research
  Institute

Goodson, Dr. Max
Dept. of Educational Policy
  Studies
University of Wisconsin

Hearn, Dr. Norman E.
Division of Plans and
  Supplementary Centers
U.S. Office of Education

Hildebrand, Dr. Edwin P.
Four-State Diffusion
  Project SPREAD
Colorado Department of Education

Hood, Dr. Paul D.
Far West Laboratory for
  Educational Research

Johnson, Mr. Donald
Duval County (Florida) Public
  Schools

Jung, Dr. Charles
Northwest Regional Educational
  Research Laboratory

Kent, Dr. J. Russell
San Mateo County (California)
  Board of Education

Kurland, Dr. Norman
Center on Innovation in Education
University of the State of New York

Lake, Dr. Dale G.
Humanistic Education
State University of New York

Lippitt, Dr. Ronald O.
Center for Research on Utilization
  of Scientific Knowledge
Institute for Social Research

Maguire, Dr. Louis M.
Research for Better Schools, Inc.

Mann, Dr. Floyd C.
Center for Research on Utilization
  of Scientific Knowledge
Institute for Social Research

Miller, Dr. Richard I.
Baldwin-Wallace College

Millgate, Mr. Irving
Xicom, Inc.

Miles, Dr. Matthew B.
Teachers College
Columbia University

Neiman, Mr. Robert
Robert H. Schaffer & Associates

Ofiesh, Dr. Gabriel D.
Center for Educational Technology
Catholic University of America

Reilly, Dr. Anthony J.
Center for Research on Utilization
  of Scientific Knowledge
Institute for Social Research

Rogers, Dr. Everett M.
Department of Communication
Michigan State University

Schaible, Mrs. Lucille
Educational Change Team
University of Michigan

Simches, Dr. Raphael F.
Division for Handicapped Children
New York State Education
  Department

Spack, Dr. Elliot
Mineola (New York) Public Schools

Sproule, Mr. George
Office of Student Organizations
University of Michigan

Taylor, Dr. Robert E.
Ohio State University

Towne, Dr. Douglas
Bureau of Educational Research
  and Services
University of Tennessee

Tye, Dr. Kenneth
Institute for Development of
  Educational Activities, Inc.

Walz, Dr. Garry
School of Education
University of Michigan

Ward, Dr. Joe H.
Southwest Educational Development
  Laboratory

Ward, Dr. William T.
Department of Education
Macalester College

Wolf, Dr. William C.
School of Education
University of Massachusetts

In addition several persons who were not able to attend gave us inputs of their ideas. These include:

Brickell, Dr. Henry
Institute for Educational
  Development

Clark, Dr. David L.
School of Education
Indiana University

Fish, Dr. Lawrence D.
Northwest Regional Educational
  Laboratory

Gephart, Dr. William J.
University of Wisconsin

Goldhammer, Dr. Keith
School of Education
Oregon State University

Hansford, Mr. Bryon W.
Colorado Department of Education

Hindsman, Dr. Edwin
Southwest Educational Development
  Laboratory

Riendeau, Dr. Albert J.
BAVTE/DVTE
U.S. Office of Education

Schmuck, Dr. Richard
Center for the Advanced Study of
  Educational Administration
University of Oregon

Sullivan, Mr. Neil
Massachusetts Department of
  Education

Watson, Dr. Goodwin
Union for Research and
  Experimentation in Higher
  Education
Antioch College

Joyce Kornbluh, the Center for Research on Utilization of Scientific Knowledge's editor, provided many helpful suggestions and checked the manuscript at various stages. Editorial assistance on Part Two, Chapters VII and VIII, was also provided by Roberta McConochie.

Many thanks are due to Rita Weigers of the Center who typed all drafts of the manuscript, tabulated responses, and handled all the detailed arrangements for CECAT, before, during, and after. It is rare indeed to find such warmth and efficiency combined in a single person, and the success of the project can be credited in no small measure to her efforts.

Most of the work reported herein was supported by the Office of Education, U.S. Department of Health, Education and Welfare pursuant to Contract Number OEC-0-8-080603-4535(010). Contractors undertaking such projects under government sponsorship are encouraged to express freely their professional judgment in the conduct of the project. Points of view or opinions stated do not, therefore, necessarily represent official Office of Education position or policy. Financial support was also provided for both the CECAT and the writing of this volume by the Kellogg Foundation through an institutional grant to the Center for Research on Utilization of Scientific Knowledge, Institute for Social Research, The University of Michigan. This volume is part of a larger report on the training, development, and support of knowledge linkers in education submitted to the U.S. Office of Education in December, 1971. Section I of that report summarizes the process of development of a Handbook for the Linker-Change Agent and the subsequent CECAT. Section II is an evaluation of the Handbook (entitled THE CHANGE AGENT'S GUIDE TO

INNOVATION IN EDUCATION*) by educational change agents and specialists in various positions. Section III is an evaluation of CECAT, itself. The other major products of the project are included as attachments to that report, namely: "Guide to Innovation in Education," and Checklists on Change Process to accompany the Guide.

A few copies of the report and most attachments will be made available to interested persons through the Center for Research on Utilization of Scientific Knowledge. Inquiries should be addressed to the author.

---

*This volume is often referred to in the text as "A GUIDE TO INNOVATION," or sometimes simply as the "GUIDE."

CONTENTS

INTRODUCTION

This book is intended for use by change agents and change agent trainers in all levels of education and in other human service areas where specialized resource helping and linking roles are being developed. Part One will provide a framework for the design of programs to train change agents in the skills of helping and of resource utilization, and Part Two will present some alternative models of such training programs. Readers who are in any way involved in the promotion, design, or leadership of such a training program should find both Part One and Part Two useful. First, this work will provide them with an orientation to training content and structural issues *before* beginning to design a program; second, it will serve as a reference on program components *during* design; and third, it will be useful as an evaluation checklist *after* a program has been drafted and put into operation. Those who are themselves change agents and participate as trainees in the multitude of "change agent" training programs that are now becoming available should find Part One valuable background reading prior to their training experience. It will provide them with the rationale for such training programs and will give them an indication of what the trainers are trying to do, what types of learning experiences will be offered, and what types of outcomes can be anticipated. It should also help prospective enrollees to judge which programs are most relevant to their own needs.

A. Why Do We Need Training on Helping and Resource Utilization?

We live in an age of expanding resources and expanding awareness of problems. However, it is also widely believed that we are entering a period of crisis in which resource capabilities will reach their limit while demands on resources continue to escalate. Regardless of the dimensions or apocalyptic potential of this crisis, there is some consensus on the need to close the gap between available resources (knowledge, technology, products, services, facilities, etc.) and known human problems and needs.

Both the *problem* and the *opportunity* are before us. On the one hand, there is a rising tide of needs and expectations, proclaimed by many as an impending series of crises (urban, ecological, population, etc.). On the other hand, in this century there has been a fantastic acceleration of knowledge building (there are more scientists alive in the world today than the total number who have ever lived up to now), and in the growth of technological know-how. Man's capabilities to create, communicate and store knowledge have never been so great, and they appear to be expanding.

The question of the use of these capabilities to meet the rising tide of need therefore becomes ever more insistent. Indeed, in the last generation there has emerged a very special branch of social science concerned with the communication and effective utilization of knowledge. We are slowly moving toward a new conception of a professional discipline concerned primarily with the *process* of change. It rests on the assumption that social progress can be planned and engineered so that it is more reliable and more beneficial to more people. This new concept of "planned innovation" stresses the importance of realistic diagnosis of needs, adequate resource retrieval, collaborative planning and solution building, and systematic design and evaluation of alternative solutions.

"Strategy" is a key aspect of this new concept of innovation because it is now recognized that change will only lead to real progress if it is brought about in an orderly sequence of goal-setting, planning, and systematic execution. Clearly, therefore, there is a need for educators to spell out in detail their "innovative" plans and activities in terms of overall *"strategies"* and the explicit sequences of action steps (*"tactics"*) that make up these strategies.

There are some resources already available to us in building such strategies. Lippitt, Watson, and Westley in THE DYNAMICS OF PLANNED CHANGE (1958) made available the first coherent conception of the social "change agent," a person who had the skills necessary to help a client work out problems in an integrated step-by-step sequence. These authors pulled together much of the behavioral and social research on the consultation process, human relations, organizational development, and group dynamics to show how such a change agent might be effective in working with individuals, groups, organizations, and total communities.

Bennis, Benne and Chin (1961) added to the growth of this movement by publishing a comprehensive set of readings from 74 social scientists under the title THE PLANNING OF CHANGE. For the first time they demonstrated that a significant new professional discipline was growing around this concept.

A rather different notion of "change agent" was expounded by Everett Rogers (1962) in his integration of several hundred research studies on THE DIFFUSION OF INNOVATIONS. Rogers' change agent concept was rooted in sociological studies of the "county agent" in the U.S. Department of Agriculture's Cooperative Extension Service. This county agent was not only a counselor and diagnostician to individual farmers with individual needs but also a conveyor of new facts and practices based on the agricultural research and experimentation of the Land Grant universities.

By the late 1960's, Havelock, et al. (1969) were proposing a fusion of these two traditions in a new concept of the change agent as process helper and knowledge linker. It seems evident that the sets of skills envisaged, namely interpersonal and inter-group relating, consultation, need definition, diagnosis, problem-solving, resource acquisition, dissemination, and utilization, are going to be needed by the educators of the future at various levels and in various role categories.

The knowledge base for resource utilization change agent training is fairly well summarized in two works by Havelock and colleagues. The first, PLANNING FOR INNOVATION, synthesizes and summarizes relevant research and theory from more than 1,000 sources. Together with other research summaries by Rogers and Shoemaker (1971), Watson (1969) and others, it gives ample testimony to the theoretical and empirical substance of this field. Several authors, including Havelock, have also attempted to develop practical guides or manuals for change agents based on this body of knowledge and following in the tradition of Lippitt, Watson, and Westley. The 1970 experimental version of the Havelock volume, A GUIDE TO INNOVATION, has been used as the basis for a model training program design for state education agency change agents. This design is presented in Chapter IX of this work.

This outcropping of publications is encouraging news to those who want to close the knowledge gap, but it is also obvious that print materials do not stand by themselves. They must be accompanied by training in the specific skills described in such guides and manuals. The "planned change" specialists are very few in number and, if their ranks do not grow rapidly, there is no hope that their message will have any significant impact.

Some training programs have been undertaken in the recent past. Of special note were the Cooperative Project for Educational Development (COPED) (see Watson, 1967) and its successor, the instrumented and packaged teacher training workshop "Resource Utilization and Problem-Solving" (RUPS) developed by Charles Jung and colleagues (1970) at the Northwest Regional Educational Laboratory. Similarly packaged and unitized training programs are also under development for information specialists at the Far West Laboratory for Educational Research and Development (1971). Numerous training programs are also now coming on the market to train educators in systems technology, program planning, and so forth. Many of these programs provide at least a partial answer to the need.

B. Why Do We Need a Training Manual?

Because so many programs and pieces of programs are under development or freshly on the market, there is a special need today to provide prospective trainers and program developers with some guidelines on training in the specific contexts of resource utilization and change agentry. It was for this reason that we assembled 50 nationally recognized leaders of research and training on educational change at Clinton, Michigan, in the spring of 1970. This volume, in large part, contains the collective wisdom of this group. Participants in the conference were carefully chosen to represent a *range* of orientations toward change agentry and toward training.

The conference was divided into three phases. In the first phase, participants discussed the content of training, i.e., the research findings and theory which form the basis of sound practice in diffusion, utilization, planned change, organization development, and related fields. We asked the question: Is there a substantial knowledge base and a coherent concept around which training can be developed?

In the second phase, the conference turned from the content to the process of training: What were some sound principles of training that should be incorporated in training programs? In the third and final phase, we tried to put content and process together as we worked in several small task force groups to design model programs for particular types of trainees and training goals.

C. Organization of the Text

The organization of this book follows the organization of the conference in general outline. Part One is concerned with the theory, goals and structure essential to program design. Chapter I will be concerned with outlining the principal content areas that relate to the concept of change agent from a variety of perspectives.

Chapters II and III will provide some suggestions on how to select training goals and what principles to include in a good training design. These sections are based on discussions in the second phase of the conference when training process issues were discussed.

Chapter IV provides a framework with eight design features that ought to be incorporated in any viable plan and suggests how such an outline can be used to develop training programs to meet various objectives.

Part Two suggests how model training programs could be put together for various types of objectives. Chapters V through VIII present outlines of several potential programs generated by our conference task force groups, and Chapter IX presents a more detailed training model for a particular type of role (change agents in state education agencies) as an example of how any design might be flushed out.

Taken together, the volume contains a number of ideas, suggestions, frameworks, principles, and strategies at several levels of specificity applicable to a wide range of change agent skills and situations. For this reason it should be a useful aid and reference source to trainers, trainees, training program developers, and change agents at large.

PART ONE:

HOW TO DESIGN
A TRAINING PROGRAM

I

OUR CONTEMPORARY KNOWLEDGE OF THE CHANGE PROCESS

During the 1960's, dozens of books and hundreds of articles were published dealing with one or another aspect of the change process. Many of these writings were reports on empirical research, many more were comments or observations on one or another strategy or theory of change, and a few were comprehensive summaries of existing knowledge and theory. Evidence of this great outpouring of research and theoretical literature can be found in several bibliographies which appeared in the second half of the decade (e.g., Kurland and Miller, 1966; Stuart and Dudley, 1967; Havelock, 1968; Rogers, 1968; Spitzer, 1968; Havelock, Huber, and Zimmerman, 1969; Skelton and Hensel, 1970).

It is not our purpose here to provide any comprehensive summary of the knowledge represented by all these works except to say that they represent an impressive and profound corpus with very high relevance to the improvement of educational practice.

In order to develop a clear and holistic conception of the change process and of the roles which specialized change agents might play in that process, a few key works are of special importance. Rogers and Shoemaker (1971) give the best current summary of empirical research on the diffusion of innovations; Bennis, Benne, and Chin (1969) provide the best reader in the field of planned change and incorporate theoretical and empirical articles from leading authorities who represent a range of perspectives; and Havelock and collaborators (1969) provide a comprehensive review and summary of most of the available literature, theoretical as well as empirical. Both Rogers and Shoemaker and Havelock, et al. concluded their works with a series of principles or propositions which roughly represent the current "state of the art" fact and wisdom concerning change. No one list of propositions can be truly comprehensive on such a broad topic but it can provide a useful starting point for building the content of training programs for change agents.

As noted earlier, the 1970 conference on change agent training began its deliberations by reviewing the existing knowledge about change that could be incorporated in training. These discussions were guided by a list of 32 propositional statements derived from the literature and endorsed as "important" or "essential" by all those participating in the conference.* Each statement was used as the basis of a small group discussion led by a participant who felt a special interest in the topic. Participants were also encouraged to generate additional propositions which they felt represented significant facts or observations on the change process from their very diverse viewpoints. The result was a truly comprehensive listing of "contents" for developing a training curriculum on the management of innovation in education and in other fields.

Most of these statements and observations are presented below in summary, grouped according to the major *perspectives* on the change process which Havelock identified in his 1969 review.

A. Change as a Problem-Solving Process

Overview

This orientation rests on the primary assumption that innovation is a part of a problem-solving process which goes on inside the user. Problem-solving is usually seen as a patterned sequence of activities beginning with a *need*, sensed and articulated by the client, which is translated into a *problem* statement and *diagnosis*. When he has thus formulated a problem statement, the client-user is able to conduct a meaningful *search* and *retrieval* of ideas and information which can be used in formulating or selecting the *innovation*. Finally, the user needs to concern himself with *adapting* the innovation, *trying out* and *evaluating* its effectiveness in *satisfying* his original need. The focus of this orientation is the user, himself, his needs and what he does about satisfying his needs. The role of outsiders is therefore consultative or collaborative. The outside change agent may assist the user either by providing new ideas and innovations specific to the diagnosis or by providing guidance on the process of problem-solving at any or all of the indicated stages. Figure I.1 illustrates this relationship.

At least five points are generally stressed by advocates of this orientation: first, that *user need* is the paramount consideration and the only acceptable value-stance for the change agent; second, that *diagnosis* of need always has to be an integral part of the total process; third, that the outside change agent should be *nondirective,* rarely, if ever, violating the integrity of the user by placing himself in a directive or expert status; fourth, that the *internal* resources, i.e., those resources already existing and easily accessible within the client system, itself, should always be fully utilized; and fifth, that *self-initiated and self-applied innovation* will have the strongest user

---

*See preface for list of participants.

FIGURE I.1
THE PROBLEM-SOLVER VIEW OF THE CHANGE PROCESS

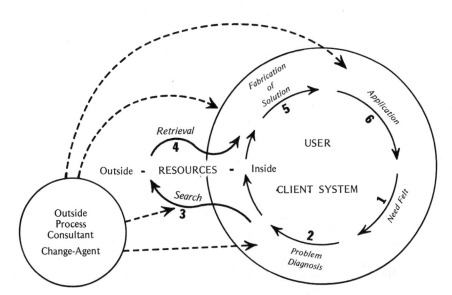

commitment and the best chances for long-term survival.

A few of the major advocates of this orientation are Lippitt, Watson, and Westley (1958), Goodwin Watson (1967), Charles Jung (1967), and Herbert Thelen (1967). Most of those who belong to this school are social psychologists in the group dynamics-human relations tradition.

Propositions Derived from Problem-Solver Perspective

"1. The *user's need* is the paramount consideration in any planned change activity."

How participants rated this point on a pre-conference inquiry form:
   26 "essential"
   15 "very important"
    7 "somewhat important"
    0 "not important"

Only two conferees questioned the validity of the proposition.

Also implied in this statement is the idea that a change agent needs to begin by defining the "user" for his change efforts. In some cases, this "user" will be a particular individual but it could also be a group, an organization, a community, or perhaps even a whole society. The proposition also had to be qualified by the fact that users are not always *aware* of the real needs they have. Hence, Hansford* notes that change agents must expend considerable effort on creating an awareness of need.

"2. Users' needs cannot be served effectively until an effort has been made to translate and define those needs into a *diagnosis* which represents a coherent set of problems to be worked on."

How participants rated this point:
17 "essential"
23 "very important"
9 "somewhat important"
1 "not important"

No conferees questioned the validity of this proposition.

This diagnosis should probably include and be based on a definition and clarification of the user's and the change agent's values. Diagnosis must be integrative. Furthermore, a prime responsibility of the change agent is to teach and share his diagnostic skills with as many members of the client system as possible (Ellis*).

"3. *User-initiated change* is likely to be stronger and more long-lasting than change initiated by outsiders."

How participants rated this point:
20 "essential"
16 "very important"
4 "somewhat important"
0 "not important"

Seven conferees questioned the validity of the proposition.

Even if change is not user-*initiated*, at least user *involvement* must be real; user commitment and involvement are vital to implementation. User involvement is especially important in need-stating and trust-building; it may be less important in the creation and development of the innovation itself. On the other hand, when innovation is perceived as imposed from above, serious disequilibrium in the form of sabotage and strikes may result.

"4. The user system should have an *adequate internalized problem-*

---

*All starred references in this chapter are CECAT contributors; see preface for full list of contributors.

solving strategy, i.e., an orderly set of processes for need sensing and expression, diagnosis, resource retrieval and evaluation."

How participants rated this point:
13 "essential"
23 "very important"
13 "somewhat important"
 1 "not important"

No conferees questioned the validity of the proposition.

Too many educational systems tend to be *reactive* problem-solvers when they should be *proactive*; i.e., they respond only to political and social coercion and then only after their problems have reached a level of painful and destructive crisis. Miles* notes the importance of developing *institutional* provisions for problem-solving at the user level, especially in schools.

"5. Change agents work more effectively if they employ a non-directive strategy."

How participants rated this point:
 3 "essential"
12 "very important"
16 "somewhat important"
 2 "not important"

Fourteen conferees questioned the validity of the proposition.

The problem-solving perspective has roots in psychotherapeutic counseling, mental health consultation and, to a large extent, in the "client-centered" counseling approach espoused by Carl Rogers (1951). According to this view, the change agent should not impose his own views of the problem or the solution on the client. Rather, he should assist the client in defining the problem for himself and working as his own problem-solver. The change agent, according to this view, can do this by taking the role of a sincere and active listener, encouraging the client to articulate his thinking and feeling, and allowing him to hear himself. This was clearly a controversial item for our change experts for, while 15 strongly endorsed it, 14 doubted its validity. This suggests that the "when, where, and how" of the non-directive approach needs to be spelled out clearly before it can be accepted as a general principle of change agentry.

"6. Change agents are primarily helpful as process consultants and trainers, helping users understand the human relations of decision-making and changing."

How participants rated this point:
   8 "essential"
  11 "very important"
  20 "somewhat important"
   0 "not important"

With 8 doubting its validity, this item was the second most controversial of the 32 propositions rated by the conferees.

This view probably had its zenith in the mid-1960's, but it is today somewhat in eclipse. Many conferees felt the need for the contemporary change agent to be an advocate and an activist partisan in many situations, particularly when he perceived a gross disequilibrium of power.

B. Change as a Research-Development-and-Diffusion Process

Overview

The most systematic conceptual categorization of processes related to educational innovation is that evolved first by Brickell (1961), and later by Clark and Guba (1965), under the heading "Research, Development, and Diffusion." This orientation is guided by at least five assumptions. First, it assumes that there should be a *rational sequence* in the evolution and application of an innovation. This sequence should include research, development, and packaging before mass dissemination takes place. Second, it assumes that there has to be planning, usually on a massive scale over a long time span. Third, it assumes that there has to be a *division and coordination of labor* to accord with the rational sequence and the planning. Fourth, it assumes a more-or-less *passive but rational consumer* who will accept and adopt the innovation if it is offered to him in the right place at the right time and in the right form. Fifth and finally, the proponents of this viewpoint accept the fact of a high initial development cost prior to any dissemination activity because of the anticipated long-term benefits in *efficiency* and *quality* of the innovation and its suitability for *mass audience dissemination*.

Prototypes of this RD&D model are presumed to exist in industry and agriculture. Figure I.2 provides an outline of its major components.

In broad terms, RD&D is itself a grand strategy for planned innovation, but, in practice, this model has been spelled out in a number of different forms, each of which stresses one or another of these steps. A few of the most commonly expounded variants are listed below.

Development of High Performance Products. Many authors see RD&D as a process whereby ideas and tentative models of innovations can be evaluated

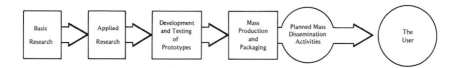

and systematically reshaped and packaged in a form that ensures benefit to users and which eases diffusion and adoption. In this process, most of the *adaptation* and translation problems of the user are anticipated and adjusted for. The final outcome is therefore *"user-proof,"* guaranteed to work for the most fumbling and incompetent receiver. To some degree, the regional laboratories of the USOE have been established to carry forward this strategy of high performance product development (Boyan, 1968).

Information System Building. Sometimes the "product" of development will itself be a system for diffusion and innovation. Some of the regional laboratories are experimenting with the design and creation of information systems which take into account the many known barriers and translation problems that separate researchers and developers from potential users (Far West Laboratory, 1968). These experimental information systems, when fully developed, will presumably have the same "user-proof" characteristics as the other high performance products discussed above. Hence, they will form a new and effective channel for the continuous funnelling of innovations and innovative ideas to practitioners.

Engineered Diffusion Projects and Programs. A few thoroughly planned and systematically executed and evaluated diffusion projects can be cited from the literature, but in spite of tremendous variations in design and context, they may be classified together as one "strategy" on the basis of certain common elements: e.g., (1) careful advance planning, (2) innovation packaging, (3) careful identification, selection, and preparation of the target audience, (4) multi-media presentation (written and oral material, group discussion, demonstration, etc.), (5) some sort of active user involvement, (6) systematic follow-up, and (7) experimental evaluation and documentation. The most successful program of this kind was developed by Bell Laboratories to diffuse transistor technology to other industries. Well documented recent ventures of this general type are Richland's (1965) "traveling seminar and conference for the implementation of educational innovations," and Glaser's (1965) project to diffuse results of a successful vocational training program for the mentally retarded. Probably the most outstanding *failure* of this strategy is that reported by Cumming and Cumming (1957). A well conceived and well designed program to diffuse new mental health concepts to a Canadian community backfired in large part because of the disturbing nature of the information itself.

Administered and Legislated Change. One presumption that is sometimes implicit in RD&D strategies is that the resulting high performance product can reasonably and legitimately be diffused through legislative or administrative fiat. If the leadership has assurance from evaluation data that the innovation will be successful and beneficial, then it may feel that it is on safe ground in deciding that all the users under its direct control shall receive it. This is a very common "diffusion" pattern for innovations. Examples range from safety devices required in automobiles to desegregation guidelines for school systems.

Fait Accompli. Related to the above is what Watson and Glaser (1965) call the strategy of innovation by *"fait accompli."* When anticipated initial resistance to an innovation is extremely great, the change agent may opt for immediate installation without consultation or the building of advance awareness. The presumption in this case is that the actual benefits from use of the innovation will be so great and so apparent *after trial* that the long-run good of the user will be served. (The initial "fait accompli" by legislated authority may, according to Glaser, be followed by local level problem-solving stimulated by the requirement to "implement.") Racial integration of the armed forces by President Truman was cited as one example where "fait accompli" strategy succeeded.

"Systems Analysis" Approaches to Innovation. "Systems analysis" usually refers to a systematic strategy of innovation which begins with the careful construction of an optimum but detailed *ideal model* of the problem area. Comparison of this ideal model with current operational reality highlights various shortcomings and focal points for change effort. The problem foci are then systematically tackled on a priority basis so that steady progress is made in approaching the ideal.

Propositions Derived from the RD&D Perspective

"1. Successful innovation usually requires formal *planning*, short-term and long-term."

How participants rated this point:
29 "essential"
12 "very important"
5 "somewhat important"
0 "not important"

Four conferees questioned the validity of the proposition.

In leading a discussion of this topic, Per Dalin* of the Organization for Economic Cooperation and Development, Paris, made the following points. First, planning of a rational RD&D sequence with a straight-line chronology is far different from planning in a multiple interest and power group context. Both types are important. Secondly, planning at the national level must take into account a multiplicity of overlapping roles and groups from the minister of education to the individual pupil. Decision-making influences many people outside the classroom.

Any major educational change probably requires long-term planning, ten years lead time or more. Case studies indicate that comprehensive structural changes in the Swedish system required 23 years for full implementation. For curriculum changes, a 10-year cycle may be possible.

Effective planning, according to Dalin, must be *integrated*, taking into account social, cultural, economic, and political factors. It must also be system-oriented, continuous, continuously evaluated and revised, and it must be democratic, i.e., those affected must be involved to the fullest extent feasible.

"2. Innovation is made more effective if there is a rational *division of labor* to carry out the necessary functions of diagnosis, information retrieval, research, development and application."

How participants rated this point:
12 "essential"
11 "very important"
15.5 "somewhat important"
2.5 "not important"

Five conferees questioned the validity of the proposition.

This proposition has to be tempered by several qualifications. First, the level and scope of the innovation have to be considered; local innovations of small scope presumably require less division of labor, less specialization, and less organizational separation than national or statewide innovations.

Second, most innovation requires some involvement by all parties at each stage; researcher, developer, evaluator, change agent, practitioner, and user.

Third, there are some competencies that can be specified that are common to various change agent roles (Goodson*).

Finally, the costs vs. the benefits of elaborate division of labor for particular projects need to be assessed; most organizations do not have the time, resources, and interest to perform all the tasks implied in an RD&D approach.

"3. Effective utilization of complex innovations must be preceded by coherently *coordinated research, development, and evaluation.*"

How participants rated this point:
   13 "essential"
   15 "very important"
   14 "somewhat important"
    3 "not important"

Four conferees questioned the validity of the proposition.

An important qualification to the above statement is provided by Kent*: "The question of values, philosophy, and goals, and how they are involved in the change process in education has to be considered in depth. Basic conflicts regarding what should be researched, disseminated, and adopted must be resolved before scientific techniques of diffusion can be applied. There is a general implication that there are vast storehouses of knowledge somewhere within resource systems and that the major problem is diffusing this information widely to users. In education, this is not the case; the usefulness of innovations must be tested and determined 'on the consumer line' by the user system."

"4. Innovation is more effective when innovators start out by stating their objectives or desired outcomes in behavioral terms."

How participants rated this point:
    9 "essential"
   20 "very important"
   12 "somewhat important"
    2 "not important"

Six conferees questioned the validity of the proposition.

The proposition, though somewhat controversial among our experts, represents an important tenet of current educational R&D orthodoxy. Kurland* notes the importance of developing a clear view of the goal or the "desired future state of affairs" at an early point in the change strategy. Millgate* adds that the concept of "change agent" requires a highly developed sense of *personal* objectives ("Who am I?") and a skill to identify objectives in complex situations.

"5. Innovation is more effective when evaluation, preferably in formal quantitative terms, is employed at each step of development, diffusion, and installation."

How participants rated this point:
  8 "essential"
28 "very important"
11 "somewhat important"
  1 "not important"

Only one conferee questioned the validity of the proposition.

Gephart* notes that "the change agent must be capable of assessing the methodological adequacy of the research done to test an innovation." Hood* adds to this the idea that the change agent has responsibility to pass these same skills on to users. "The change agent must be able to use himself and to train the user to use quantitative procedures for evaluating and testing alternatives."

"6. Innovation is more effective when it is guided by an analysis of the cost-to-benefit ratio of specific alternatives."

How participants rated this point:
  2 "essential"
21 "very important"
17 "somewhat important"
  2 "not important"

Four conferees questioned the validity of the proposition.

Several experts saw a major need for selectivity either by the user or some middle man such as a change agent. Mann* suggested the need for "a hard-nosed team constantly reviewing literature to evaluate research and sift out the junk." There is a special need for such tough-minded expertise when the evidence is conflicting and the issue controversial (as in the Jensen report). However much we want change, we have an obligation to prohibit "bad" change.

Glaser* makes a similar point: "Change agents need to be trained to ask critical questions about innovations or proposed solutions to problems, and to gain skill in evaluating alleged evidence; i.e., under what conditions does the innovation appear to work well, has it been cross-validated, what are its cost-benefits in comparison with alternative solutions, etc."

Even when the change agent wants to assume a strongly partisan role in change, he needs to be able to call on these skills. Gephart* makes this point: "In my opinion, part of the change agent's role involves the advocacy of an innovation. However, the change agent must be able to judge the soundness of the innovation he advocates. If he is not skillful at this he will lose his linkage with the user. That is, if he advocates innovations which do not work for a user, that user will not seek his aid when another problem needs resolution. To avoid such mistakes, a change agent must be able to assess the methodological adequacy of the research done in the field tests of the innovation. This does not mean that he has to be trained as a researcher. Evaluation of a process is not the same as doing that process. The activities in which you engage in evaluating the methodological soundness of a completed piece of research are not the same activities that are performed in doing that research. Thus, we need to instruct the change agent so he is capable of the evaluation of the methodological adequacy of research done in the testing of an innovation."

C. Change as a Process of Social Interaction

Overview

A third view of the change process places emphasis on the patterns by which innovations diffuse through a social system. A large body of empirical research tends to support five generalizations about the process of innovation diffusion: (1) that the individual user or adopter belongs to a *network of social relations* which largely influences his adoption behavior; (2) that his *place in the network* (centrality, peripherality, isolation) is a good predictor of his rate of acceptance of new ideas; (3) that *informal personal contact* is a vital part of the influence and adoption process; (4) that *group membership and reference group identifications* are major predictors of individual adoption, and (5) that the rate of diffusion through a social system follows a *predictable S-curve pattern* (very slow beginning followed by a period of very rapid diffusion, followed in turn by a long late-adopter or "laggard" period).

Although the bulk of the evidence comes from rural sociology, these five propositions have been demonstrated in a remarkably wide range of situations in every field of knowledge and using every conceivable adopter unit including individuals, business firms, school systems, and states.

Figure I.3 suggests the type of variable usually considered by the social interactionists. In education, major advocates of the S-I approach have been Mort (1964), Ross (1958), and Carlson (1965).

Because of the strong empiricist orientation of the S-I approach, it has generated relatively few explicit strategies or action alternatives. S-I theorists generally prefer to sit back and ponder the "natural" process without

FIGURE I.3
THE SOCIAL INTERACTION VIEW OF THE CHANGE PROCESS

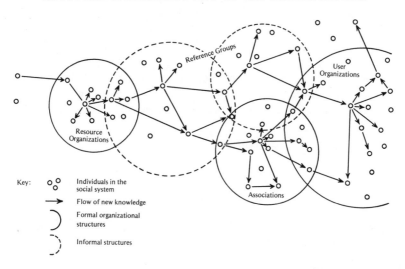

Key:

- ○ ○ Individuals in the social system
- → Flow of new knowledge
-) Formal organizational structures
- ⁻) Informal structures

meddling in it. Nevertheless, four quasi-strategies can be identified with this school.

Natural Diffusion. One derivation from S-I research suggests that innovations will diffuse through a natural and inevitable process. After a very extended early period of testing, development, trial and error, and sporadic localized adoption, innovations diffuse in a remarkably regular pattern. Indeed, when 10 to 20 percent have accepted an innovation, the forces of social interaction are such that the vast majority of the rest of the society will soon follow (Rogers, 1962).

Natural Communication Network Utilization. Most change agents undoubtedly rely on S-I principles in planning and carrying out dissemination activities. Such a strategy would include identification of opinion leadership and circles of influence within the social system, and the channeling of information to such key points.

Network Building. More ambitious and self-conscious applications of S-I principles are found in such massive diffusion networks as the Cooperative Extension Service (Sanders, 1966) and in the marketing networks of large commercial enterprises, notably drug companies. These systems use informal contact by agents or salesmen, enlisting of natural opinion leaders as "demonstrators," and group meetings of various sorts as integral parts of an innovation diffusion program.

Multiple Media Approaches. Effective commercial marketing practice is consonant with S-I findings not only in utilizing the social interaction network but also in employing a variety of media to approach the user, including mass media advertising, package advertising, salesmen, demonstrators, neighborhood "parties," free home trials, etc. S-I research suggests that different media are effective at different stages in the adoption process (awareness, interest, evaluation, trial and adoption) [Rogers, *op cit.*]. Hence, a successful program would involve the phasing of different media approaches to synchronize with progressive stages of user involvement.

Propositions Derived from the Social Interaction Perspective and Research

"1. Effective dissemination and utilization are facilitated by informal *opinion leaders*, particularly when these opinion leaders are innovative in orientation and have considerable influence over a large number of colleagues."

How participants rated this point:
    10 "essential"
    32 "very important"
     8 "somewhat important"
     0 "not important"

No conferees questioned the validity of the proposition.

As a cautionary note, Rogers* warns that the opinion leader can be "worn out" as an effective promoter of change if he becomes too closely identified with outside change agents and becomes too isolated from his followers. Opinion leaders also need to be able to filter out innovations which might upset their relationship to followers. In other words, they may be interested only in those innovations which are compatible with the maintenance of their position in the community and among their colleagues.

"2. The adoption of new ideas and practices is strongly influenced by the perceived norms of the user's professional *reference group*. If the new behavior is seen as desirable or representative of the best practice 'in my profession,' it is more likely to be adopted."

How participants rated this point:
     8 "essential"
    28 "important"
    13 "somewhat important"
     0 "not important"

No conferees questioned the validity of the proposition.

It is thus vitally important that change agents make accurate assessments of the norms and reference groups of those they are trying to influence. This may further suggest that change agents working at different levels, e.g., the university, the federal government, the state system, the local school, may need to be appreciative or at least understanding of the very different norms, languages, and habits of thought that characterize these levels.

"3. Informal *person-to-person* contact is an important factor in effective dissemination, particularly when the user is at the trial stage."

How participants rated this point:
14 "essential"
27 "very important"
7 "somewhat important"
0 "not important"

Only one conferee questioned the validity of the proposition.

This proposition requires a number of qualifiers. First of all, research studies show that personal contact is more important for late adopters; early adopters and opinion leaders are more able and willing to use impersonal sources such as the mass media. It may also be that the media are having increasing impact, a trend which might threaten traditional opinion leaders who rely on personal contacts to maintain influence. *"Sesame Street"* was cited as a possible example in which media has successfully leapfrogged over the interpersonal network to influence directly millions of mothers and children.

Personal contact may also be more necessary when strong opinions are involved and significant knowledge and attitude change are required.

"4. Individual *adoption behavior follows a sequence* which includes the steps of 'initial awareness,' 'interest,' 'evaluation,' 'trial' and 'adoption'."

How participants rated this point:
11 "essential"
13 "very important"
15 "somewhat important"
3 "not important"

Three conferees questioned the validity of the proposition.

According to William Wolf*, who is completing a major study on innovation diffusion, there are only two distinguishable stages in educational change which he calls: (1) awareness-interest and (2) trial-adoption.

He notes that educational organizations rarely use feedback and rarely drop an innovation once they have tried it (i.e., "trial" is really "adoption").

Another important qualification is that innovation adoption in schools is a *collective* decision process; hence, a psychological model of acceptance (A-I-E-T-A) may not be entirely relevant. Collective adoptions may require a different sequence and, in complex organizations, the "stages" may be represented in different persons or roles.

In his latest book on the *Communication of Innovations* (1971), Rogers devotes a separate chapter to analysis of such "collective" and "organizational" adoption decisions.

> "5. Users who have close *proximity to resources* are more likely to use them."

How participants rated this point:
   7 "essential"
  19 "very important"
  15 "somewhat important"
   4 "not important"

Three conferees questioned the validity of the proposition.

Conferees felt that proximity problems in terms of *geography* can be overcome and are being overcome increasingly in this age of rapid transportation and tube communication. However, the *psychological* distances between researcher-and-practitioner, specialist-and-generalist, and "them"-and-"us" are more difficult to overcome with technology. In some respects, e.g., old-young, black-white, we may be moving farther apart psychologically.

It was also noted that "closeness" has its problems in the form of jealousy, and the comfortable conformity and complacency of those who have been too long in close proximity to each other.

> "6. To achieve utilization, a *variety of messages* must be generated pertaining to the same innovation and directed at the potential user in a *purposeful sequence* on a *number of different channels* in a number of different formats. The resource system must act synergistically, bringing together a variety of messages and focusing them *in combination, in sequence, and in repetition* upon the potential user."

How participants rated this point:
  16 "essential"
  20 "very important"
   8 "somewhat important"
   1 "not important"

Only one conferee questioned the validity of the proposition.

"Synergy" is a complex idea which summarizes a good deal of research on change. Individual change efforts at one point in time rarely have impact by themselves. Users usually respond only after repeated inputs from diverse sources. The key concepts here are (1) redundancy, (2) diversity, and (3) synchronicity. We can plan the first two, but orchestrating the whole process so that the user feels the synergistic impact is another story. It is the communicator's dream.

D. Change as a Linkage Process

Each of the three views of the change process discussed up to this point provides us with valuable insights and useful guideposts for developing a comprehensive view of the whole, but each leaves much to be desired when viewed separately. Clearly, there is a need to bring these three viewpoints together in a single perspective that includes the strongest features of each. Havelock has put forth the concept of "linkage" as a possible unifying and integrating idea.

The concept of linkage starts with a focus on the user as a *problem-solver.* We must first consider the internal problem-solving cycle within the user as it is depicted in Figure I.1 (see above). The user experiences an initial "felt need" which leads him to make a "diagnosis" and a "problem statement." He then works through "search" and "retrieval" phases to a "solution," and finally to the "application" of that solution. But, as we see in turning to Figure I.4, the linkage model stresses that the user must be *meaningfully related to outside resources.*

FIGURE I.4
A LINKAGE VIEW OF RESOURCE-USER PROBLEM-SOLVING

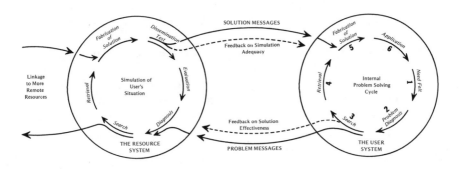

The user must make contact with the outside resource system and interact with it so that he will get back something relevant to help him with the solution process. The user must enter into a *reciprocal relationship* with the resource system that corresponds to what is happening in the user. In effect, resource systems and resource persons must *simulate* or recapitulate the need-reduction cycle of the user; they should be able to (1) simulate the user's need; (2) simulate the search activity that the user has gone through; and (3) simulate the solution-application procedure that the user has gone through or will go through. It is only in this way that the resource person can come to have a meaningful exchange with the user.

This reciprocity with the user includes testing the adequacy of the simulation model, itself. Only through an interaction and a feedback from the user can the resource person learn whether or not his model of user-behavior is correct. At the same time, the user should be learning and beginning to simulate resource system processes such as scientific evaluation and product development. Only through understanding, appreciating, and to some degree emulating such processes, will the user come to be a sophisticated comsumer of R&D.

The development of reciprocating relationships goes beyond the point of improving individual *problem-solving* processes toward the creation of a stable and long-lasting *social influence* network. This collaboration will not only make a solution more effective, but, equally important, it will build a more effective relationship - a relationship of trust and a perception by the user that the resource is truly concerned, that the resource will listen and will have a quantity of useful information to pass on. The reciprocal and collaborative nature of this relationship further serves to legitimize the roles of consumer and resource person and it builds a *channel* from resource to user.

Linkage is not simply a two-person interaction process however; the resource person, in turn, must have access to more remote and more expert resources than himself, as indicated at the left hand side of Figure I.4. In his efforts to help the user, the resource person must be able to draw on specialists, too. Therefore, *he* must have a way of communicating *his* need for knowledge (which, of course, is a counterpart of the user's need) to other resource persons and these, in turn, must have the capacity to recapitulate this same problem-solving cycle, at least to a degree. Only in this way will they be able to develop a functional relationship with each other.

Therefore, an effective change process requires linkage to more and more remote resource persons, and ultimately these overlapping linkages form an extended series which can be described as a "chain of knowledge utilization"[1] connecting the most remote sources of expert knowledge in the university with the most remote consumers of knowledge (see Figure I.5).

---

[1] See Havelock et al. (1969) Chapter 3 for an analysis of this idea.

FIGURE I.5
THE MACROSYSTEM OF USER-RESOURCE LINKAGE: SOCIETY
AS A PROBLEM-SOLVING SYSTEM

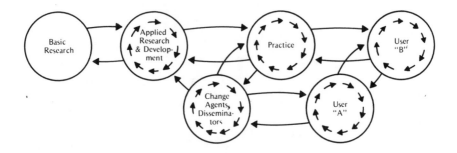

It is possible to identify and differentiate within our total society a variety of knowledge-building, knowledge-disseminating, and knowledge-consuming *subsystems*, each with its own distinctive protective skin of values, beliefs, language, and normative behaviors. These could be referred to as the "research subsystem," the "development subsystem," the "practice subsystem," and the "user subsystem." At a gross level, the prime task of knowledge utilization is to bring these great subsystems into effective linkage with each other; the kind of reciprocal simulation-and-feedback relationship described above needs to be established at the interface between systems. Linkage between systems is the essential process in any effort at planned social change.

All subsystems of the society must be able to simulate each other's problem-solving process and exchange messages concerning needs, problems, and solutions; but the efforts of all need to be coordinated and facilitated in accordance with an evolving concept of what the total dissemination and utilization system should become. This concept of a "total system" must be clearly oriented toward a definition of "the public interest" which safeguards, as much as possible, the special interests of the subsystems involved.

What are the subsystems involved and how adequately do they relate to one another now? Figure I.6 suggests some of the key linkages required in institutional terms. This figure poses some interesting issues. (1) How do consumer *needs* get articulated and communicated to the "experts" in the universities, in the professions, and other potential "resource" organizations? Does the existing system provide adequately for two-way communication? (2) Does the existing system contain all the elements that are *really* required for problem-solving and self-renewal to meet the total educational needs of the society now and in the future? New subsystems have been created recently such as the "regional laboratories," presumably to fill a gap in the system. Was there such a gap and do they fill it? These are the kinds of

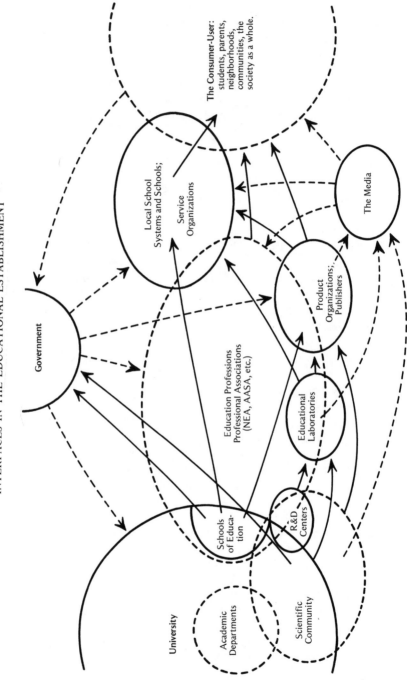

FIGURE I.6

AN INSTITUTIONAL FRAMEWORK FOR VIEWING CRITICAL CHANNELS AND
INTERFACES IN THE EDUCATIONAL ESTABLISHMENT

The Consumer-User:
students, parents,
neighborhoods,
communities, the
society as a whole.

Local School
Systems and Schools;

Service
Organizations

Government

The Media

Product
Organizations;
Publishers

Education Professions
Professional Associations
(NEA, AASA, etc.)

Educational
Laboratories

Schools
of Educa-
tion

R&D
Centers

University

Academic
Departments

Scientific
Community

questions that we must keep asking if we are concerned about the evolution of an effective national renewal system.

Obviously, not all change change agents will have a focus of concern at the national level. However, it is important for change agents at all levels to have some vision of the total resource picture relevant to the client situation in which they are working, and of the particular role that they can or should play within a total problem-solving context: local-regional-national. Figure I.7 suggests how various levels and functions might ideally relate to one another. Problem-solving goes on at all levels simultaneously and the cycle at each level from local to national may have analogous components even though at the individual level they are all within one person's head and at the national level they may each be sprawling and complex institutions as outlined in Figure I.6.

Figure I.7 also suggests several *alternative* change agent roles or functions, e.g., diagnostician, (lower circles); information specialist and solution builder (left-side circles); evaluator; system monitor, innovation manager, process helper or facilitator (center circles). Each of these roles could be actualized at the local, regional, national, or even international level.

There appears to be a growing consensus among students of educational change that problem-solving human relations approaches and rigorous system analytic approaches have to be brought together at the local level before a truly satisfactory educational change model can evolve. Dale Lake,* for example, reports that he and his staff at the State University of New York in Albany are building a model which expands the basic problem-solving model "by attending much more to management information systems, system analytic and system synthetic skills." They are also developing strategies to implant all these skills into schools and organizations. Similarly, Jung* and associates at the Northwest Regional Laboratory are now collaborating with R.E. Corrigan Associates to bring together their "Resource Utilization and Problem-Solving" training package with a PPBS systems training approach. Other such fusion efforts are taking place at many centers across the country.

In reviewing the different perspectives toward change summarized by Havelock, et al., Gephart* makes a good summary observation: "A model is possible which merges the RD&D, S-I, P-S, and Linkage models without doing injustice to any of the four. The citation of strengths and weaknesses of each of these four provides the basis for this combination. RD&D concentrates on the nature of the innovation and the work necessary to develop and diffuse it. The other three do not have this focus as directly. Since some aspects of the change process are determined by the nature of the innovation, this type of focus cannot be eliminated. S-I concentrates on the network through which information spreads. RD&D contains some of this in the 'D' but does not have the degree of clarity of S-I. P-S and Linkage models also

FIGURE 1.7

WORK ON EDUCATIONAL PROBLEMS GOES ON SIMULTANEOUSLY
AT DIFFERENT LEVELS

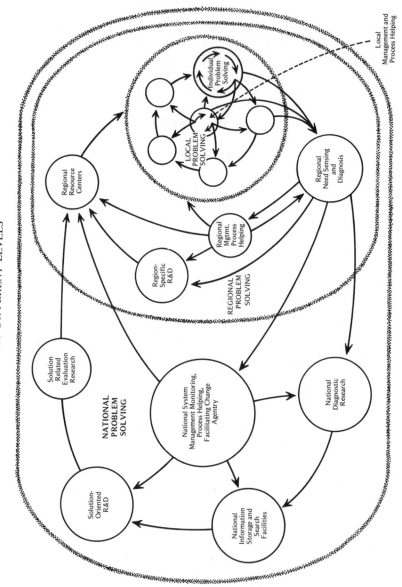

assume a network but to a lesser degree than the S-I model. The P-S model focuses on the adopter or utilizer of knowledge with an intensity not displayed in the other three. The Linkage model seems to emphasize factors that must be considered within and among the research component, the communication network, and the user. It does not seem to attend to other aspects of those components. By merging these four models, a more comprehensive system is represented."

Propositions Derived from the Linkage View of Change

"1. To be truly helpful and useful, resource persons must be able to *simulate the user's problem-solving* processes."

How participants rated this point:
  17 "essential"
  21 "very important"
  6 "somewhat important"
  1 "not important"

Four conferees questioned the validity of the proposition.

Millgate* notes that it is nearly impossible to simulate user problem-solving if you are not the user; but an important task of change agents is to make the user system conscious of itself and its own problem-solving process. This is no small feat because of the tendency of most organizational efforts to degenerate from "getting the job done" to "pleasing the boss."

Because of the difficulty that most change agents have in getting "inside the skin" and truly identifying with the client, it is often vital that they make a firm contact with insiders who can work with them. Chickering* cites the case of a change agent attempting to help a small Mennonite college in Pennsylvania; he was unsuccessful until he obtained aid from a Mennonite "brother" who could operate in the *cognitive* and *affective* style of the faculty. Several conferees stressed the need for outside-inside change team building as an important aspect of change agent skill development.

"2. To derive help from resource persons (and resource systems) the user must be able to *simulate resource system processes*, e.g., to appreciate research knowledge, he must understand how research knowledge is generated and validated."

How participants rated this point:
  6 "essential"
  17 "very important"
  9 "somewhat important"
  3 "not important"

Three conferees questioned the validity of the proposition.

Clemens* states this point from a national perspective: "As we have tried to facilitate the interpretation and distillation of knowledge (both R&D and practice) in the U.S. Office of Education, we've found precious few people who can take the double perspective of the scientist and the practitioner and analyze information in meaningful ways. Presumably, this synthesis process should be engaged in by all persons attempting to utilize knowledge; but in practice, it is not happening very often. I am not sure that this synthesizing role is trainable; maybe we have to breed such animals."

Joe Ward* also puts the case in the broadest terms: "It is important," he says, "that all human elements involved in these processes should have a common model of all processes plus a model of the linkage process."

For Taylor,* this point has special implications for the undergraduate training of educators: "Appreciation of scientific tradition must be built into education undergraduates early so they learn to look toward research in developing teaching methods."

"3. Effective utilization requires *reciprocal feedback*."

How participants rated this point:
   25 "essential"
   17 "very important"
    4 "somewhat important"
    1 "not important"

Only one conferee questioned the validity of the proposition.

It may be important to distinguish here between "task" feedback and "interpersonal or socio-emotional" feedback. Both are important in developing effective linkage, but they may interfere with each other. Subcultural norms (e.g., in Chickering's example of the Mennonite College) may prohibit direct work on the interpersonal level and, on the other hand, once a norm of working on the interpersonal level is established in some systems, the work on the task "goes to hell" (Reilly*).

"4. *Resource systems need to develop reciprocal and collaborative relationships* not only with a variety of potential users but also with a large diverse group of other resource systems."

How participants rated this point:
   20 "essential"
   20 "very important"
    8 "somewhat important"
    0 "not important"

Only one conferee questioned the validity of the proposition.

One important implication of this proposition is that change agents have to be information-oriented and have to think openly and broadly about the meaning of the term "resource." Clemens* spells this out in terms of one U.S. Office of Education role: "It does seem to me, that for the short-range of five years or so, we must build our information analysis capability. Our linkers are going to have to rely on packaged or semi-packaged information which they can then reinterpret. I believe that building this 'information analysis manpower pool' is potentially one of the highest short-term payoff areas in selection and training of knowledge utilization personnel."

"5. *Users need to develop reciprocal and collaborative relations* with a variety of resource systems (cosmopoliteness)."

How participants rated this point:
  10 "essential"
  30 "very important"
   8 "somewhat important"
   0 "not important"

Only one conferee questioned the validity of the proposition.

Building on this idea, Tye* comments: "We need to develop temporary social systems to help participants deal with back-home problems by exposure to a variety of resources - including each other - and to each other in such a way that the people involved come to rely on one another as major resource persons." This approach has been developed experimentally by John Goodlad, Ken Tye and others at UCLA with what they call "the League of Cooperating Schools." Roughly similar user-resourcer cooperative networks have been developed by Bushnell* and Spack* (ES '70; An Educational System for the 70's), and by J. Lloyd Trump (The NASSP[1] Model Schools Project).

Rogers defines "cosmopoliteness" as "the degree to which an individual's orientation is external to a particular social system." (1962, p. 17) It results from experience in more than one system either through living, traveling, visiting, or communicating. Cosmopoliteness is highly correlated with innovativeness. Rogers quotes Tarde: "To innovate, to discover, to awaken for an instant, the individual must escape, for the time being, from his social surroundings. Such unusual audacity makes him super-social rather than social."

---

[1]National Associaton of Seconday School Principals.

"6. *A willingness to listen* to new ideas (openness) is an important pre-requisite to change. This applies both to resource persons and users."

How participants rated this point:
35 "essential"
11 "very important"
 3 "somewhat important"
 0 "not important"

No conferees questioned the validity of the proposition.

For the resource system, "openness" means a *willingness to help and a willingness to listen* and to be influenced by user needs and aspirations. The "ivory tower" approach, for example, closes off valuable intellectual resources from the rest of society, creating a closed system which is indifferent to the public interest. Practitioner groups such as the legal and medical professions may also close themselves off when they establish high fees and evolve service standards which are subject only to internal surveillance and internal influence. Effective resource systems are open to influence and change both from the user and from other resource systems. It is also vital that practitioner resource systems renew their skills and their competence by continuously remaining open to the newest developments of science and technology.

For the user, "openness" is not merely a passive receptivity to outside knowledge. Rather, it is an active faith that outside resources will be useful and it requires *active reaching out* for new ideas, new products, and new ways of doing things.

One implication for training is the need to develop listening skills in the change agent and to give him the ability to train others (users and resource persons) in these same listening skills.

E. Additional Propositions About Change Process
(Rewards and Reward Structures for Changing)

Ratings were also obtained on seven additional propositions which represent frequently cited axioms of planned change but which do not fit clearly into any one of the four viewpoints described above. Most refer directly or indirectly to the rewards and the reward structures with which change takes place, and all received wide endorsement from over 50 experts.

"1. *Effective knowledge utilization is a self-fulfilling prophesy:* the user's expectation that effort (in retrieval and application) will pay off is a good indicator that it will."

How participants rated this point:
 5 "essential"
 23 "very important"
 15 "somewhat important"
 0 "not important"

Five conferees questioned the validity of the proposition.
Kurland* notes the importance of building individual and group *confidence* in the capacity to produce change.

 "2. A willingness to take risks is an important requirement for successful innovation."

How participants rated this point:
 22 "essential"
 23 "very important"
 5 "somewhat important"
 0 "not important"

No conferees questioned the validity of the proposition.
Towne* expands on this idea as follows: "As well as developing new animals known as change agents, we must instill in present training programs for most educational personnel a greater reliance upon 'new' information, as well as a more positive attitude toward the 'risk' of fighting tradition." The present state of affairs creates a real dilemma for Towne: "The more innovative a person is, the greater risks he'll take, and the greater his chance for failure. The 'farther out' an innovative idea is, the less credibility it has and probably the more *adaptation* will be required." Towne wonders how many innovators are killed off by the time lag between introduction and implementation of an innovation.

Taylor* responds that the typical system has no reason to take risks on innovation ideas until they are supported by solid evidence of utility.

Ofiesh* notes that a system needs built-in rewards for risk-taking.

Related to "risk" is the problem of "accountability." Too much stress on accountability may stifle risk-taking, particularly if the change agent or the innovator is putting his person or his career on the line when he takes a risk. Shared accountability and a specification and limitation of consequences may be ways in which risk-taking can be safeguarded. Accountability may not work for system improvement if people don't have the right to make mistakes. Change requires a certain degree of error embracement.

"3. *A willingness to make an effort to adapt* innovations to one's own situation is an important prerequisite to effective utilization (a dimension of openness)."

How participants rated this point:
21 "essential"
24 "very important"
 4 "somewhat important"
 0 "not important"

No conferees questioned the validity of the proposition.

Although this proposition received very high consensus endorsement from our experts, it runs somewhat counter to the RD&D notion of user-proof innovations. Clearly, some successful innovations are not in themselves adaptable. For example, there is no way to adapt the television images and sounds that come to us in *Sesame Street*; each program is prepackaged in a fixed format as it comes to us on the screen. On the other hand, individual teachers may be able to adapt their use of the program in supplementary teaching to different audiences.

"4. Those who already possess the most in the way of *resources and capabilities* are the most likely to get even more."

How participants rated this point:
 5 "essential"
19 "very important"
15 "somewhat important"
 1 "not important"

Four conferees questioned the validity of the proposition.

The research literature in the social interaction tradition is particularly convincing in suggesting that there is a general factor of *capacity* or competence accounting for much of the variance in diffusion studies. This summary concept ties together the highly intercorrelated variables of "wealth," "power," "status," "education," "intelligence," and "sophistication" which are invariably good predictors of successful innovation and utilization. The rich have more opportunities to get richer because they have the *"risk capital,"* both figuratively and literally.

Generally speaking, the more power, prestige and capital possessed by the resource system, the more effective it will be as a resource and as a diffuser. If the resource system collectively possesses a high degree of intelligence, education, power, and wealth, it will then have the capacity to summon and invest diverse resources; it will be able to plan and structure its activities on a grand scale over a long time-span to produce "high performance products."

Likewise for the user, the ability to assemble and invest his own internal resources and to call upon outside (and sometimes very expensive) help is extremely important in successful innovation. Another ingredient of capacity, *self-confidence* (a feeling that one *has* the capacity), is also an important predictor of successful utilization. Other important ingredients are: the amount of available time, energy, education, sophistication, and size of operation.

The various components of capacity are usually measured separately in research studies of the user, but they go together so consistently that they really form a "success syndrome." This is a factor which confounds the government policy makers who try to legislate programs to aid the poor, the underprivileged, and the underdeveloped because, willy-nilly, the high capacity people are the ones who derive the most benefit; they are the ones who know how to identify, retrieve, and make effective use of the potential new resources that these programs represent. The sad fact is that "capacity" is a quality which is distributed very unfairly in nearly all societies, usually in inverse proportion to the need for it. For the change agent who wants to make an impact, there is a real dilemma here. Clearly the best return on short investment is from a high capacity user system, but the low capacity user system is the one which needs help the most.

"5. *Anticipated profit* (*reward*) is a major incentive for diffusers and users of innovations."

How participants rated this point:
   12 "essential"
   22 "very important"
   14 "somewhat important"
    1 "not important"

No conferees questioned the validity of the proposition.

Ofiesh* sees the management of the reward system as the crucial element in change, a position which is backed up by an overwhelming body of psychological research. He states the case: "I think the basic element in change in education is tied into the reinforcing agents that are available for modifying the behavior of all operational personnel, both teachers and school administrators, for example. Without the proper principles of contingency management, it is unlikely that any change model will become viable for any long period of time. The important point that should be stressed is that change agents should be familiar with the principles of reinforcement that are necessary to be institutionalized, and to establish mechanisms for the provision of such reinforcements for those whose behavior needs to be modified in the direction of the desired change and innovative practices."

"6. *Rewarding encounters with new knowledge* lead to expectations that future encounters will also be rewarding."

How participants rated this point:

    7 "essential"
  29 "very important"
   9 "somewhat important"
   1 "not important"

No conferees questioned the validity of the proposition.

This proposition is related to the above mentioned concepts of "self-fulfilling prophesy" (E1) and anticipated reward (E5). Kurland* adds the notion that these rewarding encounters should build incrementally on one another: "A succession of successful changes that build toward a large goal are more likely to last than a large, dramatic change that was not built up out of internalized success."

Watson,* on the other hand, feels there is an argument for "utopic" models to provide positive images of future potential and unfreeze traditional thinking: "The utopian model-experimental school district or college - has most promise of transcending established ways of working."

"7. New ideas and innovations which clearly contradict preexisting values will not get very far in a user system, whereas those which *appeal to cherished values* will."

How participants rated this point:

  12 "essential"
  19 "very important"
  10 "somewhat important"
   1 "not important"

Three conferees questioned the validity of the proposition.

Mann* points out that there is almost always a gap between the actual and ideal behavior of practitioners and, for that reason, a change agent can use the perception of this gap as a lever to induce change. However, confronting the client with the discrepancy between how he is behaving and how he knows he ought to be behaving is fraught with threat. Hence, the confronting change agent must also be *supportive*. Dionne* suggests that there is an element of manipulation in such "supportive-confronting." When is it legitimate for the change agent to appeal to a person's values?

Chesler* feels that the resource person should himself have clear values about how the user should use his knowledge, but he questions whether it is always wise to assume common values. Change, he says, is a political process fraught with conflicts of interest and values.

F. Conflict Theory of Change

Many participants at the conference on Change Agent Training emphasized the importance of conflict and crisis as necessary factors which have to be managed, resolved, or even utilized in order to effect major changes in education.

It appears that we are witnessing the rebirth of *conflict and crisis models* of innovation and, although these have not yet been fully articulated, they may soon receive the same formalization and elaboration that distinguishes those presented above. Conflict models, of course, are not new and can be traced back at least to the "dialectic" theories of Hegel and Marx, but the late 20th century version is likely to be quite different from classical versions.

Chesler and Franklin (1968), for example, suggest "training for negotiation" by which they mean not only how to *carry on discussion* but also how to *equalize power relations* so that genuine give-and-take bargaining is possible.

They also suggest a general strategy of "crisis intervention," by which they mean a concentration of effort by outside change agent-consultants at the time when the client system is most disrupted and, hence, most motivated to make *sincere* change efforts.

Dalin,* in reviewing the four models of change described earlier, says: "These are based on behavioral sciences which again are based on specific values and conditions. In a relatively stable democratic situation, the social-engineering process may then be adequate. I do think, however, that recent unrest and violence just shows that real changes imply major conflicts. What is then a usable approach?"

Benne* notes the potential relationship between inter-system *conflict* and inter-system *linkage*. "Collaboration," he says, "should not be treated as a given but rather as an achievement within a context of conflicting interests and orientations. A conflict dimension underlies the dialogue between and within systems; collaboration or linkage can only be achieved as a synthesis of such conflict." Change agents, therefore, need to be able to "convert win-lose definitions of exchange between systems into win-win definitions of situations." They need to be skilled at "releasing communication between ideologically divergent systems and subsystems."

Ratings of Alternative Change Models

The 50 change experts at the Michigan conference were also asked to rank their preferences among the four models described and to add additional models to the list as they desired.   The results of these rankings are summarized in Table I.1.

TABLE I.1
PREFERRED MODELS OF CHANGE (RATED BY EXPERTS
AND SPECIALISTS IN EDUCATIONAL CHANGE AT
THE MICHIGAN CONFERENCE)

	Rank			
	1	2	3	4
Research Development and Diffusion	7	6	17	10
Social Interaction	3	8	12	21
Problem-Solving	8	19	11	7
Linkage	25	11	7	1
Other[1]	7			

It seems generally clear from Table I.1 that some sort of synthesis, such as is represented in the "linkage" model, is preferred by most authorities on the change process in education, although a clear diversity of views remains. The implication we choose to draw from all this is the proposition we started with, namely: There is a *significant body of knowledge and theory which can form the basis of coherent models of training in change process.*

---

[1]Fourteen participants suggested alternative models, although only seven chose to rank them. Ofiesh proposed a "contingency management" model. Tye suggested a "political systems" approach. Dorros emphasized the need for a conflict-crisis model. Other suggestions were on the order of over-arching syntheses (e.g., Gephart) or modifications of those offered (e.g., Lake: "systems problem-solving and organization development").

II

GOALS OF TRAINING

When considering any sort of training activity, the issue of goals is paramount. We should be able to answer the question of "why" before we move on to the "who" and "how." Designs, strategies, and procedures are useless unless they are developed for worthwhile ends. Of the many ways to approach this topic, four are of particular relevance here: (A) breadth of goals, (B) relationship of training to the on-going life history of the trainee, (C) psychological wholeness, and (D) transferability. Each of these topics should be seriously considered by the training program developer, and the choice and design of training elements should be made accordingly.

A. Breadth of Goals

Those of us who talk and write about planned change and knowledge utilization often see in these processes a road to total reform, revitalization, humanization, or self-renewal of our social system. Doubtless, when we advocate process training, we envisage this training as a means to such lofty goals. Nevertheless, training itself is a means to a more immediate end, namely, creating a cadre of professionals with a new set of skills. These persons, once they have the skills, will be able to effect further changes in a larger sphere.

The point to be made here is not to discourage the contemplation of lofty long-term goals, but rather to specify what those goals are and what intermediate goals may eventuate in their fulfillment. Training program developers should be able to state their goals *both* in the broad and in the narrow, and *both* in the immediate and in the long run. Experts differ in their specifications of the optimum breadth of goals that is appropriate for training. Some say we should train only specific skills or learnings, allowing the trainee to fit them into his life and work. Others argue just as strongly that we should be building new roles which include not only sets of skills but the necessary trappings of status, identity, and social support. Still others feel that we should be remaking total organizations, training members in "families," and reshaping the structure and institutional arrangements so that they are truly self-running systems. We can't settle these arguments but some points can be made on each level of breadth.

1. Specific Skill Learning

There is much to be said for designing training around the transfer of very specific skills which can be defined in behavioral terms. All training programs, however broad their objectives, should be designed so that behaviors, skills, sets of skills, and functions can be specified. This sort of analysis clarifies the training task and makes the evaluation task considerably easier.

Beyond this, there is something to be said for the teaching of specific skills in their own right regardless of how they are grouped and whether or not they cumulatively represent a new function or role.

For example, one sub-unit of a change agent training program might be "group process analysis and feedback." This skill might be a part of a larger unit on group problem-solving. However, even if a person were not to learn group problem-solving, the skill of group process analysis would still be useful throughout his life in a variety of group situations: in his own organization, with client groups, political and church gatherings, and even in his own family. Applications of this skill will increase his interpersonal competence and his usefulness to society. All this could happen even though the trainee never integrated this skill with other group work skills and never came to actualize himself in the role of "change agent."

In a free society, it is an individual and perhaps even a private matter how specific skills are combined and used. There may be a certain arrogance in specifying what total set or mix of skills other persons *ought* to possess after training. The individual, it is said, learns by inquiry and discovery, not by direction, and what he learns is integrated in a unique way depending on his personality and past learning. We don't accept these arguments as totally valid but we recognize and respect them.

Because of the enormous heterogeneity of people's interests and situations, present and future, it is most important to build training units which can stand alone in this way. Most training programs are probably cost effective only when these many unpredictable and untraceable uses of specific skills are included in the balance. Specifying and unitizing skill training in small segments in some ways allows maximum voluntary choice for the trainee and increases the probability that at least some *learning* will take place.

2. Skill Sets and Functions

Change agentry is clearly not a single unitary skill but a set of skills that some people argue go together. It may follow that these skills should be taught in conjunction, and that the potential change agent will need to have them taught together. If this is done, trainees will presumably have an opportunity to observe and practice the skills conjunctively and will be more likely to use them this way in their subsequent work.

The arguments for function or skill set training over total role training can be made on several grounds. First of all, it follows traditional principles of "liberal education" (but not so clearly of "professional education"). Secondly, as an "add-on" function, change agentry can be taught to persons who manage or deal with innovations as part of their work. Every administrator is a change agent part of the time. So is a teacher, a physician, and a lawyer, but they act in this capacity in *addition* to their other professional tasks. Hence, a set of skills can make them far more effective without requiring them to step completely out of other roles for which they have the training, socialization, and professional competence.

3. Whole-Role Training

There is another side to the above argument, however. Just as specific skills may make more sense when they are orchestrated in sets, so skill sets may only be put to full use if they are organized into new occupational roles. A part-time change agent may find that old and new skills are incompatible, or that old role demands from his peers in the back-home setting are in conflict with the practice of the new behaviors.

Another argument for whole-role training is based on the rarity of these skills and of the training resources to teach them. It can be argued that comprehensive change agent training is such a rare commodity that it should only be provided to the most serious students who will subsequently become trainers themselves. The strategem of training trainers is one way of creating a diffusion effect so that the largest number of new change agents or persons with change skills can be developed in the shortest period of time.

On the minus side, training for new roles is far more difficult than training for specific skills or functions. Not only is more training required because there are more skills and knowledge involved, but a whole new identity needs to be developed. Also if whole-role training is to be meaningful, it must be coupled with extensive institutional support arrangements in the back-home situation. If the training is to "stick," the returning change agent must be officially *and* informally accepted in the new role by his superiors, peers, and subordinates. This is extremely difficult when the trainer graduate is returning to an organization with a long-established tradition of role relationships, such as a hospital (doctor - nurse - patient) or a school (principal - teacher - student). For example, the role of counselor has been generally accepted by educators as necessary and appropriate for all school settings but it is still a difficult and marginal role in the school structure largely because the teacher and principal roles have had longer years of acceptance by the educational establishment. Expectations regarding *who* should do what in schools, hospitals, prisons, and other established institutions have been in place for a long time. Yet those expectations must be changed if new roles are to be made viable in these settings. Careful and extensive planning and preparation are necessary both for the trainee and his colleagues in his regular work setting. The difficulty and cost of such planning and preparation should not be underrated.*

An alternative to the "new role in old organization" arrangement is the "new role in *new* organization." The change agent can often be more effective as an "outsider" than as an "insider," partly for the reasons stated above, i.e., the great difficulties in gaining acceptance for a new role in an old system with long-established traditions. However, the "outsider" notion does not remove the institutional question from change agent training because everyone needs a home-base and a colleague-system to provide security, identity, visibility, and the kinds of accoutrements that are generally required for role maintenance over an extended time period.

4. Whole-System Training and Changing

Some theorists view the training of individual skills or persons as futile without changing at the same time the total social organizational context in which they exist. Hence, they argue that people should be brought to training in organizational "families:" peers-superiors-subordinates, doctor-nurse-administrator, principal-teacher-student. Together, in the same training environment, they can role play new relationships to each other, experiment with new organizational foci, develop new shared norms of behavior based on a shared knowledge and value base, and, in short, become a new system.

There are also some negatives for whole-system training. First, it is likely to be more complicated than skill or role training; the inputs are more diverse, the outputs less certain. The methodology for this training is not well developed and evidence of effectiveness is hard to come by.

Nevertheless, the total organization approach to training is becoming increasingly popular. Blake and Mouton have developed what they call the "Managerial Grid Program" to provide such training for industry, and Rensis Likert and his associates are working on another approach to such training which they believe is applicable to schools and government agencies, as well as to business and industry.

Numerous consulting firms have been established in recent years to supply complete training packages for organizations in the area of systemic programming, planning, and budgeting. With such programs, the line between "training" and "organizational change and development" is hard to

---

*Later in this volume we will discuss a number of the factors involved in this "institutionalizing" process. A sample plan for change agents in state education agencies is offered which takes account of such needs.

draw. In any case, many of the advocates of these approaches feel that specific skill training without total system training is meaningless and practically worthless.

Even if these advocates are correct, they still do not indicate how these master trainer-organizational architects are themselves to be trained. Hence, even accepting their assumptions in the broad, we still need to think about skill and role training for those who will later do the system training.

Participants at the Michigan Conference on Change Agent Training (CECAT) had different approaches to these four levels of goals. When the conferees divided into groups to work on alternative training designs, the task force groups which they formed were based to some extent on this dimension of four levels of breadth. (See Part Two below.) The models proposed by Hood, et al., and Chesler, et al., although radically different from each other, are both "whole-system" models. Glaser and Goodson advocate a "team" approach (intermediate between "whole-system" and "whole-role"), while Benne, et al., Havelock, and Tye are considering whole-role training. Towne views training for a function as adequate.

B. Life History Relevance (How Goals Relate to What Already Exists in the Trainee)

Any training is designed to change something about the person being trained, but a training design must take account of where the prospective change agent starts and the implications of the training for the development of the person as a whole.

There are at least three points along this life-history dimension that should be considered in formulating training goals. One goal might be to provide entirely new attitudes, knowledge, or skills, inputs that are largely unique and original as far as the trainee is concerned. A second goal orientation is to provide reinforcement or additional support for attitudes, knowledge, and skills already possessed by the trainee to a greater or lesser extent. A third approach, and perhaps the most difficult of the three, is to eradicate or redirect already existing attitudes, knowledge, or skills which are deemed to be growth-inhibiting, or which interfere with movement toward a change agent function.

1. De Novo Learning

It is probably easier to *conceptualize* and explain a new role or function as something entirely new than to present it as an adaptation or alteration of something already existing. The image is clearer and sharper and the designer has a freer hand to include all the elements that ideally ought to go together.

Even for the trainee, there is something refreshing and exciting about starting out with an entirely new role model, particularly if it is seen as an add-on item which does not challenge his existing state of knowledge, skill or self-concept. There is probably some desire in all of us to be "reborn." Accentuating the newness and uniqueness of the role and the training can feed this desire.

There are some obvious flaws in such an approach, however. First of all, it is a truism that there is no such thing as a *tabula rasa*. The trainee-recruit inevitably comes to us with some past experiences and attitudes which may stand in the way of learning anything new.

It is also a truism that there is nothing entirely new, particularly in the field of training. Change agent skills such as those described in this volume have been advocated and utilized in various contexts by various people, consciously or unconsciously, for thousands of years. The "newness" comes primarily in the combining, packaging, and labelling which is provided.

2. Reinforcing Existing Attitudes, Knowledge, and Skills in the Person

From the perspective of behavioral learning theory, the most promising approach to training is positive reinforcement. Find out what the person is doing "right" and reward him for doing it.

This approach is very difficult to plan for or to organize coherently without knowing (i) what individual trainers already do that is "right," and (ii) when they are likely to exhibit such behaviors. Short of undertaking a massive screening and diagnosis of individual trainees prior to training, one viable training method might provide extremely varied situations to which the trainee could respond freely while the trainer observed his reactions and rewarded those that were directionally relevant to the change agent concept.

Such training is undoubtly effective when the situation is suitable for the right behaviors to occur, but it requires a very skillful and alert cadre of trainers.

3. Extinguishing Existing Attitudes, Knowledge, and Behaviors in the Person

Inevitably, the trainee will come to the training experiences with many types of behavior and attitudes which are antithetical to the concept of change agent which the trainers want to instill. With some trainees it may not be possible to make any progress without either eliminating, or at least inhibiting, these tendencies.

Yet, this is the most difficult sort of training to undertake. It is highly threatening to the trainee because it makes certain negative assumptions about him and his past. Negative reinforcement is also far less efficient than positive reinforcement. Finally, it may make the trainee defensive so that subsequent learning of *new* attitudes, knowledge, and skills will be more difficult, particularly if they are offered by the same trainers.

These negatives notwithstanding, many training programs implicitly or explicitly have this goal. For example, "training" for the role of psychoanalyst largely consists of psychoanalytic treatment in which the trainee first of all recognizes his "neurosis" and then works it through so that his own neurotic symptoms and thought patterns will not interfere with his understanding and interpretation of the neuroses of his future patients. Some types of group sensitivity training are similarly directed toward exposing and clearing away social behaviors that are injurious to the trainees' relationship to the group.

In setting training goals, how do we decide among these three orientations? It is easy to say "let's do all three because all three are important." This may be ideal, but it is not the practical answer. Psychiatric and human-relating training in the past have tended to focus on orientations (2) and (3), but with mixed success. On the other hand, training for "new" skills, (1), is an "old" approach that has fared no better. Therefore, if it is true that change agentry is a new concept which involves a lot of new learning for most people, then perhaps the best compromise is to provide this training in an *openly* planned training environment in which individual learners can express (and be rewarded for) those positive change agent skills and attitudes they already possess and can feel safe enough to expose some less helpful behavior patterns which might be recognized and redirected with feedback from trainers and fellow trainees.

C. Psychological Wholeness

There has been a repeated trilogy thus far in our discussion of training goals: "attitudes," "knowledge," and "skills." There is no empirical basis for affirming the validity of this attitude-knowledge-skill formula. Indeed, most psychologists are not likely to agree on what each of these terms mean. Nevertheless, it has been convenient in psychology to make a distinction between "behavior," i.e., overt and observable physical acts; "cognition," i.e., the verbalizable "thoughts" that seem to be associated with various behaviors, and "affect," the feelings of pleasing calm, excitement, anxiety, pain, etc. that seem to be associated with either the cognition or the behavior or both. Psychologists and trainers are also likely to differ in their judgments of which of these three psychological components is most important in training and learning.

Most trainers are likely to agree that what people do is more important as an outcome of training than what they say or what they feel. Cognitive training in particular has come into disfavor in recent years. It is "old hat" to fill people's heads with facts and theories, especially if they can't or won't translate them into behavior when they get back to their work setting.

In spite of these shifts in fashion, we believe that the transfer of training is most satisfactory when all three psychological elements are present in some degree. In other words, the trainee should adopt new behavioral skills but he should be able to articulate and justify these behaviors in words, and he should know why these behaviors are important. Without such knowledge, he will not be able to integrate the new skills in his everyday life; he will be defenseless when others ask for justification of his new behavior and, most importantly, he will be unable to explain and teach these skills to others.

Finally, it is important for the trainee sooner or later to develop *positive attitudes* toward these skills, to feel that they are important and valuable. Such attitudes are important for the maintenance of new skills over time because they act as internal reinforcers which continue to operate when the change agent is alone or surrounded by others who do not understand, do not accept, or do not reward him for what he does.

It is perfectly legitimate for a trainer to choose from among these three psychological elements the one he wants to stress in a training program, but he should be aware that the others also represent legitimate training goals in themselves. However, the trainer who wishes to produce learning which is wholly integrated in the psychological make-up of the person would probably be advised to work on all three levels. In describing the kinds of inputs to change agent training that a program designer might select, we will consider all three.

D. Transferability

The word "training" implies the implanting of attitudes, knowledge, and/or skills into the trainees for some good purpose or a combination of good purposes. But how far can the training program designer go in defining and subsequently measuring outcomes? This is the transferability dimension of goal definition. At one extreme, the training goal can be stated as the growth or self-fulfillment of the trainee. If the training makes him a "better person," helps him appreciate, understand, or act more fully in some aspect of life, it is successful. At the other extreme, the goal may be defined as the remaking of the social order. The immediate training experiences are intended only as a first step. Succeeding steps in which the trainees take on their new assignments, including the training of others, will eventually lead to the social reconstruction originally conceived by the planners. The training has been transferred to the trainee, the trainee's home environment, other trainees, and the society as a whole.

Most training activities are supported for their supposed instrumental value in bringing about changes, i.e., for their transfer effects not simply to the trainee but to a situation in which the trainee will be working as well. A question very often raised is: "Did it make a difference when he got back home?"

Actually, there are several levels of transfer involved in that question. For the minimum level of back-home transfer, we would ask, "Was the trainee able to retain and use what he learned for a significant period of time in his home setting?" We might also ask if the trainee was able to continue training himself in these areas, adding to and reinforcing the skills, attitudes, and knowledge already acquired. A next higher level might be, "Was the trainee able to influence others at home in some positive and predictable way?" An even more stringent "transfer" question would be, "Has the trainee been able to train others to the level he himself has achieved?" But the ultimate question of transfer is: "Has the home system changed for the better as predicted and as a result of the training?"

The further out on this transferability dimension we choose to set our goals, the more difficulty we will have in realizing them and the more difficulty we will have in *measuring* whether they have or have not been realized. Moreover, in setting more stringent transfer goals, we are probably committing ourselves to more elaborate follow-up support to the trainee and to more extensive contractual and other arrangements with the home organization and its members.

How far should a training designer go in setting transfer goals? Obviously, it is impractical to go too far because our resources are likely to be limited. As time recedes from the training event, the intervention and interaction of other forces out of the control of the program developer will make assessment of those ultimate transfer goals difficult. Somewhere, there must be a happy medium. It would seem that some degree of follow-up, assistance, and assessment is desirable if the goal is to produce "real change," but we should also recognize the impracticality and dangers inherent in over-planning.

Summary: How to Choose Appropriate Training Goals

We have suggested four dimensions along which goals might be selected or set, hinting that all were important in one way or another. Obviously, however, a training program must have limited goals. Where should the emphasis be and how should we choose?

On the "breadth" dimension, there is no clear best choice. Good arguments can be made for specific change process skill training, for change agent function training, for whole-role training, and for whole-system training. This volume focuses on training for the *whole role* of change agent, but our CECAT conferees differed in their views and preferences. Often, the scope of training will be specified in advance by the sponsoring agency and dictated by time and budget constraints. For example, the state agency change agent training design included in Chapter IX of this volume presupposes a particular experimental federal program for whole-role training which includes institutional supports, multiple training events, follow-up help, and evaluation. Training contracts and grants rarely provide the opportunity for training programs of that breadth.

In evaluating the other three goal dimensions, it might be helpful to view them as the sides of a cube (see Figure II.1).

FIGURE II.1
DIMENSIONS OF GOALS

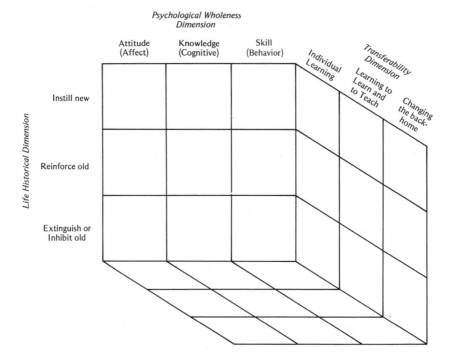

To simplify the presentation, we have reduced the many "transferability" questions to three.

First, taking the life-historical dimension, we feel that the focus should be on the "new" because there is emerging a new, exciting, and unique conception of the change agent as process helper and resource linker. Most of the requisite skills relevant to this new conception are not likely to be pre-existant in most trainees. Secondly, however, we should aim at reinforcing existing positive trends where they are evident.

Second, on the psychological wholeness dimension, it is important to see the three elements as related. We would stress the skill as paramount because knowledge or attitude without skill is likely to have no impact. Nevertheless, it is important to *know why* and to *feel* that what one is doing is right and valuable. It might be expected that trainees would come to training with a reasonably positive attitude toward the general concept. Hence, in the attitudinal domain the emphasis might better be placed on reinforcement than on *de novo* generation.

Finally, on the transfer dimension we would stress individual learning because it is the necessary first step and within the control of the trainer. We would also stress learning to learn and skill practice in teaching others what one has learned. To the extent appropriate, the future back home change activities should also be previewed and prepared for in the training event.

These suggested emphases will not be appropriate for all trainers in all situations. The important point to remember is to *consider* where you are and where you want to be on these dimensions in making your choice of training goals.

III

SOME PRINCIPLES OF GOOD TRAINING DESIGN

In Chapter I we were able to point to a growing body of research and theory about the change process. There is an equally impressive knowledge base on the process of training itself. Some of this information is experimental research on training; some of it reports on practical experience, and a good deal of it is derived from basic research on learning. It is not our intent to review that material here. Rather, we would like to offer a number of summary statements on principles of training that were discussed at the Michigan conference and which were derived generally from the experience and research of the training specialists who were present. The list below is not exhaustive but it may serve as a convenient guide and checklist for the trainer or training program developer. Later in Chapter IV we will illustrate how this list of general principles could be used to generate and evaluate more specific program features.

A. Structure

A training program is a system with goals, a division of labor (trainer-trainee), a temporal sequence, and a definable set of training activities or experiences, etc. The extent to which these systemic elements can be structured in an orderly and rational manner will have much to do with the program's eventual success. Several important aspects of structuring design include: (1) planning, (2) defining objectives, (3) specifying learnings that should meet objectives, and (4) specifying the sequence of training activities that should lead to the desired learnings.

"Planning" is perhaps the key word. A training program without a plan is impossible to prepare for and impossible to evaluate. Good planning insures that a training project will not exhaust its funds too soon, will not schedule events too soon or too late, will bring the right mix of resources, trainers, and trainees together at the right place and the right time.

Good planning also facilitates meaningful *flexibility.* It helps us assess a program's progress as well as indicating any necessary adaptations which should be made in the original plans which do not contradict our objectives. With skillful program planning, program objectives themselves can be evaluated and changed, consciously and deliberately.

Another important aspect of structuring is sequencing, the arrangement of individual activities in a step-by-step series which logically leads to the program's goal. Again this sort of structuring may facilitate flexibility: we can skip steps when it seems appropriate and still be aware of where we are. We can rearrange the order of events while still keeping track of what has not been covered. In short, the integrity of the program can be preserved.

B. Relevance

A training program should incorporate "relevance" in at least four ways. First of all, it should be relevant to the objectives. The objectives, in turn, should be relevant to some real social need. Third, the training should be relevant to the trainees' back home situations and, fourth, the training should be relevant to the needs, wishes, and background of the trainee himself.

In the actual design of training activities, experiential involvement and realism are important factors in success:

> "The more similar the conditions of the training setting to the back home setting, the more likely will be the application of new skills and orientations back home. This is a major rationale for the use of simulation techniques in training."
>
> (Jung, 1970)

C. Specificity

Related to both structure and relevance is the principle of specificity. Goals, learnings, and training activities should be specified as much as possible and, where appropriate, stated in behavioral terms. Without some specification, it is impossible to plan meaningful programs, assess relevance of particular elements, and evaluate outcomes. Specificity also facilitates flexibility and conscious choice among alternative elements. It may also allow program simplification since many elements with different rationales often turn out to have similar or identical behavioral or operational specifics.

D. Generality

It may seem strange that two seemingly antithetical concepts are offered as important principles of training program design, but there is a real sense in which programs must be general as well as specific. Harrison and Hopkins, in describing a design for cross-cultural training of Peace Corps volunteers, put the case very well:

"It is easy to provide trainees with experiences and problems to solve. It is more difficult to think through the learning and adaptation processes that must take place in this experience, to help trainees devise ways of collecting data on them, and to aid trainees in conceptualizing the processes so that they may be applied in overseas situations which on the surface may seem to be radically different from the projects assigned during training. This form of elaboration requires the trainee to take account of the training experience, to dig into it rather than float on its surface, to formulate hypotheses and questions. Without such elaboration, experiences are not converted into learning. Trainees should receive assistance in conceptualizing and generalizing their experience. It is impossible to reproduce or simulate or even to know precisely what conditions will be faced by trainees in an overseas situation. Crude simulations may be the best available. The *processes* of diagnosing and taking action on a problem are similar in the training and application situations, but the content of the problems are different. Unless the trainee has help in abstracting the process from the particular events he experiences, he will face difficulty in translating what he has learned into usable form."

(Bennis, Benne, and Chin, 1969)

The task of translating program concepts into "usable form" actually requires both generalization (from specific training experiences) and specification (back home application from the training program generalizations). Learning is effectively internalized when the trainee is able to go from the specific to the general and back to the specific with ease.

Generality is an important design principle in another sense. Trainees will have very diverse backgrounds regardless of how carefully they are selected and they will be returning to very diverse work settings. Thus, training content must be general enough in its applicability to benefit a range of people and situations.

E. Reinforcement

Reinforcement, or reward for appropriate response, is probably the oldest and most well-founded principle of learning in animals and humans. Training designers should be continuously conscious of this principle and should look for times, places, and situations in which effective positive reinforcements can be applied. As Jung (1970) states:

"It can be critical that the individual recognize reward for

changing. If the individual is not able to identify the positive
effects resulting from his changes, he may revert to earlier
behaviors, assuming his efforts have been irrelevant."

Specific experiences and the training event as a whole should be seen by
the trainee as beneficial, worthwhile, and to some extent enjoyable. He needs
to "feel good" about it so that he will further his training and encourage
others to undertake similar training.

F. In-Process Evaluation and Feedback

Good planning, specification, and structuring of training activities allow
the evaluation of program elements while the training is still going on.
Trainers and trainees need knowledge on whether to go ahead, repeat, or
reorganize parts of the training program. This "knowledge of results" is a
crucial aspect of reinforcement for trainer and trainee and is the basis for
rational decision-making. However, to be most effective, feedback must be
immediate.

In-process evaluation can and should be built into the training experience
as a whole. Like the training itself, evaluation should be relevant (to the
training and the trainee) and specific. However, to be relevant and specific, it
may also have to be *self-administered* in part or in whole. As Jung (1970)
states:

"Most individuals are more active in a training situation when
they are provided knowledge and criteria of competence to apply
to themselves and each other than when they are being directly
supervised and evaluated by an expert."

Training activities should also be designed to include longer term
(summative) evaluations to help designers and trainers make future training
events more effective.

G. Openness and Flexibility

While a training event should be planned and structured in advance, it
should also be continuously responsive to the unanticipated needs of
individual trainees and to unanticipated circumstances. Recognition and
some accommodation to trainees' initial expectations is especially important
in setting the tone of the training event. If, for example, trainees have been
told that there will be no "T-groups" the trainer should not ask for
participation in some event which might be construed as a "T-group" unless
the trainees agree to such activity. Mutual influence and the appearance of

initial influence are both important aspects of openness. As Jung (1970) states:

> "In training situations, helpees allow influence from the helper to the extent that they see themselves able to influence the helper -- e.g., the relationship needs to be reciprocal, not dependent one way or the other."

Sensing resistance and responding to it openly may also be important for the success of a training event (Jung, 1970).

> "Resistance to change is most often based in legitimate concerns for maintaining the system. Recognition of such legitimacy and openness to include resistors can facilitate a change effort."

Training events should also be designed to make maximum use of experience, skill, and varied backrounds of trainees as *resources*. Hence, there should be openness to the trainees as potential trainers and contributors to the total experience. This sort of sharing rarely takes place unless the trainers make explicit efforts to creatively involve trainees as active resources.

Finally, training designers should be open to and actively seek out the experiences of others who have designed or participated in similar events in the past, so that past mistakes can be avoided. Reports on past training events and advice from the trainers and trainees involved can contribute a great deal to the success of newly-planned training programs.

H. Linkage

The above point fits well into the concept of "linkage;" the developers of training should make sure that they and their trainers are adequately linked to appropriate resources and resource persons.

Linkage is also an important principle to apply within the training design itself. For example, we have already mentioned the need for reciprocal relations between trainer and trainee. It is also important that trainers be well linked to each other so that they can coordinate and complement each other's skills. The same applies among trainees. Part of the training should take place in pairs, trios, and quartets, giving the trainers and trainees multiple opportunities for interpersonal contact, sharing, and mutual help. Close working relationships among trainees not only reinforce learning, but also build a sense of common fate, a shared identity around the new concept of "self-as-change-agent."

The linkage concept also applies to the content of training itself. We have already noted the need for linkage of the here-and-now experiences on the training site to the back home realities that must be faced later. We have also noted the need for linkage among the components of the training design, e.g., between objectives and training elements, specifics and general learning, and the training and life space of the trainee.

I. Involvement

The training experiences should have the power to capture and hold the attention of the trainees. This usually means that the trainees need to actively utilize many of their sense and behavioral skills in the program. There should be reading *and* writing, listening *and* telling. When trainees cluster in subgroups, they should be encouraged to rotate through various group task roles such as chairman, observer, recorder, summarizer, etc.

Other well-known involvement techniques include role playing and simulation.

J. Cost Effectiveness

Training designs should generally aim at providing the greatest benefit to the largest number of trainees at the minimum cost. Although there is no rigid formula for balancing benefits and costs, realism and pragmatism are important in considering the budget, the number and quality of trainers and trainees that can be involved, and the time available for training. It is also important to build transferability into as many aspects of training as possible. The trainee who can train a dozen others is just about 12 times as cost-beneficial as the man who learns himself but isn't able to pass it on.

Another implication of the cost-effectiveness dictum is to choose prospective trainees carefully with an eye to transferability and long-term value; this means choosing individuals with some degree of leadership in their home setting in addition to competence and openness to learning. It may also mean choosing younger trainees over older ones on the assumption that they have more remaining years to practice their new skills.

K. Redundancy

Any effective communication has a great deal of redundancy built into it and this principle applies doubly to a complex communication activity such as a training program. Never assume that a message will be heard and learned in one presentation. Important points should be made again and again via different media in different contexts. If the message is important, the trainee should hear it, read it, watch it, recite it, write it, and do it.

Summarization is one obvious and important way to apply the redundancy principle. A common rule of speech-making is to "say what you are going to say, say it, and then say what you have said." Trainees should be given previews of what they are about to experience, and later should be reminded and encouraged to recall what they have learned as it becomes relevant and timely.

L. Synergy

Learning seems to take place most forcefully when a number of inputs or stimuli from different sources converge on one point. This is the principle of synergy. The simplest example of synergy occurs when two separate individuals give the same piece of advice. Two inputs from two different sources are far more persuasive than the same input from only one source. In a sense, synergy produces validation of experience.

One implication is that training programs should not rely primarily or exclusively on any one medium or communication device. Several media should be employed, preferably in concert; these may include readings, films, formal talks, informal exchanges, simulations, role plays, posted newsprint summaries, small and large group discussions, and even field trips and live-in experiences where appropriate and feasible.

On the other hand, these diverse media should be employed purposively to the same ends with a good deal of built-in redundancy.

M. Train for Psychological Wholeness of Learning

In the discussion of training goals, we introduced the notion that attitudes, knowledge, and skills need to come together (a kind of synergy) if the learning is to be adequately internalized. Here we suggest that inclusion of all three aspects of learning is an important principle in program design. Jung (1970) makes two observations:

> "Neither the learning of new knowledge nor changes in attitude are necessarily related to changes in behavior. One study showed no significant relationship between what teachers honestly believed in and thought they were doing in their classrooms as compared to what either trained research observers or their children saw them doing."

On the other hand, he adds:

> "A major false assumption implicit in many training events is that people learn simply by doing. It is, rather, being able to see oneself attempting to do that is the feedback which provides learning. Experience without feedback guarantees nothing."

N. Train for Transferability

In the section on goals and in much of the foregoing, we have stressed the notion of transferability. Jung (1970) notes the importance of this principle in training program design:

> "Unless there is some chance for trying out and practicing behavior under back home conditions, literally or by simulation training, an individual who may show change at the training site will not be likely to transfer it to his back home setting."

O. Compatibility

Training should be compatible with the trainee's personal history, previous learnings, expectations, and probable future work situation. Jung (1970) makes the point:

> "Individuals typically have multiple group roles and loyalties. Learning or practice of new orientations or skills may be resisted if the individual perceives that it will raise conflict in his multiple loyalties. A simple example would be the individual who resists learning and new professional skill for fear his increased professional value may bring increased demands that will take him away from his family role."

It is not very easy to follow the compatibility principle without having a great deal of background and diagnostic knowledge of individual trainees and their circumstances. However, it is probably wise to "dry run" training ideas and elements with representative members or leaders of the trainee population. This stresses the importance of including representatives of both trainees and prospective client systems as participants in the planning of training events.

IV

A FRAMEWORK FOR TRAINING DESIGNS

Training designs will vary greatly in detail depending on the scope of the change for which the program is designed (see Chapter II on Goals). The eight elements of a framework suggested below pertain primarily to whole-role training. Hence, they fall short of system-changing and go well beyond what would be required to train for a specific skill. The key point we wish to make in the analysis which follows is that such training must be seen in a social and temporal context that extends far beyond the training event itself. *Prior to training*, various planning and recruiting activities should take place, establishing a clear rationale and a need for the role to be trained for, identifying and recruiting the right kind of trainers and trainees, and specifying attitudinal, knowledge, and behavioral outcomes desired. *Following training*, there must be adequate preparation of the social environments to which trainees will be returning, monitoring and evaluation of progress in the new roles over time and, finally, reassessment and redesign of the entire training process based on this evaluation. Obviously, most training programs will fall far short of meeting all these provisions adequately and, indeed, some provisions may *not* be very important or relevant in some cases. In this section, we provide a comprehensive outline which can be used as an evaluation checklist or yardstick for various role training programs. The eight elements to be analyzed are as follows:

A. DEFINITION AND RATIONALE FOR THE ROLE
B. CRITERIA FOR TRAINEE SELECTION
C. OUTCOMES EXPECTED OF TRAINEES
   . . . Attitudes and Values
   . . . Knowledge
   . . . Skills
D. WAYS TO PROVIDE TRAINING TO ACHIEVE THESE OUTCOMES
E. WAYS TO SET THE ROLE IN AN INSTITUTIONAL CONTEXT
F. CRITERIA FOR PROGRAM SUCCESS
G. EVALUATION PROCESSES FOR A TRAINING PROGRAM
H. UTILIZATION OF EVALUATION

A. Definition and Rationale for the Role

A large number of authors at various times have proposed new specialized roles for education but few ever proceed beyond the talking stage or beyond the most limited and localized adoption. In the last half centruy, the guidance counselor is probably the only new role which has gained widespread (but certainly not universal) acceptance. Indeed, the literature on counseling and counselor training is filled with references to the difficulty, instability, and marginality of the role.

Nevertheless, there will be continued and intensified discussion of new roles as demands for change, innovation, and upgrading of educational systems continues. A review of a number of change role concepts is provided by Havelock in PLANNING FOR INNOVATION and four generic change agent types are suggested in the Introduction to the GUIDE FOR INNOVATION. For easy reference, the pages where these concepts are introduced are reproduced below.

What is the Role of the Change Agent in the Change Process?*

If change in a particular client system is seen as a step-by-step problem-solving process starting with a disturbance (need, pain) and concluding with the resolution of that disturbance, we can represent the helping roles played by outsiders as indicated by the four outside circles in the figure. Regardless of his formal job title and his position, there are *four* primary ways in which a person can act as a change agent. He can be:

1. *A CATALYST*
2. *A SOLUTION GIVER*
3. *A PROCESS HELPER*
4. *A RESOURCE LINKER*

These four change agent roles are represented symbolically in Figure IV.1.

1. The Change Agent as CATALYST**

Most of the time most people do not want change; they want to keep things the way they are even when outsiders know that change is required. For that reason, some change agents are needed just to overcome this inertia, to prod

---

*Exerpted from Ronald G. Havelock, GUIDE TO INNOVATION IN EDUCATION to be published by Educational Technology Publications, Inc. in 1973.

**Adapted from Havelock (1973), *op. cit.*

FIGURE IV.1
FOUR WAYS TO BE A CHANGE AGENT

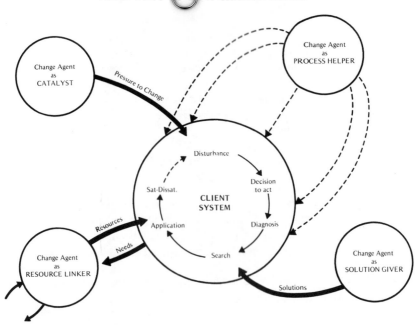

and pressure the system to be less complacent and to start working on its serious problems. In education today this role is often taken by students, concerned parents, or school board members. They do not necessarily have the answers, but they are dissatisfied with the way things are. By making their dissatisfaction known and by upsetting the "status quo," they energize the problem-solving process; they get things started.

2. The Change Agent as SOLUTION GIVER *

Many people who want to bring about change have definite ideas about what the change should be; they have solutions and they would like to have others adopt those solutions. However, being an effective solution giver involves more than simply having a solution. You have to know when and how to offer it, and you have to know enough about it to help the client adapt it to his needs.

3. The Change Agent as PROCESS HELPER *

A critical and often neglected role is that of helper in the processes of problem-solving and innovating. Because clients are not experts on the "how

---

*Adapted from Havelock (1973), *op. cit.*

to" of change, they can be helped greatly by people who are skilled in the various stages of problem-solving. The process helper can provide valuable assistance in:

a. showing the client how to recognize and define needs
b. showing the client how to diagnose problems and set objectives
c. showing the client how to acquire relevant resources
d. showing the client how to select or create solutions
e. showing the client how to adapt and install solutions
f. showing the client how to evaluate solutions to determine if they are satisfying his needs

4. The Change Agent as RESOURCE LINKER *

Effective problem-solving requires the bringing together of needs and resources. "Resources" can be of many kinds: financial backing, knowledge of solutions, knowledge and skills in diagnosing problems, formulating and adopting solutions and expertise on the process of change itself. Resources may also consist of *people* with time, energy, and motivation to help. A very special and underrated change role is that of the "linker," i.e., the person who brings people together, who helps clients find and make the best use of resources inside and outside their own system.

These four "types" hardly exhaust the range of possibilities, however. Moreover, they are not necessarily mutually exclusive. A training program could be designed to combine "catalyst," "process helper," and "linker" roles as "functions" in a larger role concept. Indeed, the notions of "evaluator," "system analyst," "planner," or "implementer" may represent additional functions that could be combined in one "change agent" training program.

Regardless of the combination of functions included, a good role rationale statement should include evidence on five points.

1. Coherence of the role concept
2. Distinctiveness
3. Need
4. Feasibility of training
5. Adoptability of the role

1. *Coherence of the role concept:* The functions or skills described should hang together and form a coherent whole, preferably based on prior conceptualization and research. Presumably, combinations with inherent contradictions such as "negotiator-advocate" or "evaluator-supporter" would either be ruled out or shaped to account for incompatibilities.

---

*Adapted from Havelock (1973), *op. cit.*

2. *Distinctiveness:* What is proposed should be clearly different from existing roles and/or roles proposed in other programs under different labels. In some of the training models proposed in Part Two of this report, distinctiveness of role is spelled out partly in terms of *function* but also in terms of *level* (e.g., national, state agency, local school district, school building).

3. *Need:* The introduction to this report suggests some reasons why change agent roles are needed now in education. Educational manpower need surveys have been undertaken which suggest specific needs for disseminators, evaluators, and developers. More broadly speaking, much has been written in the recent past on various educational crises which are either current or pending. The general need for change and improvement of educational practice is not hard to justify. It should not be difficult to further justify the need for change *process* specialists based upon the information contained in Chapter I.

4. *Feasibility of training:* A design should indicate what resources are available for carrying out the training. Such resources would include relevant research and development literature and products, a pool of potential trainers with adequate skills, understanding, and appreciation of the need, and a sponsor willing to support the program financially and to sanction the installation of trainee-graduates.

5. *Adoptability of the role:* Finally, there should be enough general recognition of the need for this sort of role within educational establishments to permit the installation of the graduates at various sites with reasonable chance of success. A prestigious sponsor can do a lot to create legitimacy but the need for the new role must also be reasonably apparent to members of those institutions which will subsequently be the role "adopters." Such institutional readiness has at least four dimensions:

   a. ·perception of need for role
   b. recognition of the role concept as developed and labelled by the program
   c. willingness and ability to provide local financial support over time
   d. openness to change

Creating a new role is an act of social engineering in the truest sense. The diagrams below may suggest some of the problems. We will never be introducing a new role into a social vacuum; there will always be a pre-existing structure or network of relationships between pre-existing roles, sometimes protected by considerable power, prestige, and thousands of years of tradition. In deciding that a new role is needed, we are presuming that a real gap exists in this network, not in terms of social relationships but in terms of functional relationships to serve the system's goals. Hence, even though we may be filling a functional gap, we are at the same time disrupting an existing set of relationships and forcing on the system a new set of relationships (see Figures IV.2 and IV.3).

FIGURE IV.2
THE PROBLEM OF CREATING A NEW ROLE

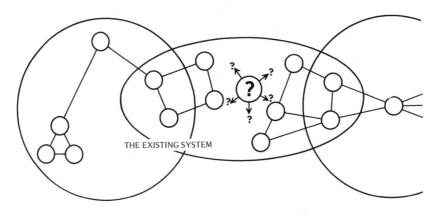

THE EXISTING SYSTEM

FIGURE IV.3
THE NEW ROLE AND THE ROLE SET

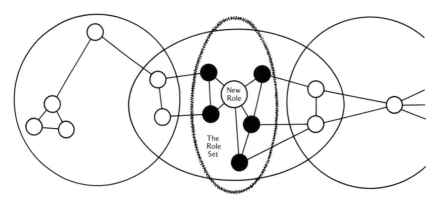

New Role

The Role Set

Role theorists have used the term "role set" to define the group of individuals with whom a particular role holder must relate most closely in his everyday work. The role set is very important to a role holder because through their perception and behavior they convey to the role holder an image of himself. If they deny his existence or refuse to treat him as a distinct entity, he is powerless to act and will ultimately fail in the role. For this reason, any good role training design must (a) define the probable role set for the trainee and (b) indicate the ways in which the role set will be led to accept the role.

The Value of Role Training

This listing of requirements for a good role rationale might lead one to believe that whole-role training is too difficult and too cumbersome a goal for which to plan. Therefore it is important to keep in mind some of the very considerable advantages of whole-role training. In the first place, roles are frequently necessary to institutionalize important new social functions. People charged with only part time and partial responsibility for complex functions are less likely to fill them proficiently over extended periods of time. A role serves institutionalization in at least four important ways:

1. it focuses attention and visibility on the functions;
2. it provides clarity to the functions for both the role holder and those who relate to him;
3. it reduces overload on the person(s) fulfilling the functions; and
4. it reduces some of the training costs because fewer persons require complete training for the functions.

B. Criteria for Trainee Selection

The reputation of a training program probably depends as much upon the quality of its recruits as on the quality of its training. The recruiter will be searching for candidates who have certain backgrounds, traits, and talents which *predispose* them to the kinds of roles for which the training is designed. Some of them, in fact, may be qualified to receive their diplomas when they show up at the door.

On the other hand, a *strong* program ideally should be able to take recruits of diverse backgrounds with a low initial knowledge-skill level and transform them into qualified role holders.

The key conditioning factor which forces us to steer a course between these two extremes is *availability* of recruits. A training program needs trainees; hence, if the entry requirements are set too high, they will have to be violated to admit candidates and, in the process, the integrity of the program design may be damaged. If, on the other hand, they are set too low, the program may fail because of the incompetence of the trainees; moreover, as the "graduates" attempt to install the role concept in their back-home setting, their fumblings may well be attributed to the program or to the whole idea of the new role.

These problems and risks are accentuated when a new and innovative role development program is initiated. This will undoubtedly be the case for "change agent," "linker," "disseminator," or "information specialist" training over the next decade. Innovative programs will probably attract people who are themselves innovative, creative, searching for something new, dissatisfied with the status quo and probably slightly over-qualified in some respects for the jobs they are in right now. These attributes are mostly assets as qualifications for training. But there is another side to it; such individuals are also more likely to be marginal to their home organizations, non-representative, and perhaps low on influence. This innovativeness makes them mavericks or oddballs; the risks they necessarily take as innovators sometimes lead to visible failures which others take as signs of weakness or incompetence. Adding to these problems is the fact that some will be truly incompetent misfits who are eagerly shunted into training programs by their peers and employers when the opportunity arises. A *very strong* program can take such people and give them a new lease on life, a clear and strong new self-image with a set of specific and useful skills to go with it, but the state-of-the-art of change agent training has not yet reached that point.

These are the general considerations that should be uppermost in the program developer's mind as he starts to lay down entry criteria. What are some of the specifics?

Background, Traits, and Characteristics

Rogers and Shoemaker (1971) summarize the empirical research evidence on what makes a change agent effective. Some of the positive attributes which they list are particularly important in developing selection criteria for trainees:

1. *"The extent of change agent effort."* This might suggest the suitability of traits of persistence, high energy, and commitment to work.

2. *"Empathy with clients"* and "client orientation rather than change agency orientation." The trainee should then possibly have an attitude of commitment and dedication to the client and consumer groups whom he will later be serving (e.g., the poor, the hard-to-employ, students, or whatever).

3. *"Credibility in the eyes of his clients."* The meaning of "credibility" will vary greatly with different clients. In any case, the trainee should not be identified with a reference group which marks him as biased in the eyes of clients. Drug salesmen are viewed by physicians as being of very low credibility because of their economic dependency on the firms they represent. The same might be said for persons representing educational textbook publishers or advocate groups of various sorts. However, the most important factor in credibility is the trainee's reputation

for past success or failure as a change agent or simply as an effective person in his work.

4. *"Higher social status among clients."* People who are looked down upon for whatever reason are likely to have a tougher time as change agents. Traditionally, age (older), sex (male), education (high), and economic standing (wealthy) have been associated with high status but this will also vary from group to group. One problem with recruiting innovative people as change agents is the possibility that they might have low social status in the eyes of others (the great silent majority) in their system.

5. *"Higher education and literacy."* Aside from its status benefits, education also has some primary benefits related to effectiveness: education presumably makes one aware of more problems, more alternative solutions, and more resources. It also makes a person more able to utilize resources that are available, particularly if they are in written form, and better able to *articulate* needs, resources, and solutions to others. Above all, a change agent will have to *defend* and continually re-explain and rejustify his role to his role set, to various authorities and to clients. A good educational background will likely (but not necessarily) help in these efforts.

6. *"Cosmopoliteness."* A term used by diffusion researchers to indicate gregariousness and frequency of contacts with persons and organizations outside one's place of work. Good change agent trainees are likely to have had a *variety* of experiences in various roles, in different types of organizations, in different places. They are more likely to attend professional meetings and conferences, to be demonstration site visitors, and travellers. No one of these attributes is a reliable index of a candidate's suitability for training, but evidence of two or three of these attributes in a man's history will suggest a cosmopolite orientation.

7. *"Homophily with clients."* Rogers defines homophily as "the degree to which pairs of individuals who interact are similar in certain attributes." In other words, a trainee should be similar in key respects to the people he is going to be serving later as change agent. If he is going to be working with Blacks he should probably be Black; if he is working with youth he probably should be young; and so forth. How far one should go in using homophily as a criterion will depend on the clients one has in mind and on their tolerance for "differentness." Some training programs specify particular clients who have a great deal of psychological investment in one or two traits or attributes. This might be in being "Black," "poor," "female," "Jewish," "a priest," or "M.D." If this aspect of identity is very salient in the situations in which the change agent is likely to be operating, he should probably

share the characteristic in question. There are two primary reasons for this. First, he will possibly have a greater capacity for empathy with the client, and second, he will be *seen* as having such capacity and therefore will be given a fair chance at being accepted and listened to.

Attitudes and Values

Although it is rather difficult to screen candidates on such a basis, it is likely that several attitudes and values predispose individuals toward being good change agents. Some of the attitudes can be developed or reinforced by the training experience itself, but there has to be a foundation on which to build. The Michigan Conference generated a number of ideas about what such attitudes and values might be for the prospective educational change agent. Here are some examples:

Concern and interest in educational progress.
Belief that educational progress can be made more effective by understanding and changing the process.
Belief, or willingness to believe, that new roles can be a useful part of such change.
Interest and willingness to assume such a role.
Interest and willingness to assume role of trainee.
General interest in continuing personal growth: self and others.
Probably should not be a zealot for particular educational causes, philosophies or products.

Knowledge

A training program should not assume prior knowledge of the change process, although such might be desirable, and it should not make too many assumptions about a candidate's preparedness in specific areas. On the other hand, there are some topics with which candidates should be at least generally familiar. These might include the following:

1. Understanding of what constitutes human values and needs, the heirarchy and relative importance of different needs and values to different people.
2. A very broad acquaintance with scientific values and methods and the rationales behind them.
3. A broad acquaintance with the U.S. educational scene, the structures and norms of educational establishments: local, state and national.
4. A broad understanding of the problems and needs of education.

Skills

The primary aim of most training programs is to provide people with new behavioral skills of various sorts. At the same time, such training must presume the prior existence of skills on which the new ones are to be built.

Above all, change agents must be able to *relate to people* at various levels in a system, sometimes in situations of great ambiguity where they are likely to be the recipients of suspicion and hostility, where their words and deeds are likely to be misperceived, distorted, and exploited. Therefore, prior skills are most crucial in the areas of *human relations* and *communicating*. The training itself may provide a number of new skills in these areas but the trainee will probably need to show some skills in this area before training begins. At the most basic level, he must be able to read, write, listen, and talk with above-average proficiency, and he must be able to do so in a variety of situations with a variety of materials and styles; he probably needs to be able to communicate effectively both orally and in writing to people of varying status. These skills are not so common. Most of us have some difficulty communicating and relating to people of very high or very low station. The ideal change agent, on the other hand, is not fazed by power and prestige, his own or anyone else's; he can talk down or up as person-to-person.

Along with relating and communicating skills is likely to come some evidence of leadership ability. The change agent, because he moves in an ambiguous, confusing, and somewhat disorganized social space, must himself be an organizer; he must be able to put people together in teams to work on problems. Some sign of this organizational and leadership ability should be evident in the candidate's background.

C. Outcomes Expected of Trainees

The program plan should specify how the trainee will be different after training than before training. Broadly, there are three ways he can change:

1. he can have new or changed *attitudes and values*
2. he can have new or changed *knowledge*
3. he can have new or changed *skills*

Depending on the goals of the training, these outcomes may be specified *only* in terms of attitudes or only in terms of behaviors or knowledge acquired. However, most programs will have a number of expected outcomes in all three categories. It is especially important that outcomes be directly related to the definition and rationale statement for the role (#1 above) and that they build realistically on the trainees' probable qualifications at the point of entry (#2 above).

What are the desirable outcomes of training for "change agents?" Chapter I of this manual lists a number of facts and theories about the change process that might be relevant. Several of the major books in which change process or change agent concepts are explained or discussed could also serve as a basis for beginning to derive a list of outcomes. Whichever source we draw on, we should, ideally, design a change agent training program which aims at making trainees into *masters of the change process.* This mastery might be exhibited in any or all of the following ways:

1. attitudes and values relevant to the change process
2. interest and involvement in change processes
3. knowledge and understanding of the change process
4. understanding and skill in *how to gain further* knowledge of the change process
5. skills in carrying out change projects and consultations from initiation through installation phases
6. skills in informing, inspiring, and training others with respect to changing and the change process.
7. understanding and skill in analyzing and evaluating change processes

Note that in the above list, we have added growth and self-renewal of the change agent himself (#4) and diffusion of the change process (#6) as important skill areas. We feel that any good training design should speak to these issues specifically.

The sessions of the Michigan Conference on Change Agent Training produced many ideas about desirable outcomes of training programs. The following list, though not complete or exhaustive in any sense, reflects some of these discussions:

1. The Change Agent Should Have These Attitudes and Values:

Primary concern for benefit of the ultimate user (usually students and communities in the case of education).

Primary concern for benefit of society as a whole.

Respect for strongly-held values of others.

Belief that change should provide the greatest good to the greatest number.

Belief that changees have a need and a right to understand why changes are being made (rationale) and to participate in choosing among alternative change means and ends.

A strong sense of his own identity and his own power to help others.

A strong concern for helping without hurting, for helping with minimum jeopardy to the long- or short-term well-being of society as a whole and/or specific individuals within it.

Respect for existing institutions as reflections of legitimate concerns of people for life space boundaries, security, and extension of identity beyond the solitary self.

2. The change agent should know these things:

That individuals, groups, and societies are open inter-relating systems.

How his role fits into a larger social context of change.

Alternative conceptions of his own role now and his potential role in the future.

How others will see his role.

The range of human needs, their inter-relationships and probable priority ranking at different stages in the life cycle.

The resource universe and the means of access to it.

The value bases of different subsystems in the macrosystem of education.

The motivational bases of different subsystems in the macrosystem.

Why people and systems change and resist change.

How people and systems change and resist change.

The knowledge, attitudes, and skills required of a change agent.

The knowledge, attitudes, and skills required of an effective user of resources.

3. The change agent should possess these skills:

How to build and maintain change project relationships with others.

How to bring people to a conception of their priority needs in relation to priority needs of others.

How to resolve misunderstandings and conflicts.

How to build value bridges.

How to convey to others a feeling of power to bring about change.

How to build collaborative teams for change.

How to organize and execute successful change projects (e.g., Stage I-VI of A GUIDE TO INNOVATION).

How to convey to others the knowledge, values, and skills he possesses.

How to bring people to a realization of their own resource-giving potential.

How to expand people's openness to use of resources, internal and external.

How to expand awareness of the resource universe.

How to work collaboratively (synergistically) with other resource systems.

How to relate effectively to powerful individuals and groups.

How to relate effectively to individuals and groups who have a strong sense of powerlessness.

How to make systemic diagnoses of client systems and how to generate self-diagnosis by clients.

Even these lists are probably too general to constitute behaviorally specific outcomes, but they may at least point the direction in which the program planner should go. No one actual program would be able to include all the desirable attributes of an ideal change agent as outcomes. However, it is good policy to start by generating a very large number of possible outcomes and then to rate each in priority terms, perhaps arriving at two final lists of (a) minimal outcomes expected, and (b) maximal outcomes hoped for. The latter list would provide a useful framework or checklist for subsequent evaluation of trainee's performance. Some graduates would presumably move by personal preference and ability toward one set of outcomes, while others would move toward a different set. A very large and comprehensive list provides a means for tracing these alternative paths, no one of which is necessarily superior to another.

D. Ways to Provide Training to Achieve Outcomes

In Chapter III, we provided a partial listing of principles of training design that might guide the development of an actual program. The design itself should incorporate most such principles along with specifications of:

1. the training experiences to be arranged;
2. the materials which need to be purchased, written, compiled, or developed to be given to trainees with training;
3. the timing and sequencing of training sessions; and
4. the setting(s) in which the training is to take place.

Of the many ideas about training activities advanced during the Michigan Conference, a number were incorporated in the Task Force Reports (see Part Two), but, for some readers, a listing of the more salient and generally favored elements may be useful. Twenty-six program features are provided below in the form of propositional statements. Each is followed by a series of numbers which refer to the 15 principles of Chapter III. Although the two lists are somewhat redundant, this second set of statements tries to be more specific and refers to the training procedures used, rather than to the design of the program as a whole.

Features that should be incorporated in the training	Rationale (from Chap. III*)
1. Knowledge inputs should be matched with behavioral. Behavioral inputs should be matched with knowledge.	2, 4, 8

2. Trainees should have experiences which integrate all their knowledge and skill learnings.
e.g., a) case study reading and analysis
  b) case simulation
  c) case expectation and direct experience
  d) actual case analysis and reporting
	13, 14

3. Trainees should simulate experience of their future "role set" (see page 64).	8, 14
4. Variety of case materials and activities should match variety of experience in roles.	8, 14
5. Training should be rewarding at all levels.	5
6. Training should build sequentially and logically on itself.	1, 8
7. Training should be non-terminal (mechanisms for continuing education should be built in).	7, 8, 10, 14
8. Training events should be extended over time in work experience to allow integration into everyday life.	10, 13, 14, 15
9. Trainees should be trainers to each other.	10, 11, 12, 13, 14

---

*The principles reviewed in Chapter III were as follows:

1. Structure	6. In-Process Evaluation and Feedback	11. Redundancy
2. Relevance		12. Synergy
3. Specificity	7. Openness and Flexibility	13. Psychological whole-ness
4. Generality	8. Linkage	
5. Reinforcement	9. Involvement	14. Transferability
	10. Cost-Effectivensss	15. Compatibility

Features that should be incorporated in the training	Rationale (from Chap. III*)
10. Trainees should be self-analysts and evaluators.	2, 6
11. Trainees should be contributors to research and development on their role.	2, 6, 7
12. Trainees should become a social system.	5, 8, 9
13. Trainees should participate in design of own training.	2, 7
14. Training should always include knowledge and skills in acquiring more such training.	8, 10, 14
15. Training should cover all expected outcomes.	1, 2, 3
16. Training should lead to self-actualiztion of trainee.	4, 5, 9, 15
17. Training should lead to feeling of accomplishment by trainee.	5
18. Training should lead to enhanced sense of identity of trainee.	2, 5, 9, 14
19. Training should lead to greater desire to learn.	9, 10, 14
20. Training should lead to greater understanding and concern for the human condition.	2, 8, 9
21. Understanding of installation problem should be included in training.	1, 10, 14, 15
22. Understanding of rationale for role and larger social context should be included in training.	1, 2, 3, 4
23. How to create or acquire role support materials (handbooks, guides, reference, diagnostic, self-evaluation tools, procedures) should be included in training.	8, 14
24. Understanding and skill in explaining role to others should be included in training.	8, 11, 14

*The principles reviewed in Chapter III were as follows:
1. Structure
2. Relevance
3. Specificity
4. Generality
5. Reinforcement
6. In-Process Evaluation and Feedback
7. Openness and Flexibility
8. Linkage
9. Involvement
10. Cost-Effectiveness
11. Redundancy
12. Synergy
13. Psychological wholeness
14. Transferability
15. Compatibility

25. Understanding and skill in handling those threatened by and/or attacking the role should be built into training.

    5, 14

26. Training should lead to social visibility and public recognition of achievement and qualification (degree, certificate, title).

    5, 9, 14

E. Ways to Set the Role in an Institutional Context: Installation

A role training program must make concrete provisions for returning the graduate to a home setting and insuring his placement and support in the new role over time. For a new role of "change agent," shrouded in ambiguity and threat for many in the home organization, the installation task is both very difficult and very necessary.

Conditions Which Must be Met in the Installation Design

An installation design must include provision for at least six conditions:

1. maintenance and reinforcement of the *identity* of the graduate as a *change agent.*
2. fundamental *security* for role maintenance in terms of financial, psychological, social and legal support over time.
3. specified *limits* on role tasks and expectations to prevent overload or exploitation.
4. *freedom* to perform in the role in a way compatible with personal needs and aspirations of the graduate, including mobility and a chance to experiment with various facets of the role without the threat of premature interference or punishment for failure.
5. *rewards to the change agent* for being a change agent.
6. *rewards to the role set* for accepting the graduate as a change agent.

There are a number of ways in which these six principles can be incorporated in an installation program. The seven types of arrangements listed below could be used in various combinations depending upon the opportunities provided by the situation, the program sponsor, and the goals of the program.

Arrangements for Installation

1. A Contract With the Home Organization

It is sometimes possible and usually advisable to spell out a written contract with the agency which will be the home of the newly trained change agent. This contract should specify the minimal conditions for role viability in economic and legal terms. A contract never can guarantee success of the new role but it can help provide fundamental security and legitimacy to the role holder. It serves as a last line of defense in a showdown and may also help to keep the role definition clear and clean in the eyes of the change agent and the organization leadership. Nevertheless, a contract should not be so tightly written that it limits the life space of the change agent. It should also include some sort of escape clause for both parties in the event that the situation should prove too difficult.

2. Preparation of the Role Holder

As noted previously, the training experience itself should include much consideration of what will happen when the graduate returns to the work situation. Of particular importance is providing training in how to continue self-training. A program could also include arrangements for testing, qualifying, and certifying graduates. These formal arrangements may help to legitimize the graduate and shield him initially from suspicions of incompetence. Lastly, it may be important to give program graduates material supports in the form of specially prepared notebooks, handbooks, and reference tools relevant to the type of change agent role they will be filling. If such materials are available, they serve to reinforce identity, to aid in continuing study and practice in the role, and to show to the change agent and others that he is indeed a specialist with special knowledge and expertise on the process of change.

3. Preparation of the Role Set

When a new person comes into an organization with a new title and a new job to do, he sets off tremors of concern among the others in the organization with whom he is functionally related. They will be asking themselves questions such as: "Will he have power over me?" "Will he interfere with my work?" "Will he take over responsibilities that I had before he came?" "Was he brought in because the boss thought I was inadequate?"

There is probably nothing that can be done which will completely eliminate all these questions. The members of a role set only learn to accept a new role over time; after extended interactions, they will come to realize from experience that the person is more helpful than harmful to them and their work.

Nevertheless, a training designer should at least consider the possibility of preparing the members of the role set to receive the graduate. This preparation could come in the form of advance information or even some sort of training if role set members are accessible and the training budget is adequate. Information should be explicit and aimed at answering the probable concerns of the role set. Role set members might be shown some of the training materials, the training design, and the installation contract, if any. They should also be given clear signals from the organization leadership that the new role is endorsed and sanctioned at the highest level *and* that the concerns of the other members of the organization will be heeded. Ideally, members of the role set should be given an opportunity to express their concerns openly to the leadership, to the graduate, and to the training staff. This information is helpful not only for its cathartic effects but also because it can provide guidance on redesign of the program, adaptation required by the graduate, and the types of support behavior that the leaders will have to provide.

4. Building a Role Maintenance Team

Role installation has to be a cooperative effort on the part of a number of people inside and outside the receiving organization. It is usually desirable, therefore, to have the graduate create a small committee of individuals to whom he can report periodically to discuss his progress and who can provide advice on problems, new directions, and ways to adapt his role to the system. Such a team might include one or two colleagues of equal status, someone of senior or leadership status, and someone from outside (e.g., another graduate, a trainer, or some other "expert").

Such a team would serve to enhance and clarify self-identity and function. It would also help to involve the system in recognition and utilization of the role.

5. Role Monitoring and Adjustment Mechanisms

The above suggestion of a "maintenance team" might fall into a broader category of monitoring and adjustment of the role. Much of this monitoring and adjustment can be accomplished by the role holder, himself, if he is self-critical, sensitive, and secure. However, the training program should help him by giving him tools for monitoring his own performance and for assessing the reactions of others toward him (e.g., the leadership, subordinates, the role set, and clients).

Outside evaluation with feedback to the role holder is an alternative approach. It has the advantage of offering objective "quality control" data to the program sponsor, but the disadvantage to the role holder of surveillance with the implication that he may sometimes be seen as incompetent or inadequate to his task. Outside evaluation ought to be useful to the change agent, himself. Therefore, he should have something to say about what goes into it and who gets it.

6. Creating Role Partnerships

A training program should establish some sort of "buddy system" for graduates. One way to do this is to insist on at least two candidates from each home organization who can go through all the training experiences together. If this is not possible, then it is at least desirable to put trainees together in pairs or trios which communicate and share problems regularly over time after training has ceased.

While they are in training, these pairs or trios should practice communication with each other and should build *expectations* of future continuing contacts.

7. Building a Role Reference Group

A major outcome of a successful training program is a group of people who now have a shared experience and to some degree a shared identity, but typically this shared identity dissipates rapidly as the trainees return home. The design of change agent training should anticipate this problem and incorporate features which forestall it. The "buddy system" mentioned above helps to do this, but there are other mechanisms which may be employed as well, e.g., reunions, a newsletter which circulates among all graduates and to which all contribute, annual events and joint enterprises of various sorts; all these contribute to a continuing sense of membership in a special group with a special identity and a special mission.

F. Criteria for Program Success

A program can be considered "successful" if it has provided benefits to clients or to the society which outweigh the costs of the training. In practice, however, we are rarely able to measure such benefits, while the costs are sometimes all too evident. Nevertheless, there are several levels of operational criteria which can be applied to indicate some sort of "success."

At the lowest level we can measure trainer and trainee satisfaction with the training, itself. At a somewhat more rigorous level we can acquire some measure of the trainees' *actual* attitudes, knowledge, and skills at various times subsequent to training. These measures should, of course, reflect the expected outcomes (see Section C, above) on a point-for-point basis. Either the minimal or the maximal attitudes, behaviors, and skills could be used as performance criteria.

At an even more rigorous level we could examine the behavior of the trainee *in the role* over time: Is the trainee able to gain acceptance from his role set? Is he able to develop projects and programs as anticipated in the training program "outcomes?" Is he able to hold his job? Can others explain what he is doing?

At an even higher level we could look for evidence of transfer of attitudes, knowledge, or skills from the trainee to others. For example, are others in the client system learning about the change process? Are they becoming more competent in carrying out change or managing innovations? Is the client system as a whole developing a self-changing and growth capacity?

Finally, at the highest level we can ask the ultimate question: Does this training, role behavior, and transfer of attitudes, knowledge, and skill do anybody any good? Is the world better for it in some way? In a most limited sense, the world is better if the trainee, the role set, the client system or the society is "satisfied." Usually, however, we try to look for harder evidence than this: Is the client system more productive? Have costs been reduced? Has efficiency been increased? Is the total system functioning "better" in some way? Have we added measurably or significantly to the life, liberties, happiness, or self-actualization of people?

It should be evident from the foregoing discussion that a wide range of success criteria are possible, some more impressive than others, perhaps. The most important points to remember, however, are the following:

1. think through, choose, and specify the criteria you want to use; and
2. try to fit the criteria to the role definition (Section A), the outcomes expected (Section C), and the training provided (Section D).

G. Evaluation Processes for a Training Program

If possible, a training design should include a formal and specified procedure for evaluation. Such evaluation is important and useful in a number of ways. First, it requires program developers and trainers to plan and think clearly about what they want to achieve and how they can do it. Second, it provides information to sponsors and policy planners on whether or not such programs should be continued, repeated, terminated or modified. Thirdly, if it is so designed that the trainer can receive feedback during training, it can allow for in-process program improvement. Finally, it can give the trainee feedback and reinforcement on his own behavior.

Four Evaluation Stages: Context, Input, Process, Product

Daniel Stufflebeam and his associates at Ohio State University advocate a system analytic view of evaluation. They note that any type of programmatic activity can be analyzed in four ways: first, the "context," i.e., the environment or the problem setting in which the program is developed and for which it presumably is to be relevant; second, the "input," meaning the resources, plans, and people who go into the program; third, the "process," i.e., the actual activities that go on in the program, the ways in which the people and resources interact and are transformed; and finally, the "product:" the outcomes, consequences, and impacts on the environment that ensue from the activity.

In a program to train change agents, these four evaluation stages might be specified as follows:

1. *Context Evaluation:* an assessment of the current educational scene including surveys or estimates of needs for change, availability of innovations, availability of manpower in various categories, current levels of proficiency in change process, and the needs for new roles, new skills, etc. The context evaluation answers the overall question: Is there a need for this sort of training?

2. *Input Evaluation:* an accounting of the trainers and trainees who enter the program, the characteristics of the training plan, the financial resources budgeted and provided, and the provisions made in advance for installation. The input evaluation should be designed to answer the questions: Is this type of training feasible? Are the various conditions for program success present? Have we done a good job of planning, designing, funding, staffing, and recruiting?

3. *Process Evaluation:* a day-by-day monitoring and analysis of the training activities and subsequent installation efforts. This phase of evaluation answers the questions: Did the program proceed as planned? What actually did happen during training and during installation?

4. *Product Evaluation:* the impact of the program on the trainees, the client systems, the society. This last phase is probably what many people think of as "evaluation." What was the end result? Which of the anticipated or hoped for outcomes (see Section C) were actually achieved?

Principles of Evaluation Procedure

Regardless of the stage, evaluation for a training program should ideally meet the following ground rules:

1. It should be designed and reported as relevant feedback to some speci-

fied individuals and/or groups (trainers, trainees, program designers, policy makers, funders, users, etc.). An evaluation which is only filed away is a waste of time and money for everyone.

2. It should be cost-beneficial; if it costs more than the program itself and ties up many man hours for staff and trainees, then it should be reexamined.*

3. It should be relevant to the rationale, intended outcomes, and success criteria of the program.

4. It should allow comparative judgments leading to rational decision choices (e.g., "program X" produces more learning than "program Y," or "program X produces more learning than no program at all").

5. It should represent meaningful input to research, development, diffusion, and utilization (i.e., it should be multi-purpose).

Measurement Techniques

There is probably little that we could or should add to what may be found in various texts on data gathering in the social sciences. It is important to stress the great variety of measures available and possible and the dangers of too much reliance on any one of them.

It should also be stressed that methods should be simple to administer, use and explain. Neither trainee nor trainer will have much patience for evaluations which are not relevant and which don't make sense to them. This applies also to the technique of "log" keeping or record keeping in the home setting. This sort of information, *if it can be collected,* is potentially very useful, but the graduate may not see it that way if it has not been adequately explained to him, if he has not had practice in doing it, and if he has not seen how it can be used to help him.

Another measurement issue in evaluation is "unobtrusiveness," i.e., how much is the subject aware that he is being evaluated. Obviously, self-ratings, paper-pencil tools, and interviews are highly "obtrusive." This is good in the sense that the trainee is put on notice that he is expected to perform well in the role; he is also given cues as to how he should perform. On the other hand, obtrusive measures are highly vulnerable to biasing effects; trainees will do anything or say anything they can to make themselves look good, short of outright lies, if they feel that their livelihood is at stake. Evaluation should be non-threatening and objective at the same time. There is probably no way to reach this goal unless (1) data are anonymous to everyone except the trainee, or (2) they are collected without the knowledge of the trainee. The latter is clearly unethical if the information *can be* used to the detriment of the trainee at any future time.

---

*On the other hand, if the primary purposes of the project are research or development on training this may be appropriate.

Another step which is sometimes taken to make evaluation more objective is to segregate evaluators from trainers and trainees. This approach also has pitfalls in that evaluators may not be involved or identified adequately enough with the program to understand its objectives and how results are manifested. In this case, they would not be able to collect relevant and meaningful data. A second problem is the social *distance* created between evaluators, trainers, and trainees which makes later utilization of results more difficult. Hence, even if an evaluation team is hired or contracted separately, it should work to develop a trust relationship with the trainers and trainees as a first order of business.

H. Utilization of Evaluation

A complete program design might or might not include an evaluation procedure. If it does, it should also include some indication of how the evaluation will be used once it is made: possible audiences for the information, how it might be transmitted to them, and what they might do with it.

There are at least seven primary audiences for evaluations of training programs:

1. the program developers: for redesign of the program or future programs;
2. the trainers: so they can do a better job now or in their next training assignment;
3. the trainees: so they can understand the experience more fully, make up for deficiencies and confirm or disconfirm subjective feelings about the value of the program;
4. the program sponsor and potential sponsors of future programs: so they can decide whether their resources are well spent and whether they should continue sponsoring similar programs;
5. potential recruits to training in future programs;
6. members, especially leaders, of the organizations which host the change agents (i.e., as certification that the change agent is what he is purported to be);
7. researchers and developers who are concerned with the change process, training, and role development.

How evaluative information is conveyed to these audiences will depend upon the audience to some extent. As a minimum, there should be a research report which gives the basic facts in summary form. Such a report would probably have most meaning for those closest to the experience (trainers, trainees, program developers), or those most steeped in methodology and most able to absorb research "reports" (researchers and developers).

For other audiences there should also be simpler summary documents, well illustrated, with a minimum of extensive tabular presentations and with a minimum of specialized or technical language.

Beyond printed media, the plan might include presentations at professional meetings, special conferences, and special issues of appropriate journals and magazines.

Whatever the form of these dissemination efforts, they should include well-reasoned attempts to *derive action implications* for the audience toward which they are directed.

PART TWO

ALTERNATIVE TRAINING MODELS

INTRODUCTION

The Michigan Conference on Change Agent Training produced many ideas about change and about training during its first two days. These ideas have been incorporated in much that has been said in Part One. However, the conference came to a focus in the third day on the task of creating alternative models of training for different concepts of "change agent." Members of the conference spent some time forming into task groups according to their personal views of what should be trained for at what level and in what way. The potential alternatives are, of course, staggering and those that were chosen do not represent any systematic attempt to cover all possibilities. In some cases, the "teams" turned out to be individuals who wanted to work alone to develop one concept; in other cases, they were pairs or small groups.

One task force report was not a change agent training program as such, but was, rather, a descriptive paper designed to acquaint change agents in education with the use of power and dissemination functions of educational professional associations so that these might be utilized to effect change. This report is presented in the Appendix.

The other ten task force reports which were produced may be grouped into four general categories of training programs: 1) programs to train school systems to develop a self-renewal capacity, 2) programs for change agent linkage of school systems to resources, 3) programs to effect political and structural changes in school systems, and 4) programs to improve the effectiveness of other educational agencies. In addition to these ten reports, we have developed one model in much greater detail for training change agents in state education agencies. This is included as a sample of what each task force report might look like if fully developed. The orientation of each of these models is summarized in the table which follows.

As this table indicates, some of the reports developed programs to train change agents from outside the client system, while others developed programs designed to train some or all of the members of the client system to act on a permanent basis as their own change agents. Two reports (Glaser and Goodson; Towne) combined these two orientations.

For those programs which conceived the role of the change agent to be an outside resource, the agent is sometimes described as acting in a general knowledge linker role, while at other times he is described as having a more specialized mission.

The relationship of the agent with the client varied from one report to another. One report (Tye) considered the role to be of a temporary nature, with the change agent moving on to other school systems once his mission was accomplished. Two reports (Glaser and Goodson; Towne) considered

ORIENTATIONS OF THE TASK FORCE REPORTS

TASK FORCE REPORT	TRAINING FOR OUTSIDE CHANGE AGENT			TRAINING FOR CLIENT SYSTEM PERSONNEL		SCHOOL SYSTEM IS CLIENT		OTHER SYSTEM IS CLIENT
	Agent as general knowledge linker	Agent has specialized role	Agent-client relationship	All members of client system	Special group in client system	School system as a whole	Special group within school	
Chapter V: Programs to train school systems to develop a self-renewal capacity								
A. The School-Community Resource Team -Glaser & Goodson	X RUS		temporary: on call		X S-C team	X		X community
B. The Knowledge Utilization Function/Role -Towne	X RUS		temporary: on call	X		X		
C. Minimal Training System for Self-Renewing Schools -Hood, et al.				X		X		
D. Integrated Model of Counselor Behavior -Walz, et al.					X counselors	X		
Chapter VI: Programs for change agent linkage of school systems to resources								
A. The Knowledge Utilization Specialist Team and Leader -Wolf	X KUS team & leader		permanent: regional service				X administration	X trainers of educ. practitioners
B. Teacher Trainers -Ellis, et al.	X-teacher trainers		permanent: reg. serv.				X teachers	

Chapter VII: Programs to effect political and structural changes in school systems	A. The Political Linkage Agent -Tye	X PLA	temporary			X	
	B. Change Through Crisis -Chesler, et al.				X-ADORAG; social architect	X	
Chapter VIII: Programs to improve the effectiveness of other educational agencies	A. Macrosystems Model -Benne, et al.	X interface	permanent				X-USOE & State Depts.Educ.
	B. "Delivery" Dilemma of State Departments of Education -Millgate & Lippitt			X			X State Depts. of Education
Chapter IX: Sample Model of a fully developed training design	Change Agent Training for State Education Agencies (SEACAT) -Havelock				X-general process consultant		X state ed. agencies

that the initial relationship of the change agent with his client would be intensive, but that once the client system had received training and guidance in managing change it could take over most of the knowledge utilization functions for itself. The change agent would remain available but would be called in only in complex change situations. Two reports (Wolf; Ellis, et al.) conceived of the change agents as permanently serving school systems within a specified region but without primary ties to any one client system. These agents would be housed in the State Departments of Education and would be responsible to them rather than to the client systems. Another report (Benne, et al.) designed the change agent role as a permanent interface between two systems which interact on a regular basis.

Most reports were concerned with situations in which the school system or certain groups within the school were the clients. Only two task force reports (Benne, et al.; Millgate and Lippitt) were concerned exclusively with other educational agencies as the direct clients. Like the Millgate and Lippitt model, our SEACAT model is also concerned with the State Education Agency as the direct client. Our model resembles the Millgate and Lippitt model in that it calls for the training of personnel from within the State Education Agency for the purpose of improving the internal capacity of that agency to carry out the knowledge utilization process. Unlike the Millgate and Lippitt model, we propose to train only one, or preferably two, members of each agency. These individuals will then perform as general process consultants within their agency on a permanent basis. It is hoped, however, that these trainees will be able to transmit much of their learning experience to other members of the agency so that all members will work in concert to increase knowledge utilization within the agency and throughout the state system.

Framework of the Papers

All task force design teams were asked to formulate their models to correspond roughly to an outline of seven key design elements:

1. "define the change role and provide a rationale"
2. "preconditions for selection and training"
3. "outputs from training: knowledge and skills"
4. "ways to provide required training (e.g., timing, scheduling, types of materials, types of experiences)"
5. "criteria for success in the role"
6. "evaluation process," and
7. "how to set the role in an institutional context."

Note that these seven categories correspond to the "framework" analysis presented in Chapter IV. However, the conference did not have the benefit of that sort of detailed analysis of components and many participants chose not to follow the entire outline in a point-for-point fashion.

V

SELF-RENEWAL WITHIN THE SCHOOL SYSTEM

Four of the task force reports fall in the category of training programs which are designed to improve the capacity of the school system to diagnose its own problems and to utilize resources to meet the needs and realize the potential of the system itself and all the individuals within it. All of these models have the school system as the primary client, and all of them propose the training of all or some of the school personnel to act as permanent change agents within the system. Two of them also propose the training of an outside change agent to assist during the phase of system training. Table V.1 indicates the focus and goals of each of these programs in brief outline form.

The first two papers in this group (Glaser and Goodson; Towne) are similar in that they call for the training of a Research Utilization Specialist (RUS) who will help the client school system in its attempt to develop skills and mechanisms for the planning and management of change programs. The role of the RUS is in both cases considered to be a temporary one, with the agent moving on to other client systems once the original client has established a certain level of proficiency. The agent is, however, to remain available for assistance to the client system in future complex change situations. Both cases also call for the training of members of the client system but, whereas the Towne model suggests the training of all members of the school system, the Glaser-Goodson report suggests the training of a team of key school personnel and community leaders to manage future change programs. In both models the training of the change agent and client personnel is designed to take place concurrently and collaboratively after an initial intensive training program for the RUS.

The role of the RUS and the outputs of training which are suggested in the two papers have a somewhat different emphasis, however. The Glaser-Goodson report calls for a broad view of the role of the RUS as a catalyst, process helper, knowledge linker and assistant to the client in adaptation and implementation of solutions. Therefore, in addition to training in systems performance indicators and the planning and management of change processes, the need for an understanding of areas such as the dynamics of social systems, human motivation, and value considerations is also stressed.

TABLE V.1
PROGRAMS TO TRAIN SCHOOL SYSTEMS TO DEVELOP
A SELF-RENEWAL CAPACITY

REPORT	CLIENT	GOAL OF TRAINING MODEL	CHANGE AGENT ROLE
A. The School-Community Resource Team -Glaser & Goodson	A School-Community System	Link research findings with users in school and community. Train a school-community resource team (S-C Team) and a Research Utilization Specialist (RUS).	*RUS* 1. Catalyst 2. Process helper 3. Knowledge linker 4. Adaptation-implementation helper *S-C Team* 1. Self-help in planning and managing change.
B. The Knowledge Utilization Function/Role -Towne	Users of educational knowledge - schools or individuals.	Train all educational personnel in knowledge utilization. Train a Research Utilization Specialist (RUS) to help in complex change processes.	*RUS* 1. Interface between resources and user. 2. Help client in information retrieval and utilization. *All Educational Personnel* 1. Information retrieval and utilization.
C. Minimal Training System for Self-Renewing Schools -Hood, et al.	The School	A rational approach to self-renewal of schools through Planning, Programming and Management (P,P&M).	*All School Personnel* Each staff member has an allocated function; all functions together comprise the P,P&M process.
D. Integrated Model of Counselor Behavior -Walz, et al.	Schools and students	Develop a model of counselor behavior which will utilize resources to help each person or institute to realize its full potential.	*Counselor* 1. System diagnosis 2. Performance appraisal 3. Out-reach to clients 4. Advocate/initiate changes 5. Environmental intervention 6. Linkage with resources 7. Evaluation

In contrast, the Towne model describes the role of the RUS to be primarily that of a knowledge linker between the client system and available resources. The model concentrates on training in seven basic elements of the process of knowledge retrieval and utilization, from awareness of knowledge resources to translation of research implications into a form usable by the client. Interaction with the client system to achieve implementation of appropriate solutions is called for, but this is subordinate to the other functions of knowledge utilization.

However, the Towne report goes further than the Glaser-Goodson report in proposing that ultimately all educational personnel should be trained in knowledge utilization as part of their pre-service education. The proposed program for the training of an RUS and the in-service training of school personnel is necessitated by the fact that present pre-service educational programs do not include training in knowledge utilization. This paper therefore also describes a pre-service training program to fill this gap. Such a program would include formal courses in knowledge utilization and the addition of experiences in information utilization within existing courses.

The model put forth by Hood, et al. does not involve the training of an outside change agent but focuses instead on the training of all school personnel. The goal of this model is the achievement of a self-renewal capacity of school systems through a rational process of Planning, Programming and Management (P,P&M). It calls for a formal training program to provide all school personnel with an orientation to this process. The process itself is described as being comprised of eight basic functions which start with the assessment of needs and end with installation and evaluation of appropriate solutions. Rather than all personnel receiving training in each of the eight functions, this model proposes that the functions should be allocated among the staff and that in-depth, on-the-job training should be provided for each individual only in his allocated function.

The training model includes completely validated packages which allow self-installation of the training program by an interested school system. The program would contain packages for orientation, skills training, and implementation of the initial organizational restructuring for allocation of functions. The program would also provide consultant support for installation and implementation of the training packages.

Walz, et al. also proposed a training program for school personnel which focuses on the training of *counselors* in various settings. It is felt that the counselor is especially suited to occupying the role of educational change agent since his ultimate goal is to help all students, and the system, to meet their full potential. In order to meet future needs, however, this task force developed the concept of an integrated model of counselor behavior. The specific behaviors which would be included in the integrated model would be based on a comprehensive search of student developmental needs and of available resources on the impact of planned intervention on these needs. It is anticipated that, in his new role, the counselor would have broadened responsibilities to conduct complete system and individual diagnoses, conduct performance appraisals, reach out to potential client populations, advocate and initiate client changes, intervene in client environment when necessary, provide linkage with resources, and conduct evaluations of his own role performance. The training program would be developed on a flexible basis to meet the needs of different counselors in different settings. It would be multiple-leveled and would be unitized and packaged for either pre-service or in-service use.

A. Training the School-Community Resource Team*

Context

Billions of dollars a year in public funds are spent in support of research, and nearly 120 million is yearly invested in educational research. A fair number of projects or studies have yielded seemingly promising findings for the improvement of educational practice -- if one can even half-believe the authors of the final reports on these studies. Yet, reading achievement and many other kinds of hoped-for educational progress by students is low. Congress, and taxpayers in general, are questioning the value of financing educational research if the seemingly valuable and applicable findings are not utilized by our school systems for the improvement of educational practice.

The concept of the educational "change agent" or "research utilization specialist" which will be presented here is one in which the agent links promising research findings with potential users in a school system and with potential users in other related community facilities. Since the school deals with only a portion of a student's interests, activities, or problems, the *research utilization specialist* can work most effectively if he has entree in, and is in close contact with, the various facilities, groups, and services which, together with the school, comprise "the community." Thus, his client will be a "school-community system" which will include interrelated social institutions such as social and recreational service agencies and police, as well as the school.

Since any program of change is most likely to be successful if those undergoing the change are involved in its planning and implementation, the total training program should involve not only the prospective change agent but also key people in the school-community system which he will serve. Thus, the local personnel trained in this program will constitute a

---

*Drafted by Edward Glaser and Max Goodson; edited by Mary C. Havelock.

school-community resource team which will continue to function as the planner and manager of change in its system after the training program has terminated and the services of the *research utilization specialist* are no longer available.

The questions which must be answered, then, are: What is the most effective role for the *research utilization specialist?* Who should be trained to serve in this capacity? How should he be trained? And how can his training be coordinated with the training of the school-community resource team?

1. The Role of the Research Utilization Specialist

Because each school-community system has its own individual problems and characteristics, the change agent cannot simply present to his client an innovation which has worked well some other place and assume that it will be happily adopted here -- or that it would be beneficial if it were adopted. Therefore, the change agent will not act merely as a transmitter of knowledge; rather, his basic objective will be to help his school-community system to adapt and adopt for its own use the knowledge and innovations which are most appropriate for it.

To meet this objective, the research utilization specialist will serve initially as a *catalyst, resource person* and *occasional "gadfly"* in stimulating the school-community system to work out and implement a change program designed to best suit its own needs. The first step in this process will be a self-examination and appraisal by the clients with the help of the change agent. As a result of this effort, they should then begin to hammer out the specifications of characteristics of optimal outcomes for the system. Next, the change agent must help his client to think through performance measures, that is, to define system goals in terms of reasonable individual action. Performance rewards must also be defined to assure that the goals outlined by key personnel will be acceptable to all individuals involved in the change program. Throughout this planning process, the change agent must also be ready to provide help in conflict resolution and problem-solving and to work out any needed collaborative arrangements among the interrelated community systems.

Once the school-community resource team has identified its urgent problems and needs and has agreed upon outcome specifications and goals, it will then be ready to begin the process of identifying solutions for those problems. The role of the change agent at this point will be to serve as a *knowledge linker,* bringing his clients and their problems together with his fund of information about new knowledge and knowledge resources in education. He will draw upon the promising research and demonstration findings distilled and made accessible by the Educational Resource Information Centers (ERIC) and upon any additional technical assistance available, and he will select from these the knowledge and innovations which are relevant to the problem at hand. The change agent can then help his clients to organize and reformulate such knowledge into a range of alternative solution possibilities from which the most promising solutions can be selected for installation into the school-community system.

During the program, the change agent is likely to encounter a minimum amount of hostility and skepticism from his clients if he is seen as serving the school-community system's own *self-interest*. The fact that the members of the school-community system play a very active role in shaping the change program will help to insure not only that they will accept and work cooperatively with the change agent but also that the changes which are finally made will be truly beneficial and will be accepted by the community as a whole. Furthermore, the training received by the members of the school-community resource team during the change program will provide them with the capability of continually re-examining their own system and engaging in further problem-solving efforts on a collaborative basis. To a great extent, the system will be able to function independently in the future, calling upon the services of a research utilization specialist only for the specific purpose of *knowledge linkage* -- or when particularly difficult or complex problems arise. Thus, training resources would basically be tied up in each particular school-community system only for the period of time designated for the training program.

2. Selection for Training

Selection of a school-community system to participate in the training program should be principally on a volunteer basis, since the primary consideration in the selection of a system is its *readiness* for change. The university or training institute which would be conducting the training program would issue invitations to school systems which meet certain prescribed suitability criteria. It is anticipated that one or perhaps two systems would be ready immediately to participate actively in the training program.

Readiness cannot be expressed simply as a willingness to join in the program. A representative group of key personnel from the school and related facilities should agree to participate and must be given enough time and freedom from other responsibilities to allow them to do so. These key personnel, the future school-community resource team, should include the city government manager; police officer; members of the school central office, including social worker, psychologist, curriculum director and guidance personnel; the principal, teachers and students from the school involved.

Initially, a consortium of five school-community systems might be formed that would include the one or two active systems that are ready to participate in the training program and also three or four other systems which are not quite ready to participate. These other school-community systems in the consortium will provide key personnel who will observe the action project and act as consultants, critics and evaluators. As these systems become ready for action, the university or training institute would introduce the training program for additional research utilization specialists as well as for the new school-community teams on an in-service basis, and it would invite additional systems to join the program.

The training institute should also establish some basic criteria for training for the role of research utilization specialist. However, as in the case of selection of the school system for participation, the selection of research utilization specialist trainees should also be principally on a volunteer basis since the primary qualification for training is *readiness*.

There are several categories of individuals who might be eager to volunteer for the training program. Among these would be *consultants* who are interested in learning more about how to serve their client systems through acting as a linking agent between existing knowledge or resources and the needs or problems experienced by the school system in everyday operation. A second source of potential trainees might be *university graduate students* who volunteer for in-service training as knowledge utilization specialists, educational change agents, or community development facilitators. It is also likely that certain *educational researchers* would be interested in learning more about how to link their research with the interests and needs of users (practitioners or teachers, and ultimate consumers, namely, students). Finally, training volunteers might come from the *user* group itself. Teachers and administrators who are interested in improving their own performance might be eager to participate in a program which would provide them with acceptable and meaningful tools for serving that interest.

It is visualized that many of these trainees would assume the role of change agent only part of the time; their in-service training would permit the continuation of their previous roles. It is hoped that by this method they would learn how to optimize the usefulness of their work for the occupants of other role positions.

3. Outputs from Training

Since the trainees will be engaged in learning how to plan and manage change programs, there are certain basic concepts of knowledge which both groups should gain from the training program. These would include, first of all, an understanding of the *dynamics of social systems* and an understanding of *human motivation* and various styles of personal functioning. A second important group of concepts would be those involved in developing *system performance indicators* which would be appropriate for *diagnosis, evaluation,* and providing *feedback* data to be used in further *planning* and *problem-solving* efforts. Concepts that are needed for *planning and managing a change process* are important for all trainees.

The research utilization specialist trainees must have a thorough understanding of the procedures of *research retrieval, analysis* and *selection of knowledge* relevant to solving a particular problem. The school-community resource team should have a general knowledge of these procedures and should know how to judge, for future problem-solving, the point at which they should call on the services of knowledge specialists or other outside sources.

The change agents should, in addition, learn procedures for planning and managing the processes involved in the diffusion of promising R&D (research and development) and E&D project experiences and knowledge to other systems in the consortium beyond the actively involved systems.

Although the content of the knowledge to be gained by the two training groups is similar, it will be put to use in different ways by each group. The change agent will approach his training experience with the objective of learning how to *help others* to develop problem-solving skills, whereas the school-community resource team will be learning techniques of *self-help* in problem-solving. This difference in the basic objectives of the two groups will be reflected in a different, though complementary, set of skills which each group should learn.

The research utilization specialist should, first of all, be skilled at *listening* and helping others to improve their listening skills and attitudes. Secondly, he should be able to help people identify and *diagnose* their own problems and needs and *analyze the system forces* bearing upon those problems and needs. Third, he should be able to serve effectively as a *resource person and linking agent* to bring information about relevant knowledge to his client and to apply coping procedures developed by others with reference to similar problems. Fourth, the change agent must be able to help his clients *develop solutions* from this relevant knowledge. Finally, he should be able to serve as a consultant in solution *implementation,* evaluation, and a cycle of continuous refinements.

The corresponding group of skills which the school-community team should learn from the training program would include: listening effectively; making a force field analysis of their own system and identifying and diagnosing their own problems and needs; developing solutions to these problems; and, finally, the ability to implement these solutions, to evaluate them and to refine them.

In addition to these skills, all trainees, change agents as well as school-community participants, should learn to become aware of *value* considerations. They should be aware of their *own values* and they should be sensitive to *value differences* as well as consensus among participants. The change agent must not make the mistake of thinking that his own values will be irrelevant to his role of helping others; nor should he, on the other hand, make the assumption that his values will be shared by his clients.

One very important outcome of the training program for both groups should be *commitment* on the part of each one to make a sustained effort for self-improvement and for more effective role performance. All trainees should recognize that the need for personal learning, as well as for system change, will continue after the formal training program has ended.

4. Ways to Provide Required Training

The university or training institute which will be providing the training will be responsible for the various aspects of the training project. It will be in charge of selecting the school systems and the trainees and coordinating the training of more research utilization specialists with increasing needs as additional school systems volunteer for active participation. It will also be up to the training institute to design and work out the details of the training program, but certain basic guidelines will be suggested here.

The training program for the change agent and for the school-community system with which he will work may be run concurrently after an initial lead-time training for the agent. Since much of the knowledge and skills needed for running a change project will be called into play in a reasonably predictable sequence over time, the training program for the change agent can be designed to keep him one step ahead of his client. By providing continuous training during the change project time, the trainer will be able to explore with the change agent trainee any special problems which may arise as he deals with his client.

It is suggested that the training of research utilization specialists be designed as a one-year internship or in-service arrangement. The first two weeks would be devoted to intensive orientation including an overview of the basic steps and components involved in planning and managing change and the time-scale of these steps in terms of the one-year program. In the second phase of the orientation, the change agent should be given intensive training in learning the concepts of group dynamics and human motivation and the skills involved in listening effectively. The orientation program should include, finally, material which will familiarize the change agent with the techniques of diagnosis and methods of helping his client make its own system diagnosis. This basic training will give the change agent enough knowledge and skills to establish a satisfactory working relationship with his client upon entry into the system and to begin the first stage of the change process, problem identification.

The remainder of the one-year training program for change agents may be designed on a less intensive basis. Two days of each week should be spent in the field working through the steps of the change process with the school system client. One day each week would be spent back at the training institute or university to continue the detailed study of the change process to keep ahead of the steps being performed in the field. In addition, part of the time spent at the university should be devoted to scrutiny of the program in action and to review discussions about progress being made and problems encountered. The change agent would devote the remaining two days of each week to his on-going job or to his other studies.

The change agent will also receive a further training experience by participating in the formal training program to be given to his client. The training program for the school-community resource team should consist of a formal program which would be coordinated with the efforts of the change agent. The formal program should be designed as a two-day workshop or laboratory training held every four months. The purpose of this workshop would be to bring together this diverse group of individuals and their change agent under circumstances which would allow them to get to know one another in a way they would not have a chance to do in their normal role settings. Knowing each other and learning the interaction pattern of the group members should provide the team with the key to their ability to work together in effective problem-solving ways.

The workshop could be structured around a set of exercises* which might include:

a. Listening exercises.
b. One-way vs. two-way communication.
c. Practice consultation skills in triads.
d. Identification of primary personal interaction style (helper, thinker, fighter); puzzle assembly exercise by groups composed homogeneously regarding styles.
e. Use of instruments of predicting (hunching about) behavior of self and others in a T-group and checking predictions against experience.
f. Use of conflict model vs. consensus model for experiencing conflict as well as collaborative-integrative behavior in a training-laboratory group.
g. Use of Erickson's eight stages of life for self-diagnosis of development

---

*Workshop exercises of the nature which we are suggesting here are being developed and are available in prototype form from such organizations as NTL, R&D Center at Wisconsin, Northwest Regional Lab, CASA (Oregon), and COPED.

stage, insight into effects of these steps as described by teachers who are experienced in various stages and exploration of inter-generation issues.

h. Use of incomplete sentences for promoting analysis and providing statements of concern for consultation and problem-solving, e.g.:

"When I enter a new group I feel _____."

"The worst thing that could happen next year in our community is _____."

"If (such and such a problem) is not solved by (such and such time) _____ is likely to happen."

i. Identification of personal-role problems and organizational problems by reflecting upon reality involving the individual.
j. Selecting problems on priority basis and making a force-field analysis.
k. Locus of decision-making, comparing actual with ideal.

The results of the entire change program will depend greatly on how well the participants can translate the workshop experience into on-the-job behavior. If they are successful at this, they will be well prepared to cooperate with each other and with the research utilization specialist as he leads them through the steps of the process of learning how to determine and meet their own system objectives.

5. *Criteria for Success in the Role*

How successful the RUS is in carrying out his defined role can be judged on the basis of three criteria. First, the school system should meet its own hammered-out program objectives and its own (agreed upon in advance) specifications for an optimal outcome system. Performance criteria will need to include process and time dimensions along which specific controls can be defined.

Second, the RUS should perceive himself as having developed significantly in knowledge, skills and value clarification.

Third, the members of the client system with which the research utilization specialist has worked should rate him as having been effective in his role.

6. *Evaluation Process*

There are four means by which the effectiveness of the change process itself can be evaluated. The first of these is to gather and interpret data with reference to client system performance before, during and after the intervention or service of the research utilization specialist.

Second, the degree of corrective action taken on problems which the people in the system have identified should be described and, if possible, measured.

The third means is to measure response to feedback information about system performance.

The final means of program evaluation is to survey the perceptions and feelings of all component groups in the system (i.e., administrators, teachers, students, parents, and community facility personnel) before and after the consultation intervention.

7. How to Set the Role in an Institutional Context

To insure that the role of the research utilization specialist is viable and effective for solving the problems of one particular school-community system and for linking new knowledge with potential users, careful planning and arrangements must be made on a continuing basis.

First of all, it is important that the needed system support from the U.S. Office of Education and the training institution be developed through detailed planning before the training program is launched.

Second, the contractual understanding and relationship among the consortium of school-community systems should be designed to maximize the chances that initially inactive members will volunteer to become active members within a reasonable period of time. The participation of key personnel of the inactive systems as observers, critics and consultants is of importance in this regard. It will help them to gradually become involved in the program and to consider the advantages which active participation could bring to their own systems.

A reasonable time-scale for the eventual activation of these passive systems should be set up and made clear in advance by the training institute. This time-scale should indicate a range of expectancy rather than setting a rigid cut-off date to permit the school systems to judge their own readiness and to volunteer at the appropriate time. The training institute must make long-range plans on a somewhat flexible basis and be ready to begin the training of additional research utilization specialists as the need arises.

As the initial training program is completed, the research utilization specialists who have completed their one-year programs will be ready to go into other client systems. The training institute will have a small but continuing commitment to these agents to keep them up-to-date on new knowledge and resources in education and to be available to consult with them as they encounter unfamiliar problems with new clients.

In addition, the training institute must make plans which will go beyond the training program as designed for the school-community systems in the initial consortium. Soon after the program is launched, arrangements must be made to include new school systems or to form a new consortium so that the training program can operate on a continuing basis.

Finally, as the training program expands to include more systems, it will be necessary, for geographical reasons, to join with other universities or institutes to provide the required training. Arrangements for this expansion of the program should be made well in advance.

B. Training for the Knowledge Utilization Function/Role*

Context

Information retrieval and utilization cannot be considered simply as a *role* to be carried out by a specialist, but must also be recognized as a necessary *function* of all personnel involved in a change process. Therefore, we should consider the training of individuals other than knowledge utilization specialists who will function as knowledge retrievers and utilizers as a part of their respective roles in the field of education.

To the extent that the change process incorporates the decision-making process, it incorporates the function of information retrieval and utilization. A change which is brought about without the utilization of a decision-making process is an irrational *imposed* change and runs counter to all basic principles of social action within our present culture. Such a change does not require information retrieval and utilization, but, rather, it only involves "1984" type training and harsh external sanctions. If we agree that the change process should center about rational and sound decisions, it must involve the function of *complete* retrieval and utilization of information.

Information may be derived from many diverse sources, and this information will vary in its degree of accuracy and validity. Availability of information increases with time but, at any one point in time, we are limited to the quantity and quality of the information then available. If a decision is made at time "X," it is made with incomplete information as judged by time "X" plus "Y" when the decision is implemented. Rather than this factor depreciating the necessity of information retrieval and utilization, it illustrates the need for all change process personnel to be capable information-retrievers and utilizers to foster self-renewal and alteration of the implemented change.

There is no single individual involved within the change process who does not already utilize some system of knowledge utilization. A major difficulty existing at the present time, however, is the internalization of this function within individuals. All persons rely upon such knowledge utilization processes in an unconscious manner, but each does so with varying degrees of

---

*Drafted by Douglas Towne; edited by Mary C. Havelock.

success. If the function were a more conscious effort, a more objective view could be taken regarding its effectiveness.

No matter how much training an individual receives in knowledge utilization, he must still realize that he contains only a discrete portion of the available and relevant information. If he decides to rely solely upon the information and knowledge within himself, he must accept the possibiity of and responsibility for a decision based upon incomplete information. Such accountability must be clarified and appreciated.

1. The Function and Role of Knowledge Utilization Specialist

The alternative to each individual acting as his own information system is the involvement of a knowledge utilization specialist in the change process. When the change process is judged to be of sufficient magnitude, a specialist in this field can aid and supplement the other personnel and processes; but it is necessary in each case to illustrate and justify the effectiveness and usefulness of involving a knowledge utilization specialist. To the degree that the change process requires that decisions be based upon external information as well as internal information to be adequate, the process requires expertise in the function of information retrieval and utilization.

The basic need is to clearly delineate the elements of the process of change and to specify the relationship between these elements and the various procedural steps involved in knowledge utilization. In addition, it is necessary to understand when and how each individual is to be involved in the various steps of this function or role. For example, the expert resource would deal with more abstract or science-based knowledge, whereas the user would be more involved with practical and specific knowledge of circumstances in his immediate work environment. The change agent would play the role of linker at the interface between expert and user system.

2. Selection for Training

All educational change agents and all educational personnel who are involved in a change process should be trained in the field of knowledge retrieval and utilization. The training program will have the greatest success, however, if the trainees already posess an awareness of this function and its importance. Therefore, some means must be found of developing this awareness in the prospective trainees prior to specialized training.

For future educational personnel the means of providing this awareness is clear; it should be developed as part of the pre-service education for all prospective educational personnel. There is no cause for concern that such training will be superfluous since virtually everyone who enters the field of education will at some point be involved in a change process.

3. Outputs from Training

The process of knowledge retrieval and utilization can be divided into seven basic elements or steps and a training program should provide expertise in each of these areas. By the end of the training program the trainee should be able to:

a. *Identify* and *specify* the types of knowledge and data potentially relevant to the specific problem.
b. Maintain awareness of *direct* and *indirect* sources of such data and knowledge.
c. *Search out* and *retrieve* unknown and known sources of directly and indirectly relevant information.
d. *Critically analyze* these identified sources and glean the essential knowledge from the larger information corpus.
e. *Derive implications* from the available knowledge which are relevant and meaningful to the problem. This implies a listing of alternative implications to be utilized in the decision-making process.
f. *Translate* these obtained implications into terms understandable by the "user." Depending upon the degree of sophistication of the knowledge, a "translation linker" may or may not be required.
g. *Interact* with the client system to assess the utility of the knowledge, recycle the process as needed and implement continued knowledge utilization practices.

4. Ways to Provide Required Training

In essence, three separate training programs must be designed. The first would provide pre-service education to all potential educational personnel. The second would provide in-service education to change process personnel as an integral part of the change process, and the third would be a "crash" program for the change agent or agency prior to the initiation of a change process. The programs for the change personnel and the change agents would provide experiences in each of the seven elements described above, while the pre-service program would concentrate on the areas of search, retrieval, analysis and interpretation.

a. Pre-Service Education

As an integral part of the undergraduate programs of all potential educators, there should be learning experiences available which require the student to retrieve, analyze and interpret information from diverse sources. In the present system our students are too often "fed" pre-digested knowledge from only two sources: the all-knowing professor and the textbook. In neither instance is the student encouraged to question these sources in a critical manner or to search out alternative sources. In even fewer instances is the student led through a simulation of the processes by which the professor or the textbook become the "valid" source of knowledge.

Such experiences should be built-in at all points throughout the educational system. They are especially critical in professional courses but at the present time they are lacking even here. With the rapid growth of educational knowledge it seems far more important to teach the *process* of information utilization for continuous learning than to teach the derived conclusions and implications contained "within" existing professors and textbooks. These derived conclusions and implications will soon be out of date and by the time the student becomes a practicing educator they will be even more out-dated.

Scheduling of these learning experiences should take two forms. It seems perfectly feasible to implement a "course" on information utilization immediately preceding the practicum experience of the student. Such an experience might be a formal course in which each student utilizes his own field of specialty for the content. It could also be designed as an adjunct to an existing course and could supplement the course through a greater experience in the process of information utilization.

In addition to these specialized experiences there should be a required experience in information utilization within each existing course. What is implied here is *not* the usual required term paper which relies upon the library as the only information source, nor is it the term paper which merely parrots information obtained upon a certain subject.

The types of materials utilized in such training would be diverse. They would range from the theoretical document and the cookbook-oriented text to the emotion-laden mass communications. Many of the same techniques may be used in dealing with the information gathered from all these sources, but the student should be aware that, in some respects, there are critical differences. For example, information from people is usually fleeting and is not available for "rereading."

Experience should also be provided in the use of process materials necessary to carry out the search, retrieval, analysis, evaluation and interpretation. Such materials would include directories, thesauri, search forms, interview schedules, and descriptive statistical computational guides.

The types of experience should range from descriptive narratives of completed processes, through simulated experiences, to real experiences. The experiences should be designed to illustrate both the positive and the negative aspects of the information utilization function, since it is better to learn from unsuccessful exercises in a controlled, non-costly experience than later in a real-life situation.

b. In-Service Training for the Knowledge Utilization Function

As an integral part of a change process all personnel involved in the change should receive training which will equip them with the skills and knowledge needed to perform the function of knowledge retrieval and utilization. Training should be spaced over the period of the change process so that instruction is given in each of the seven basic steps of the process (as detailed under "Outputs from Training") just prior to the actual performance of that step in the school setting of the trainees. Specific types of instruction and materials are appropriate for training in each of these seven steps.

i. *Identify* and *specify*. First, instruction should be given in the procedures to be used in making a diagnosis, and guidelines for using these procedures should be presented. Next, exercises in problem identification and clarification should be carried out, using both simulated and real situations.

ii. *Awareness*. Instruction should be given in the use of the technique of "brainstorming" and the trainees should be given a chance to experiment with this technique in guided exercises. Then directories of information sources should be presented and directions should be given explaining how to use these.

iii. *Search* and *Retrieve*. The trainees should first carry out search and retrieval exercises on a simulated problem area. Next, case studies or reports on real situations should be given, presenting the trainees with real problems which need to be solved. Then the trainees should be given an opportunity to perform actual searches of data, documents and people to find information relevant to the solution of these problems. Guides which detail the procedures involved in information collection should be supplied to aid the trainees in this search. For this experience it is important that the trainees be provided with adequate resources in terms of time and money.

iv. *Analyze*. Evaluation guides should be provided which list and explain basic criteria or assumptions which are inherent to each type of information. Then simulated experiences in the analysis of information sources should be presented illustrating both correct and incorrect methods. Finally, the trainees should be guided in performing group exercises in the critical analysis of information and information sources.

v. *Derive Implications*. The trainees should engage in group activities involving diverse individuals in the process of interpretation of relevant knowledge. It will become apparent that a range of alternative implications may be derived for any problem and the group should learn how to summarize and report these findings. They should also be given instruction in the writing of reports.

vi. *Translate*. Exercises in eliminating verbal misunderstanding should be performed; Rogers' exercise* would be particularly appropriate. Semantic differential and word association exercises may be used to identify and resolve cognitive disparity. The trainees should, finally, receive training in role playing in order to learn to appreciate the problems of communication between persons occupying different roles.

vii. *Interact* and *Recycle*. Trainees should be given instructions in self-analysis, interpersonal communication (both verbal and non-verbal) and group dynamics. They should perform exercises in each of these three areas in order to develop awareness and sensitivity in their interaction with others.

c. Crash Training Program for the Knowledge Utilization Role

Educational change agents should also receive thorough training in each of the seven steps of the knowledge utilization process, and their training should be very similar to that outlined above for educational personnel involved in a change process. The basic differences between the two programs would be in terms of time and scheduling.

The crash program for change agents would be given prior to initiation of a change process rather than as a part of the process, and it would be given as an intensive program of relatively short duration. In this program change agents should acquire a general appreciation of all aspects of the knowledge utilization function and role.

Although simulation of role performance would be desirable before the change agent enters a real change situation, it might possibly involve too much time. If such is the case then it would be important to recruit a trainee who already has some experiences in the role of "interfacer" between user and knowledge resources.

5. Criteria for Success in the Role

Whether or not the role of knowledge utilization specialist has been successfully performed by the change agent may be judged on the basis of his performance in each of the seven steps of the knowledge utilization process. Certain criteria should be met relative to each of these steps.

a. *Identify* and *Specify*. It must be demonstrated, by means of diagnostic procedures, that the appropriate data, documents and individual *types* of information relevant to the problem are specified in discrete terms.

---

*See Part Two, Chapter IX, Attachment to Unit #7 by Floyd C. Mann.

b. *Awareness.* Awareness is exhibited by demonstration, through listing, of all potentially useful sources of information, both direct and indirect. This awareness should include data, documents and individuals *inside* and *outside* the client and change agent systems.

c. *Search* and *Retrieve.* It must be demonstrated that complete and valid searches of the data, document and individual sources inside and outside the client and change agent systems have been completed.

d. *Analyze.* The relevant knowledge should be grouped according to the category from which it was drawn. (A 3x2x2 matrix will thus be formed: data/document/individual; inside/outside client system; inside/outside change agent system.) A critical analysis is demonstrated by defending, for each of the 12 categories, the inclusion and the exclusion of information gathered from the search and retrieval.

e. *Derive Implications.* The "chain of reasoning" through which the derived knowledge has led to the stated implications should be explicated. A measure of success is the number of *different* implications derived and the clarity of assumptions and rationale involved in each.

f. *Translate.* The measure of success here is the observed congruency between the client's and the resource person's interpretation of the knowledge.

g. *Interact* and *Recycle.* The degree of reprocessing which can be illustrated is the measure of success here. Both the reprocessing which is done with the aid and assistance of the change agent and the reprocessing which becomes a continuing behavior of the client system should be considered in making this judgment.

6. Evaluation Process

The success of the entire change process depends upon effective execution of each of the seven steps of the utilization process. Therefore, an outside evaluator should assess the degree of success of each of these steps.

a. *Identify* and *Specify.* The documentation of this process as prepared by the change agent should be analyzed, and the change agent should be interviewed so that he may explain and clarify the procedures utilized.

b. *Awareness.* The data, document and people sources which were identified should be compared with the sources available.

c. *Search* and *Retrieve.* The completeness of the search and retrieval may be evaluated by making a sampling analysis to compare the amount of relevant information which was found with the amount of relevant information which was *not* found. Efficiency of the operation may be evaluated by making a similar sampling analysis, comparing the amount of relevant information which was selected.

d. *Analyze.* A sampling analysis should be made to determine the quality of the utilization of obtained information; that is, it should be determined whether relevant and valid information was used or not used, and whether irrelevant and/or non-valid information was used or not used.

e. *Derive Implications.* It should be determined whether or not chains of reasoning were logical and appropriate. An additional evaluation measure here is the number and diversity of implications derived.

f. *Translate.* The success of the translation activities can be evaluated on the basis of the degree to which the chains of reasoning were agreeable to and congruent with the client system. It must also be established whether or not implications were apropriately weighed and whether the selection of a solution was made on a rational basis. The final measure of success here is whether or not an implication *for* action has been implemented *in* action.

g. *Interact* and *Recycle.* An evaluation must be made of the documentation of recycling activities. In this process an increasing degree of specificity should be exhibited. It is also important to assess the amount and quality of continued interaction between user and resourcer. Finally, and most importantly, the amount and quality of continued knowledge utilization activity practiced by both user and resourcer must be evaluated over time following the conclusion of the original change process.

7. How to Set the Knowledge Utilization Function/Role in an Institutional Context

In the program which we have outlined here, all personnel involved in a program of change in a school system will receive training in how to perform the function of knowledge retrieval and utilization. If they have received pre-service training in these functions, as advocated here, they will be familiar with the rationale of such a training program and minimal resistance should be encountered. If, however, the personnel who are to be involved in the change program have not received pre-service education in this area, it would be wise to start the program with an additional initial workshop. This event could be used to acquaint the personnel with the reasons for the proposed training program, and it would give the personnel an opportunity to air and dispel any doubts they might have about it.

The fact that all change personnel will be involved in a knowledge utilization training program should make the introduction of a specialist into the system easier. The change personnel should be equipped to make rational decisions as to when the services of the specialist are necessary and how they should be used. His role should be readily accepted and he should not find it necessary to devote too much time to justifying his existence to those with whom he will be working.

C. Minimal Training System for Self-Renewing of Schools*

Context

Any large organization will find itself constantly in the process of making decisions, instituting new programs, and adapting to changing conditions. Such activities are basic to the survival of an organization as an effective part of society. The agency should therefore not be in a position of relying substantially on outside sources for help in carrying out such basic self-renewing activities. Rather, the organization ought to have the internal capacity to make itself self-renewing through a planning, programming and management (P.P.&M.) process.

Although this type of organizational competence is necessary for any large agency, it is especially necessary in our school systems. Public education is one of the key self-renewal mechanisms of society and must have its own internal self-renewal capacity. This capacity should be conceptualized as a set of functions within the institution rather than the special role of one or two individuals.

The goal of the training program to be proposed here is to achieve a general understanding of the P.P.&M. process throughout the school district and to train members of the system to apply P.P.&M. skills to their jobs. The entire body of school personnel must function as agents of change on a continual basis. Therefore, the only realistic way of approaching a training program for change in education is to view the challenge in terms of training all school personnel rather than a select cadre of change agents. It is necessary to support such a program with trained consultants who, in turn, can be considered as "change agents." For our present purpose, however, we will regard such consultants as a part of the proposed training program and we will not discuss their own training specifically.

The need for such a rational approach to change in the local educational agency is imperative. Experience has taught the school administrator that elements in a school slystem are so *interrelated* that dysfunction in one area perturbs the entire system. Therefore, the administrator needs an effective means for looking at the dynamics and status interactions of all subsystems in his district.

System analysis is such a technique. It is not perfect, but it is undoubtedly the best proven set of heuristics now available for a system which is complex

---

*Drafted by Paul Hood, Russell Kent, Donald Johnson, Louis Maguire and Joe Ward; edited by Mary C. Havelock.

and dynamic. The process of analysis (including educational P.P.&M.) cannot provide substantive answers to the administrator's questions, nor does it constrain use of any available set of techniques or strategies, such as human relations training, conflict resolution, or crisis coping. But analysis does permit a wise *choice among alternatives* and the planned, appropriate employment of *procedures* and *monitoring of effect* throughout the system.

Further, this technique deals with predictive models, not descriptive models. It permits identification of real, significant *constraints* and *resources* which condition choice. Further, it permits prediction of *probable outcomes* if various change strategies are employed, so that rational choice and allocation are possible.

This approach depends heavily on *validating procedures* derived from system analysis and from the technology of training. A package which provides for implementation and maintenance of an entire training and organizational change program must be developed, refined, and validated. Such a program must respond to all important requirements and must utilize all relevant techniques and resources.

A program of this type will enable the managers of educational enterprises to *get more done* with given resources and with *fewer risks*. It will also enable them to avoid or anticipate and minimize the effects of undesired consequences.

This approach is probably the most cost-effective method for creating a significant advance in the capability of the more than 5,000 moderate and large school districts of the United States to survive, respond effectively to societal needs, and accomplish self-renewal of their operations.

A corallary to the last point is that this approach is undoubtedly the most promising for creating a *searching, receptive* and *effective climate* for the wise employment of the output of educational and other RD&D investments. It creates an informed, critical, and capable user of RD&D products.

1. The Roles and Functions Involved in the P.P.&M. Process for Self-Renewing Schools

The process of planning, programming, and management within a school district should not be considered as a *role* to be performed by any single individual. Rather, the school system and the personnel in it must posess a *set of functions or capacities* to make the organization self-renewing by a rational P.P.&M. process. There are eight basic functions which must be performed in order to carry out this process:

   a. Assessing needs.
   b. Setting priorities.
   c. Selecting and/or designing alternative solutions.

d. Testing of options.
e. Installing validated options.
f. Monitoring, modifying and improving.
g. *Continually redetermining the relevance to redefined goals.*
h. The capability to set priorities, plan and manage all of the above.

These functions constitute a coherent and necessary set for the school. For the individuals, these functions may be allocated in various sub-sets with different emphasis. For example, one person may be particularly skilled in planning and have only a general familiarity with the other functions.

We may define a *role*, on the other hand, by the set of skills which it requires. An analyst, for example, must have the ability to define a problem, define a mission, identify resources, constraints and alternatives, and select alternatives. The analyst must have *proficiency* in these skills, whereas the other staff must have an *orientation* permitting them to cooperate and coordinate with the analyst.

In addition to roles *per se*, we may also describe *types* of roles. The key administrative and leadership positions are role types filled by *persons who request work and interpret its results.* Specialists are those who do the staff work. The role of school leaders is to participate, provide input, react to output, and operationalize the plans and programs. Others, such as teachers, students and community members, fill a necessary function by having an orientation so that they may effectively participate.

Consequently, there is a large number of *combinations* of roles and role types that may be defined, depending on the size and the structure of the school district. This is why we are stressing the concept of functions within the institution rather than the role of one or a few individuals.

There are a variety of organizational arrangements which may be instituted to provide for the self-renewal functions. These may range from a highly centralized P.P.&M. staff to a diffuse and widely shared P.P.&M. responsibility. If there is to be widespread participation in decision-making, then it is particularly important that there be a general understanding of the P.P.&M. process throughout the institution. It is important that the self-renewal functions operate efficiently and effectively in an adaptive way for the specific institutional context.

2. *Preconditions for Selection/Training*

A program which is designed to provide training in self-renewal capacities for an entire school system must of course deal with the existing resources and personnel. There is, therefore, no choice to be made in terms of who is to be trained. On the other hand, it is necessary to make careful allocations of functions to the existing staff before training begins.

There are a variety of strategies which may be employed in initiating the structure, but there are three general procedures which must be followed in all cases. First, the superintendent and key personnel must be fully informed on all aspects of the restructuring program and the training program itself, and they must be committed to them. Second, there must be a diagnostic effort to define *key context variables*. These would include (a) the *problem* of the system, (b) the *resources* available, (c) the *capabilities* of the personnel and (d) the *readiness* for change exhibited by the system as a whole and the personnel individually. The third procedure which must be followed is to evaluate alternative organizational arrangements, implementation strategies, and rates of conversion.

3. Outputs from Training

The goal of the training program is to provide each trainee with a general understanding of the planning, programming, and management process and with competency in the particular function allocated to him. A detailed listing of the desired output of the training program should be drawn up for each of the eight basic functions listed above in Section 1. In this report we shall simply give an example of the types of skills which might be listed for one of the functions.

For competency in *needs assessment*, the trainee should have a set of skills which would include the following:

a. Skills in collecting data and interpreting discrepancies between objectives and present status.
b. Skills in validation and prioritization.
c. Skills in relating needs to the overall situation leading to problem definition.

4. Ways to Provide Required Training

a. The Training Program

A two-part program to train school personnel in the planning, programming and management process should include a formal program and an on-the-job apprenticeship. The formal program should consist of 30 to 50 hours of training provided by colleges, universities or training institutes prior to the on-the-job application. Alternatively, it could be conducted by the schools themselves during some period of the school year, or, preferably, over an entire school year to permit skills practice. The purpose of the formal program should be to provide *familiarization* with the P.P.&M. process and *orientation* to the eight functions of the process. Practicums and simulation experiences can be used to help provide this training.

The apprenticeship would take place either following or during the formal training program. The purpose of the apprenticeship would be to create *proficiency* in specific skill areas. It is important that this be an on-the-job program in which the trainee can practice his new skills with support, guidance, and protection.

b. The Training Package

Packaging of all aspects of the training program is essential to maintain quality and economy of training. Completely validated packages should be provided to cover each of the following areas:

i. Consultant support.
ii. Organizational restructuring.
iii. General organizational orientation.
iv. Diagnosis.
v. Apprenticeship (on-the-job experiences).
vi. Implementation.
vii. Evaluation.

Those who are interested in training packages of this type should be aware of the work which is currently being done in this area as well as programs which are available at the present time. Two self-contained packages which provide the minimal formal training program are "Operation PEP"* and "SAFE"**.

Two elaborated systems are currently under development: "Administering for Change"***and "Educational Planning and Management System"****. These systems are being designed to work with and provide complete implementation packaging for installation of specific training models in colleges, universities, extension services, or by self-contained in-service arrangements. Within a period of one or two years these elaborated package components

---

*Information on Operation PEP may be obtained by writing to: Dr. Russell Kent, 590 Hamilton Street, Redwood City, California 94063.

**Information on "SAFE" may be obtained by writing to: Dr. Robert E. Corrigan, 8701 Adah Street, Garden Grove, California 92641

***Information on "Administering for Change" can be obtained by writing to: Dr. Louis Maguire, Research for Better Schools, Suite 1700, 1700 Market Street, Philadelphia, Pennsylvania 19103.

****Information on the "Education Planning and Management System" can be obtained by writing to: Dr. Paul D. Hood, Far West Laboratory, Hotel Claremont, Berkeley, California 94705.

will be available for operational testing under special conditions. Within two to five years, complete modules will be available without special restrictions, probably through commercial distributors.

It is also planned to provide for complete consultant support packages, diagnostic and assessment packages, and general orientation packages. These will probably be available in three to five years. In addition, apprenticeship and on-the-job experiences must be developed and packaged. This kind of training is critical and absolutely essential since the ultimate success of the P.P.&M. process depends on adequate performance of skills on the job.

5. Criteria for Success

The success of the training program can be judged best on the basis of whether or not the trainees have acquired the ability to apply planning, programming and management skills to on-the-job requirements. Each trainee should perform effectively in his allocated function and he should also work cooperatively with other individuals who are performing other functions in the P.P.&M. process.

In addition, the initial problems of the system as detailed by the diagnostic effort should have been corrected and the system and individuals within it should respond quickly and efficiently to new problems as they arise. In addition, the system should seek out new and better ways of doing things without waiting for inefficiencies to become problems. Only by performing at such a responsible level can the school system be considered truly self-renewing.

6. Evaluation Process

Evaluation of the training program, on the basis of the above criteria, should be made first on proficiency of in-term job training skills and later on on-the-job performance. The trainees must have the ability to develop acceptable plans and programs which meet standards of peers and superiors. The standards for trained personnel should be set at a substantially higher level than they would be for experienced but untrained educators.

In addition, a measurement of the performance of the system as a whole should be made both before and after the training program. System performance will show, first, the extent to which all school personnel have an understanding of the P.P.&M. process in general and an appreciation of the functions performed by others in the system. Second, it will show the extent to which the school system is performing in a self-renewing capacity.

Evaluation of the benefit of a training program to an institution is, of course, a highly complex problem. However, specific evaluation instrumentation is under development and undoubtedly will be more technically adequate than that available for any other model.*

7. *How to Set the Training System in an Institutional Context*

This training program will of course be inherent in the user system. There are, however, some problems in providing for implementation and packaging. In addition to the need for providing training support and adequate diagnostic and evaluation tools, the need for organizational orientation and restructuring will occur in every case.

Installation is a system-changing process, and the financial costs of restructuring must fit user requirements and capacities. Estimates for specific cases can be made at the present time by available consultants, or help may be obtained from other districts which have installed one of the minimal systems (PEP or SAFE). General methods for making cost estimates or selecting an organizational arrangement will be developed. The elaborated systems mentioned here (produced by Research for Better Schools and the Far West Laboratory) will provide for a set of alternative organizational arrangements, including an "information unit" facilitating choice and complete guidance regarding implementation and assessment.

D. Integrated Model of Counselor Behavior**

Context

Present counselor behavior is becoming increasingly inadequate in meeting the needs of people and institutions. As our society becomes more complicated, the shortage of solutions to meet our many pressing problems will become even more acute. If counselors wish to maintain their capacity to help each person or institution to realize his or its full potential, they must incorporate more effective modes of behavior into their present repertories. These new behaviors must be related to a new conception of the desired outcomes and goals of counseling as well as to the incorporation of new practices and procedures. In this paper we will put forward a proposal for a training program for counselors to add new behaviors to the counselor's

---

*For models, see the evaluation of major leadership development systems as described by Paul Hood and others in Hum RRO Publication Series: "Evaluation of three experimental systems for non-commissioned officer training" Technical Report 67-12, Alexandria, Va., Hum RRO, Sept. 1967 (ERIC Ed 017821). "Preliminary assessment of three NCO leadership preparation training systems" Technical Report 67-8, Alexandria, Va., Hum RRO, June 1967 (ERIC Ed 014653).

**Drafted by Garry Walz, George Sproule, Marlene Pringle and Jane Skinner; edited by Mary C. Havelock.

repertory. This program would result in an integrated model of counselor behavior based upon identification of school and student needs and upon full utilization of the present knowledge base and resources.

1. The Counselor Role

The concept of an integrated model of counselor behavior must be developed on the basis of comprehensive research in the areas of student or client needs and related counselor intervention techniques. We can suggest seven primary types of counselor behavior which may result from such a search.

First, the counselor should be able to carry out a more complete diagnosis than is currently practiced. He should make a systems analysis, whether he is dealing with an individual or with an institution. Counseling even in a restricted area of client needs must be related to the total life space of the client.

Second, counselors should rely less upon present testing and appraisal methods. With the change in the speed with which our society is undergoing change and the diversity of individuals now seeking counseling, tests are becoming less readily acceptable than they once were as appropriate tools for diagnosing a client's interests and potential. In particular, the culturally distinct have challenged the grounds on which the tests have operated and have disputed the assumption that all individuals have had an equal opportunity to learn and become familiar with the contents covered by tests. Others have decried not only the inadequacy of the tests but also their use in ways that have restricted entry into potentially appropriate areas and have discouraged development of the individual's potential rather than encouraging it. The current emphasis must be on measurement by performance rather than by tests. Opportunities must be provided in which an individual can have a fair chance to perform, and he must be provided with whatever assistance he needs to perform at a given rate.

Third, the counselor should make an attempt to reach out to potential clients, rather than waiting for his services to be solicited. Counselors have a responsibility to identify and interact with individuals who could make use of their services, and this applies particularly to population sub-groups. The non-directive approach may be appropriate for working with average white students who are making plans for college entrance and who have their possible options clearly in mind. A poor black youth from the inner city, on the other hand, is likely to feel that the future holds little promise for him, and he will have very little desire or motivation to seek counseling on his plans for the future.

Fourth, the counselor should be an advocate and initiator of specific desirable changes in his clients. This would include counseling in the areas of life-style planning, destiny control, self-interest advocacy, participatory governance, "significant group" relationships and the effective utilization of human and physical resources. Decisions relative to schooling and career must involve the individual's total set of attitudes and values and how these fit together into a life style. The client should become aware of how he is affected by and interacts with the personal and impersonal elements in his environment, and he should become aware of how he can control the direction of his own life.

Fifth, the counselor should take direct intervention action to change the environment on behalf of his client in certain situations. For some clients, such as the culturally distinct, it is often the environment, rather than any deficit within the individual, which interferes with desirable behavioral changes. Therefore, if the system for treatment of the individual is in fact to lead to significant behavioral changes, it is necessary that the counselor interact and intervene in the environment of the client as well as interacting with the individual hemself. This intervention may take the form of community counseling programs, family counseling, coaching on the job or a greater involvement of the counselor in the life-space of the client.

The sixth area of counselor behavior is to provide linkage with resources. Computer-assisted counseling and the use of information systems to assist clients in the identification of educational and occupational opportunities should be regularly employed. Linkage with intrapersonal, interpersonal and impersonal resources must be maintained at all times to provide the most responsible counseling possible. In addition, linkage with peers and professional organizations will be invaluable for providing a viable system of support for the role.

Finally, the counselor should seek and find the necessary feedback to evaluate his own efforts and the resultant behavior of his clients.

2. Selection for Training

Contemporary trends in counseling and education suggest that the younger generation of counselors are restlessly waiting for a new conception of their role which is more robust and more reflective of the world we are moving toward than the one we are moving from. There should be no dearth of present or prospective counselors who will be candidates for the proposed program.

In the long run, all counselors should receive training in the integrated model of behavior. Training for the counselor in the new role should be incorporated into his pre-service education. For present counselors, in-service training must be provided, and for the initial training program, the trainees should be selected on the basis of their own desire for change and the willingness of their institutions to provide support for this training.

The potential trainee system (counselor, school and community) would be informed of the "integrated model" training program and they could participate in it only by self-nomination. This nomination would require the endorsement of at least two school reference groups (e.g. the school board and the superintendent) at the initial stage of selection. This endorsement would provide at least some partial support for the counselors who would be trained and would be a start toward legitimizing the new role.

At this point there would be a contract between school board, superintendent, counselors and training agency specifying the responsibilities of the parties involved. The contract would define such matters as the number of orientation conferences to be held, what training is to be provided, the nature of consultation services of trainers, cognitive responsibilities of counselors and evaluation procedures. Built into this contract would also be specific provisions which would involve the nominated counselors in seeking and receiving the endorsement of other school and community groups after the first orientation conference.

3. Outputs from Training

The training program would provide experiences leading to proficiency in the role behaviors listed above. Particularly important will be the ability of the trainee to fully utilize all available resources and assist in the implementation of the action strategies which he advocates for his client.

In addition, the trainee should be able to articulate the rationale for the role and functions for which he is being trained. Even though the trainee is drawn from inside the system in which he will be serving after training, the introduction of a new set of behaviors will necessitate the implementation of entry strategies into the system. The trainee will have to gain acceptance from all members of the system, students and community as well as teachers and school administration.

4. Ways to Provide Training

Developing an integrated model for counselor training will require a major effort on the part of the program planners. The program must be rigorously conceived and coherently planned with built-in evaluation and accountability at several levels and stages. The program must be based on manpower needs and projections running at least a decade ahead.

Model development can be sub-divided into three main phases. The first phase should be devoted to developing the model of integrated counselor behavior. The initial task of this phase would be a search and analysis of the available knowledge resources to identify research relating to student developmental needs and the impact of differential planned interventions upon those needs. The next step would be retrieval of data from students regarding their needs and their responses to existing educational designs and practices. The first phase would conclude with the combination and integration of data from the knowledge search and experiential acquisition into a model of counselor behavior which specifies counselor roles and functions. The integrated model of counselor behavior should contain the kinds of innovations and inventiveness for the new role of counselor suggested above.

The second phase would be devoted to designing a comprehensive training program in which interrelated skills and understandings are learned in a coherent sequence. The program will also have to be multiple-leveled, providing training for the paraprofessional indigenous worker, the school-based counselor and the university-based counselor-educator and researcher. The program will have to be conceived as an in-service package and as an academic sequence with undergraduate and advanced level components. In addition, the program will probably have to be unitized and packaged so that specific elements can be put together in different combinations for the needs of different trainees in different situations.

The third developmental phase would be concerned with field testing the prototype of the integrated model of counselor behavior. This phase would be characterized by developing the new counselor approach into a functioning model to demonstrate and replicate the essential counselor behaviors. The design would utilize simulation to enable counselors to experience in a "hands-on" manner the actual behaviors and roles they would be expected to perform. The field testing would enable counselors from a wide variety of settings to respond to the appropriateness of the behaviors of the integrated counselor model. Both academics and practitioners will have to collaborate in a consortium arrangement to provide the necessary varieties of supervised field work integrated with course sequences.

A major goal in developing and testing the model would be to design a model that would be responsive to a broad cross section of the needs of schools and students. Information obtained from the field testing would be used to revise the model to make it more relevant to the needs of different student sub-groups and the constraints of varying education settings. Hopefully, 75% of the planned counselor behaviors would be of such generalizable utility that they could be adopted for local use by all of the counselor-school units in the system. Variance in counselor behavior between settings would amount to approximately 25% and the counselor behaviors in that variance would be locally designed and implemented.

Final evaluation of the program would be based on behavioral criteria emerging from the initial conceptualization.

5. *How to Set the Role in An Institutional Context*

Organizational establishments yield grudgingly to the need for structural changes but several forces are working in favor of ultimate acceptance of a variety of new and redefined educational roles. In some cases, the long-latent clash of interests between students and teachers and between students and students has surfaced, forcing schools to seek out individuals who have special skills in negotiation, group management, participation, and problem-solving. In these cases, the need for the "process expert" was accelerated dramatically. In other settings, where such crises are still latent, forward-looking administrators will be reaching out for those same process specialists to provide some preventive social medicine to the school environment.

As the establishment reaches out, the counselor change agents should be ready to serve, but they should also be ready to bargain for the kind of institutional acceptance and security that they will need in the long-run to make their roles tenable and livable.

VI

LINKING SCHOOLS TO OUTSIDE RESOURCES

Two task forces (Wolf; Ellis, et al.) developed programs to train change agents to act as permanent liaisons between knowledge resources in education and users of these resources. These two reports are summarized in Table VI.1.

TABLE VI.1
PROGRAMS FOR CHANGE AGENT LINKAGE OF
SCHOOLS WITH RESOURCES

REPORT	CLIENT	GOAL OF TRAINING MODEL	CHANGE AGENT ROLE
A. The Knowledge Utilization Specialist Team and Leader -Wolf	Local education agencies and institutes of higher education	Linkage of client systems with knowledge resources	*KUS Team and Leader* 1. Generate awareness of knowledge resources, communication channels and client needs. 2. Translate awareness into action.
B. Teacher Trainers -Ellis, et al.	Practicing teachers	In-service training of teachers by trainers operating out of State Departments of Education.	*Teacher Trainer* 1. Diagnosis 2. Linkage with resources 3. Support

In both models, the change agents are described as being housed in the State Departments of Education and their task would be to service educational agencies within a specified region much as the county extension agent services agricultural needs. They would create in their clients an awareness of the latest information on innovations in education and would help the client system to translate this awareness into action.

The Wolf model proposes that the change agent role be filled by a Knowledge Utilization Specialist (KUS) team and leader. The team members would routinely visit with the administration of local schools and with the trainers of educational personnel in institutes of higher education, and they would be on call to assist their clients when problems arose. These change agents would have a complete knowledge of educational resources and would be able to assist in applications at any level or in any area of school functioning. The team leader would be a member of the State Department of Education and would coordinate the activities of the KUS team members, as well as linking them with other resources.

The team leader would therefore need training in human interaction and the process of change, and an in-depth knowledge of current curricular, instructional and organizational matters in education. In addition, he would need to understand the functioning of federal, state and local educational agencies and other facilities such as the regional laboratories.

The team members would receive similar training, but instead of having a knowledge of federal and state agencies, they should understand the power structure and operation of the client systems within their regions.

The training program for the KUS team would combine formal campus instruction with field experience. The program for team leaders would require two years, whereas one year of training would be sufficient for team members.

The change agent role in the model developed by Ellis, et al. would be filled by a cadre of Teacher Trainers. There is no specification of a team leader in this report, but it is assumed that personnel within the State Department of Education would coordinate and direct the trainer cadre.

Rather than acting through the school administration as in the Wolf model, these change agents would work directly with teachers. Besides providing linkage with resources, the Teacher Trainers would assist in diagnosing the system and would give support to teachers who were adopting new materials or methods. In addition to scheduling frequent consultations with clients, the Trainers would also conduct periodic workshops in each client school.

In order to design a training program to meet these needs, it is suggested that a cross-discipline consultant team be established for the purpose of defining the desired behaviors of Teacher Trainers. In addition to specific training program content which may be developed by this team, it is suggested that teacher trainers should receive instruction and experience in communication, diagnosis and problem-solving, the process of change, utilization and evaluation. A training program of about 18 months duration is proposed, which would include classroom, laboratory, and field experiences.

A. The Knowledge Utilization Specialist Team and Leader*

Context

To effectively carry out their mission of imparting the knowledge and wisdom of our society to the young, educational practitioners must remain constantly aware of new developments in the field of education. These new developments include materials and methods for teachers, administrators, or the trainers of educational personnel.

Awareness of new information does not imply utilization, however, but is only the first step on the road to adoption or rejection of an innovation. Once awareness of a particular innovation exists, a judgement must be made as to whether or not there is a need for an innovation of this type, and, if the need exists, whether this particular innovation is the most appropriate one to fill the need.

Once a decision has been made that an innovation is appropriate, a number of steps may have to be taken in order to implement adoption. Training for use may need to be provided for some or all of the personnel of the school system, and adaptions of the innovation itself may need to be made.

Finally, after a significant period of use, the innovation should be evaluated. It should be established that the innovation resulted in the improvements anticipated, and that no undesirable effects were caused.

Clearly, this set of utilization activities cannot be carried out under present conditions by busy educators on an independent basis. First, there are no effective channels of communication through which an awareness of educational research can readily be maintained. Second, the task of sifting through available information on innovative materials and methods to identify potentially applicable information requires more time than the average educator can spare from his assigned responsibilities. Finally, resources to provide training in the use of innovations are generally lacking within most school systems.

In order to solve these problems, a new mechanism for effective knowledge utilization must be established within the educational system. To meet this need, we will develop in this paper the concept of the Knowledge Utilization Specialist (KUS) team, which will generate, coordinate and maintain an awareness of relevant new information among educational personnel, and translate this awareness into action.

---

*Drafted by William Wolf; edited by Mary C. Havelock.

1. The Role of the Knowledge Utilization Specialist Team

Knowledge Utilization Specialist Teams would be sponsored by and housed in the State Department of Education; they would link local education agencies and institutes of higher education with the knowledge resources of federal and state education agencies, state universities, and nearby regional education laboratories and Title III units.

Each KUS team would be set up to serve a prescribed client territory of local education agencies and institutes of higher education. The number of members in each team and the number of teams within a particular state would be determined by the needs of that state. Figure VI.1 shows the linkage network which would be provided by each KUS team.

FIGURE VI.1
LINKAGE PROVIDED BY A KUS TEAM LEADER AND MEMBERS

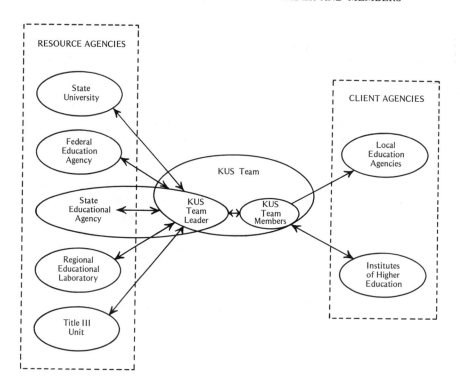

The team leader would assume the role of linkage agent between the knowledge resources and the team members, and this role would involve two main functions. First, the leader would assemble information from the five resource agencies shown in Figure VI.1, and he would transmit appropriate information to each of his team members. Relevancy of information would be determined on the basis of frequent interaction with, and systematic feedback from, each member of the team. Second, the leader would be responsible for coordinating the activities of the team members.

Team members would work directly with the administration of local school systems and with the trainers of educational personnel in the institutes of higher education. Members would be responsible for providing their client systems with information relevant to their needs, for assisting them in making decisions to adopt innovations, and for providing support during installation of innovations.

A team consisting of about ten members could serve perhaps 20-30 client systems, with each member being assigned primary responsibility for serving two or three clients. Each member would thus be able to develop a close working relationship with each of his clients, and he would be responsible for creating and maintaining in his clients an awareness of new information.

Through frequent contacts with the team leader, each member would be kept informed of innovative activities of other client systems in the region so that experiences of all the team members could be shared. Successes and difficulties encountered in the adoption of an innovation by one client could serve as an aid to the other KUS team members as they counseled their own client systems on the advisability of adopting that innovation.

Once a client decided to adopt an innovation, the KUS member assigned to that system would consult with the team leader on implementation strategies. Other KUS team members with experience with this or similar innovations might be called in as consultants. For complex implementation strategies, some or all of the other team members might be called in to provide system orientation programs or training workshops for staff skills development. The KUS team concept would thus provide maximum support both for the client systems and for the change agents themselves.

2. *Preconditions for Selection for Training*

Candidates for KUS team leadership training should have at least a bachelor's degree; some advanced training in education or administration would be desirable. Experience as an educational practitioner would be helpful, but experience related to the operation of any of the future client or resource agencies would be particularly relevant. In addition, the potential candidate should be recognized as an "opinion leader" by those with whom he has worked in the past. To locate persons who fulfill all these qualifications will clearly require an active recruiting program and a careful screening process. Not only must references be solicited from superiors, but an inquiry must also be made among the peers and subordinates of the potential candidate to assess his capacity for leadership and effective communication.

Selection criteria for candidates for team membership training may be somewhat less rigorous, and the primary requirement for training should be a bachelor's degree. It should be determined through interviews with the candidate that he communicates clearly, is able to establish an open relationship, and offers potential as an "opinion leader."

3. Outputs from Training

The KUS team leader should receive training in four primary areas. First, he should have an in-depth knowledge of curricular, instructional and organizational matters within the field of education. He should become familiar not only with the content of these areas but also with trends, applications, and sources of information about new developments. Second, he should learn about the process of change so that he will be able to function effectively as coordinator of the activities of team members. Third, he should have extensive knowledge about human interaction on individual, group, and system levels. Expertise in this area will be essential for establishing good relationships with resource system personnel and with team members. It will be particularly important for him to develop communication strategies which "turn on" team members and elicit meaningful feedback from them. Finally, the KUS leader should receive instruction in the purpose, operation, programs, and idiosyncracies of the resource agencies with which he will be dealing.

Training team members will to some extent parallel training team leaders. Members will also need to know about curricular, instructional and organizational matters in education, but this knowledge need not be as extensive as that required of the leader. Members should receive instruction in the process of change; they should learn not only how the process works but also how they may facilitate it. Training in human interaction skills should be as extensive as that for team leaders, but the focus here should be on developing communication strategies which "turn on" client system officials and elicit meaningful feedback from them. Rather than learning about resource system operations, team members should learn about the power structure, operations, and staff structure of the future client systems.

4. Ways to Provide Training

Training programs for KUS team leaders and members should be offered by an established university or school of education, and campus experience should be combined with workshop and field experiences. The program for KUS team leaders should be a two-year program leading to an advanced graduate degree; the program for the team members should be of one-year duration, leading to a master's degree. These programs might take the form outlined below:

Schedule of Events Needed to Produce a KUS Team Leader

a. Two-week summer workshop at a selected university for 10-20 trainees. Trainers would:

    i. Specify field experience needed by KUS personnel.
    ii. Describe the elements of educational knowledge communication and feedback networks.
    iii. Establish performance expectations for KUS team leader role.
    iv. Plan a program for each trainee: detail a personalized modus operandi for attaining needed skills and attitudes, explore available resources of the university and agencies within the immediate environment that might bear upon the trainee's program choices, and set forth an individualized work plan for the fall school term aimed at developing some of the needed competencies.

b. Enrollment in courses at the selected university. Courses chosen should reflect the needs set forth by trainees. Existing university offerings will meet some of these needs; however, special seminars and independent study will be needed to meet others.

c. Two-day January workshop at the selected university for same group of trainees to:

    i. Review work completed to date.
    ii. Assess individual progress in relation to overall performance expectations of the program and the individual work plans submitted.
    iii. Modify subsequent plans to reflect these assessments, setting forth a second individualized work plan for the spring school term aimed at developing additional needed competencies.

d. Enrollment in courses at the selected university (as under item b.).

e. One-week June workshop at the selected university for the same group of trainees to:

    i.   Review work completed to date.

    ii. Assess individual progress in relation to overall performance expectations of the program and the individual work plans submitted.

    iii. Modify subsequent plans to reflect these assessments.

    iv. Develop a field experience program for the second year, including simulation and other "packaged" material to be used as part of practice. In conjunction with these intentions, the following will occur:

        (a) Representatives from future resource systems will describe field opportunities for trainee consideration.

        (b) Simulation and other "packaging" specialists will describe available resources, use strategies, feedback techniques, and preparation possibilities.

    v. Set forth another individualized work plan for the second fall school term which includes several field experiences and exposure to field applications of simulation and packaging techniques. (Arrangements for field experience should be made by program personnel.)

f.   Enrollment in courses at the selected university. Most of the work at this time will be devoted to field exploration.

g. Three-day January workshop at the selected university for same group of trainees to:

    i.   Share field experiences completed.

    ii. Assess individual progress in relation to overall performance expectations of the program and the individual work plans submitted.

    iii. Modify subsequent plans to reflect these assessments and set forth a final work plan aimed at culminating the training experience.

h. Enrollment in courses at the selected university. Most of the work during the spring term will be devoted to generating and testing simulation and other packaged materials. It is hoped that these explorations will result in the evolution of a kit of materials which can be used in the KUS practice.

i.   Graduation

    i.   Certificate of Advanced Graduate Status earned.

ii. Option exists to complete doctorate while "on the job."

Schedule of Events Needed to Produce a KUS Team Member

a. Two-week summer workshop at a selected university for 30-50 trainees. Trainers would:

    i. Specify field experience needed by KUS personnel.

    ii. Describe the elements of educational knowledge communication and feedback networks.

    iii. Set forth performance expectations for KUS team member role.

    iv. Plan program for each trainee which would detail a personalized modus operandi for attaining needed skills and attitudes, explore available resources of the university and agencies within the immediate environment that might bear upon the trainee's work program choices, and set forth an individualized work plan for the fall school term aimed at developing some of the needed competencies.

b. Enrollment in courses at the selected university. Courses chosen should reflect the needs set forth by trainers. Existing university offerings will meet some of these needs; however, special seminars and independent study will be needed to meet others.

c. One-week January workshop at the selected university for same group of trainees to:

    i. Review work completed to date.

    ii. Assess individual progress in relation to overall performance expectations of the program and the individual work plans submitted.

    iii. Modify subsequent plans to reflect these assessments.

    iv. Develop a field experience program for the spring term. Representatives from future client systems will describe field opportunities for trainee consideration.

    v. Set forth an individualized work plan for the spring term which includes several field experiences. (Arrangements for field experience should be made by program personnel.)

d. Enrollment in courses at the selected university. Most of the work at this time will be devoted to field exploration.

e. Graduation.

i. Masters Degree earned.

5. *Criteria for Success in the Role*

Success of the KUS team may be judged on the basis of performance of the team itself and the client systems. Performance criteria for the KUS team should be based on competency in three areas: 1) facility with basic education concepts in curriculum, instruction, and organization; 2) facility with knowledge of change process and human interaction; and 3) the degree to which opinion leadership is exercised.

KUS team success can also be assessed on the basis of client system performance in three areas: 1) an attitude of openness and receptivity toward logical change; 2) logical change occurs on a regular basis; and 3) change incorporates new knowledge as it becomes available.

B. Teacher Trainers*

Context

A great wealth of knowledge and techniques which should benefit teachers is currently being produced in the United States. However, the existing mechanisms are totally inadequate for transmitting this knowledge on a systematic basis to practicing teachers. On the one hand, it is often hard for teachers to find the time and money to attend such programs as summer institutes which are offered by universities to up-date teachers on new materials and methods. On the other hand, there is no established network for bringing these materials to teachers.

When a teacher learns of new innovations, he often does not know whether they are applicable to his own situation, and, if so, how to go about instituting them. New ideas which a teacher might find in a professional journal are likely to need extensive adaptation before he can use them in his classroom. Indeed, the information is often presented in such a manner that its relevance is not even apparent. Similarly, new approaches which a teacher hears from colleagues in other schools may not appear to be suitable to his own classroom situation, and he has no one to call on for assistance in adapting new practices to his own particular needs.

A program is needed to bring information about new knowledge and techniques to the teachers in their own school settings and assist them in

---

*Drafted by Betty Ellis, Elliot Spack, Charles Chandler, and James Beaird; edited by Mary C. Havelock.

adapting these innovations for their own uses. We propose the creation of the role of "teacher trainer" to carry out such a program. This program could be developed to fit within the State Departments of Education and could operate in some ways like the Cooperative Extension Service of the Department of Agriculture.

This paper will develop a model for the training of a cadre of teacher trainers who will link teachers in local school settings with resources across the nation.

1. The Role of Teacher Trainer

Teacher trainers would be a part of the State Departments of Education and would routinely visit with and conduct workshops in the local schools within a specified region. This region could be an urban school district or a county-wide region in a rural area. In any case, the area covered should be small enough to allow the trainer to become familiar with the teaching needs of each school in his district.

The trainer would act primarily as a linkage agent, bringing current knowledge and techniques to schools and teachers. He will also need to be able to diagnose the classroom needs of the schools he services and he must be able to help the teachers adapt new materials for their own needs. In addition, he should help the individual teachers to utilize resources for their own purposes, and he should provide support for the teachers in their efforts to introduce innovations into the classroom.

2. Preconditions for Selection for Training

Four primary criteria may be used in the selection of individuals to be trained for the role of teacher trainer. First, the individual should be people-oriented. He should enjoy working with people and should exhibit characteristics of good communication skills; he should be good at listening as well as relating. Second, he should be able to operate at different levels simultaneously. That is, he should be able to establish good relationships both upwards and downwards. Third, he should be flexible. He should expect that different individuals will respond in different ways and at different rates, and he should be able to train teachers at a pace which is suitable for each individual. Fourth, he should have some minimal level of knowledge and sensitivity about the area of teacher training.

In addition to these four criteria, it would be desirable, though not essential, for the prospective trainer to have some experience in education both inside and outside the classroom. Clearly, someone who has had experience as a teacher is in a good position to know what types of difficulties teachers encounter in trying to introduce innovations. In addition, however, an individual with a broader range of experience, e.g. as both teacher and school administrator or as member of the staff of a State Department of Education, will have a knowledge of education needs which transcends those of the individual classroom.

In order to find such individuals, traditional methods of screening applicants will be inadequate. Personal interviews will be essential, and the recommendations of trusted people who have worked with the candidate would be quite valuable. Above all, it is important to avoid getting a one-sided or purely "academic" picture of the applicant. Considerable time and effort should be allocated to this selection procedure.

3. Outputs from Training

In order to plan the type of behavioral outcomes which the training program for teacher trainers should produce, it is first essential to know what behaviors are desired of teachers and, ultimately, of students. Several studies have been done on teacher behavior and some of these would be useful in planning the desired program. These include the study done by Heathers at the University of Pittsburgh; Frymier's study, "Model Teacher Training Efforts," done at Ohio State University; and a *Nova University* study, "Analysis of Teacher's Role in Individualized Environment."

In addition to resources from inside the field of education, information sources and planning personnel from outside the educational system are needed to plan a comprehensive program. A task force could be set up for the purpose of establishing desired behaviors of teacher trainers. This consultant team should include such specialists as anthropologists, sociologists, economists, physicists and population geographers, who would contribute ideas from their own disciplines that would constantly stimulate the system. This team would bring a broader perspective on trends in education to the planning of the program.

These approaches can result in a highly detailed specification of desired behavioral outcomes of a training program for teacher trainers, but we can mention here some general types of knowledge and skills which should be an essential part of a training experience for any teacher trainer.

In order to form a good working relationship with the teachers he is serving, the trainer agent should receive training in communication skills. He should also receive sensitivity training to gain self-awareness and to appreciate the values, beliefs and orientations of other people. In addition, he should learn team building, collaboration skills, and small group processes.

To help his client schools in analyzing their problem areas, he should also learn a variety of diagnostic and problem-solving skills. Along with this he should be skilled at observation and documentation.

To translate problem statements into action, he should know how to plan a change program, and he should be able to help the client system arrive at a consensus on desired goals. He must also know how to deal with political issues and with conflict within a system.

To bring resources to bear on the problem, he must be expert in utilization skills and skilled at applying research methodology to the classroom. He should also have skills in the area of evaluation so that he can assess the results of his training efforts.

In addition to these skills, the trainer agent should learn how to keep himself up-to-date on current research bearing upon education and he should be able to teach some of the skills in this area to his clients.

4. *The Training Program*

A complete training program could be developed which might operate over an 18-month period. This would include field experience combined with a wide variety of classroom and laboratory experiences. A most advantageous arrangement would be joint sponsorship of the program by schools of education or teachers' colleges and State Departments of Education. The institute of higher education would provide resources of personnel and materials, and the program would lead to a formal degree from the institution. Whether a new degree should be created or a standard degree in the new field should be awarded is open to question. The State Department of Education would contribute to the training program by providing some of the laboratory experiences and overseeing the field experience in a local school district. Thus, the trainee would have the opportunity to learn about the operation of the agency which will ultimately sponsor him in his work and to develop working relationships with personnel of the department.

Some materials would need to be specifically developed for this program, but there are also a great number of materials already available which could be used with varying degrees of adaptation. The National Research Training Institute has developed manuals, workbooks and mediated self-instruction materials which would introduce the trainee to research, development, and evaluation skills. The National Audiovisual Center has established the National Depository of Prototype Teachers Educational Materials; these include videotape, slides, and micro-teaching packages. These materials are valuable for feedback, self-evaluation and program evaluation. Millgate's film strips on critical thinking and the book *Values and Teaching* by Raths et al. would also be valuable source materials.

In addition to classroom experiences which would introduce background and theory to the trainees, a range of laboratory experiences should also be provided. These could include sensitivity training, simulation, role playing, psychodrama and micro-teaching. Field training would provide the trainee with experiences in observation and data collection.

Although an 18-month program can be designed to provide all the training necessary, it is also important to keep the program flexible. Some trainees may already have experience in the field; for instance, a trainee might already be quite expert in community organization and his primary need would be to learn skills in the interpersonal area. Therefore, a training program should be designed to meet only those particular aspects of the person's skills which need improvement, since a complete and well-rounded program would only be redundant for such a person.

5. Criteria for Success in the Role

The teacher trainer's success can be judged only on the basis of whether or not he has demonstrated competency in bringing about desired behavior in teachers. The success of the teacher's behavior, in turn, can ultimately be judged only on the basis of whether he has brought about desired changes in his students.

6. The Evaluation Process

Judgement as to the adequacy of teacher behavior and the success of the trainer should take place over a one-or two-year period since some of the changes that the teacher has caused in the student incubate and are not evident until somewhat later.

No evaluation plan is offered for this training model but the task force suggests R.A. Stake's *The Countenance of Educational Evaluation* as a good starting point.*

7. How to Set the Role in an Institutional Context

We have suggested lodging the role of teacher trainer within the State Department of Education to give legitimation and credibility to the role. In addition to this, credibility from outside this agency would be of assistance in giving support to the role. The American Federation of Teachers and the

---

*Stake is at CIRCE, University of Illinois, Urbana, Illinois.

National Education Association are looked to by teachers for assent and leadership. It would therefore be helpful if the leadership of these organizations were involved in periodic seminars to inform them of the activities of the teacher trainers and to solicit their opinions on possible changes and additions which might be made in the conduct of the role.

VII

EFFECTING POLITICAL AND STRUCTURAL CHANGE IN SCHOOLS

Two task forces developed training models designed to alter the political structure of school systems, placing particular emphasis on redistribution of power within the system. The goals and change agent roles involved in these models are summarized in Table VII.1.

TABLE VII.1
PROGRAMS TO EFFECT POLITICAL AND STRUCTURAL
CHANGES IN SCHOOL SYSTEMS

REPORT	CLIENT	GOAL OF TRAINING MODEL	CHANGE AGENT ROLE
A. The Political Linkage Agent -Tye	The School: 1. Political sub-system (administration and board of education). 2. User groups (community, teachers and students).	Develop a rational strategy for equalization of power between political group and user groups.	*Political Linkage Agent (PLA)* 1. Process helper 2. Catalyst 3. Solution giver
B. Change through Crisis -Chesler, et al.	A School in Crisis	Utilization of crisis to define problems and re-structure the school system.	*Advocator-Organizer-Agitator (ADORAG)* 1. Define problems *Social Architect* 1. Restructure school system to solve problems

The differences between the change agent roles and the strategies advocated in these two papers are a result of different initial school situations which are assumed as the starting points of the planned intervention.

Whereas Chesler, et al. proposed a program to utilize a crisis situation in a school to restructure the system, the Tye model is designed to avert crisis by means of a rational strategy to redistribute power within the school system.

Tye's model is built on the assumption that, at the present time, power in a school system in controlled and exercised exclusively by the "political" subsystem (administration and board of education). He feels that this inhibits change and leads to a feeling of impotence and frustration on the part of the user groups, i.e., the community, teachers, and students. The goal of this model is to equalize power between the political group and the user groups so that policy formulation can become collaborative and so that the planning and management of change can be shared by all groups.

To accomplish this goal, Tye proposes the employment of a Political Linkage Agent (PLA) who would act as process helper, catalyst and solution giver during the process of equalization of power. The PLA would remain with the client system only until an equitable balance of power had been achieved.

The training of the PLA would reflect the specialized nature of his task. He would become knowledgeable in such areas as political and social systems theory, school government, small group processes, and negotiation procedures. He should also become skilled at diagnosis of power structures, ideology analysis and the planning of cooperative models of school governance. Tye envisions the training of a PLA to be a two year program with the first year devoted to seminars and laboratory experiences and the second year to include seminars, internships and the preparation of a dissertation.

The model put forward by Chesler, et al. is designed to take advantage of all the elements of a crisis situation to restructure the school system to better meet the needs of its members. Rather than employing an outside change agent to accomplish this process, it proposes that individuals from within the system be trained to fill two types of change agent roles. It is suggested that when a crisis occurs, a training team be called in to identify members of the system who are already exercising some degree of leadership in the crisis situation and to train these individuals to be more effective as agents of change. One type of change agent role for which "natural" candidates would be identified would be that of Advocator-Organizer-Agitator (ADORAG). The individuals selected would receive training which would enable them to arrive at a definition of system problems. The training would include instruction in organization of peers, bargaining and crowd control, recognition of fundamental issues and ways to move from values to actions. The other type of prospective change agent to be identified would be the Social Architect, whose role would be to restructure the school system in such a way as to solve the defined problems. These individuals would receive training in value clarification, organizational development skills, political and decision-making skills and diplomacy.

The training program itself is expected to take one to two years, with another two years required to accomplish the restructuring of the system. A key aspect of the training program would be the development of constructive team collaboration among the ADORAG's and the Social Architects.

A. The Political Linkage Agent*

Context

Any changes which are introduced into a school system are prescribed by the policy of that system. Therefore, to assure that a program of planned change will have more than superficial results, it must be preceded by an examination of the policy which has been determined by the system. If the proposed changes do not fit within the policy guidelines of the system, then a change in policy is clearly called for. The issue which we will address here is how changes in policy formulation can best be effected.

At the present time, the political subsystem (including the board of education and top administrators) of a local educational system establishes the policy for the schools in its jurisdiction. Such policy consists primarily of the determination of values and the allocation of resources. Because the political group seeks to maintain and/or maximize its power, policy decisions are likely to be made in an authoritarian manner, with little or no collaboration with the user groups of the system (community, teachers, and students).

However, when users are not allowed to participate in policy formulation, or when users' values differ from those of the people in power, the result is likely to be intense conflict. A struggle is likely to ensue in which the users attempt to wrest power from the hands of the political group. However, an escalation of conflict as a means of equalizing power in a time of already intense disequilibrium is certain to be non-constructive and has the potential of bringing about either anarchy or tyranny.

In order to avoid such conflict we feel that it is necessary to develop planned strategies for bringing about shared power through the broadening of the base of policy formulation. A rational approach of this kind is not simply desirable; it is imperative to the survival of both local and national educational systems. Perhaps a model of an educational system based on such rationally planned strategies can serve for many other types of social institutions as well.

*Drafted by Kenneth Tye; edited by Roberta McConochie and Mary C. Havelock.

1. The Role of the Political Linkage Agent

The role of "Political Linkage Agent" (PLA) would be to serve as liaison between the local political subsystem (board of education and school administration) and the user groups (community, students and teachers). His focus would be on policy formulation, and his primary task would be to assist the school system in building mechanisms for sharing power between the political role incumbents and the user groups.

To carry out this task the PLA would function, first, as a *process-helper*. He would attempt to improve the quality of exchange between the political subsystem and the user groups and would work to overcome the gate-keeping and rigid boundary maintenance by the political incumbents. Second, the PLA would act as a *catalyst*, helping his clients to identify problems and to focus on the issue of goals. Finally, the PLA would serve as a *solution-giver*. He would be able to link his client with appropriate resources from which possible solution alternatives could be derived. He and his client should then work together to choose and adopt the alternative best suited to solving the identified problems and meeting the established goals.

2. Preconditions of Selection for Training

Although the political linkage agent will learn many of the skills necessary to his position during the course of a training program, he should ideally possess some important qualifications at the outset. Hence, the following are stipulated as preconditions for selection of candidates for training for the role of PLA:

a. *A commitment to participatory democracy.* The PLA will answer to groups that have large amounts of power in the educational system, as well as to groups that are powerless. In this role, he will be vulnerable to being co-opted by the more powerful group. To insure that the change agent answers the needs of systems on both sides of the interface, the PLA would best be committed to non-authoritarian methods.

b. *An inquisitiveness about human phenomena.* The PLA will need to look for real, often non-obvious, causes of behavior and interaction patterns. These will usually not be apparent from a cursory examination of a situation or from the immediate explanations of his clients. If the agent is to be motivated to seek out the roots of issues and opinions, he would benefit from an innate curiosity regarding interpersonal exchange.

c. *A predisposition toward interaction with others.* Since the PLA is bound to be caught in a cross fire of interests, he will need to establish and maintain good working relationships and viable channels of communication with members of the various subsystems, including those with whom he differs.

d. *Sympathy.* The PLA will need to listen sympathetically to different, often opposing, points of view. To pose solutions that speak to the concerns of diverse interest groups, he will need to understand and sympathize with a variety of perspectives.

e. *Intelligence.* The PLA will need to be quick witted, flexible and creative. He must be open to discarding some alternatives as well as seizing upon others. He must be able to analyze any given situation in a rational manner, but, in addition, he must function alertly and responsively in crisis situations. Moreover, these qualities should be apparent to members of the various subsystems to insure his credibility.

f. *Low need for personal power.* The role of PLA does not lend itself to self-glorification. On the contrary, if the PLA is successful, the subsystems will eventually be able to establish their own mechanisms for self-evaluation and self-renewal and, in so doing, they will do the change agent out of his job (and perhaps enable him to move on to other systems which need his services).

3. Outputs from Training

A program for the training of political linkage agents should, first of all, provide the trainee with some basic knowledge about the theory and operation of political systems and about the process of planned change. Second, the trainee should learn a set of skills which he may employ in bringing his new knowledge to bear on the situation of his client system.

a. Knowledge.

i. *Political Systems and Social Systems Theory and Operation.* Since the PLA will be dealing with political and social structures, he will need a knowledge of how such systems operate and why they interact in certain ways. An examination of the range of theory in this area will give him a base upon which to construct new possibilities to fit the demands of new situations.

 ii. *School Government: Superordinate Political Systems (e.g. state legislature, state boards of education) and Subordinate Social Systems (e.g. schools, support systems).* To work effectively with these groups, the change agent will need to know the history and rationale of the structure and interaction of such systems as well as the types of issues which affect them.

 iii. *History and Philosphy of Education.* A study of these areas will provide the PLA with an essential background knowledge. He will gain from this a feeling for the types of approaches which have been used in the past to solve problems in education. He will become familiar with successes and failures in applying different theories and practices of education to different school situations.

 iv. *Organizational Theory and Operation.* A knowledge of organizational psychology will be extremely helpful in assisting the PLA to appraise the system's situation, difficulties and strengths. Findings in this area may provide *methodology* for coping with the situation as well as specific *solution alternatives* which may be introduced to improve it.

 v. *Small Group Theory and Operation.* Knowledge in this area will enable the PLA to understand and evaluate the interaction patterns, both interpersonal and intergroup, of the members of his client system. It will also provide him with valuable insights into his own interaction with his clients.

 vi. *Resource Systems.* The PLA will need to be familiar with appropriate resources upon which he may draw in carrying out planned change; he must know where to find them and how to use them. He might consult a variety of centers, groups or materials depending on the situation (e.g. ACLU, policy centers, Educational Research Information Centers).

 vii. *Negotiation Procedures.* For achieving consensus on goals, problem diagnosis and solutions, the PLA will need to have a knowledge of the procedures which may be employed in arbitration. Ultimately, the success of the change effort will depend on effecting agreements among subsystems.

b. Skills.

 i. *Diagnosis of the Client System's Formal and Informal Power Structures and Extant Channels of Access to the Political Subsystems.* Before the PLA can hope to institute any changes in the distribution of power, he must first analyze the existing structure of both the user and political power systems. He must identify not only the formal leaders, but also the informal opinion leaders within each group. In addition, he must determine whether there are persons outside the system who are influential in the determination of policy.

ii. *Analysis of the Subsystems' Ideologies.* Skills in determining the value stance of his client will be essential to the effective functioning of the PLA. He will need to find out the values, beliefs, interests, preferences and opinions of members of both the political system and the user system in order to deal effectively with them.

iii. *Diagnosis of User's and Political System's Demand and Support Patterns.* The PLA will need to know what resources (human, material and financial) are available to each of the subsystems of his client and how these resources are utilized in carrying out policy. This will give him an indication of how effectively these resources are being used at the present time, as well as informing him on what may be available to him as he begins to formulate a plan for change.

iv. *Examination of Each Subsystem's Conversion Processes, Structurally and Functionally.* The PLA must be able to diagnose how each subsystem actually goes about converting policy into action. He must find out which individuals are responsible for instituting changes once policy decisions have been made, the extent to which lower level personnel are involved in the planning of change programs, and the methods used to persuade affected persons to adopt the change. Only after determining the present state of affairs can the PLA begin to make recommendations to improve these procedures.

v. *Group Operation and Group Problem-Solving.* The PLA will need to operationalize his knowledge in this area. He will need to be a process observer, advocate, and arbitrator in the context of small group meetings with members of the various subsystems.

vi. *Planning Alternative Models of Cooperative Governance Based on Data and Needs.* Once the PLA has extracted information from the systems regarding interests, goals, structures and history of interaction, he will need to propose alternative solutions which answer the problems of the various interest groups and which contribute to their growth.

4. *Ways to Provide Training*

The training program suggested here lends itself to a graduate program designed to educate prospective political linkage agents in areas relevant to the development of cooperative school governance. A two-year program could be designed in which the first year was devoted primarily to seminars and laboratory experiences. The second year would include seminars, internships, and the preparation of a dissertation.

a. Types of Materials.

i. *Research and Theory.* Materials should be included which cover the range of topics described above as the desired "knowledge" outputs of training. One broad area to be covered is the theory and operation of small groups and of larger political and social systems, with special attention being paid to materials on the educational system in particular. In addition, materials on negotiation procedures and educational resource systems should be incorporated in the curriculum.

ii. *Case Studies.* Appropriate case study materials would include examples of community conflict, school board decision-making, decentralized decision-making, and power utilization.

iii. *Problem-Solving Frameworks.* Havelock's (A GUIDE TO INNOVATION IN EDUCATION, 1973) analysis of the process of change would provide valuable theoretical background and practical guidelines.

iv. *Diagnostic Instruments.* Existing diagnostic instruments which might be utilized include those appropriate to (1) power structures (Kimbrough, Ralph B. "Power Structures and Educational Change," 1967); (2) ideologies and beliefs (Gallup)*; (3) demand and support patterns (Tye)**; and (4) conversion processes (Scribner).***

v. *Group Decision-Making Simulation and Evaluation Material.* Examples of useful items in this category might include "Truck Driver," "Walk on the Moon" and "IPA."

vi. *Negotiation Procedures.*

b. Types of Experiences.

i. *Seminars.* The seminars should cover the materials listed above under "Research and Theory," "Case Studies" and "Problem-Solving Frameworks." Readings and films should serve to stimulate discussions of the materials being covered.

---

*Gallup, George, "Third Annual Report of the Public Attitude Toward Public Education 1971," PHI DELTA KAPPAN, September, 1971, Vol. 53, p. 33+.

**Tye, Kenneth, "Conceptual Framework for Political Analysis Public Demand and School Board Decisions," Unpublished Dissertation, Los Angeles, California: University of California, Los Angeles, 1968.

***Scribner, Jay D., "The Politics of Education Reform: Analyses of Political Demands," URBAN EDUCATION, January, 1970, Vol. 4, No. 4, pp. 348-374.

ii. *Laboratory Experiences.* First, trainees should participate in exercises which demonstrate group operation, problem-solving and decision-making. Second, they should be trained in the use of diagnostic instruments; and, finally, they should participate in negotiation simulations and should learn techniques of handling confrontation situations.

iii. *Internships.* Each trainee should serve as an intern, both within a political subsystem (school board, administration) and within a user group (community action groups, teacher groups, student groups). This on-the-job training should involve practice in the use of diagnostic tools and laboratory experiences.

iv. *Dissertation.* The trainee's experiences as an intern would provide the content for a dissertation which would analyze the host school system in terms of its power structure and its policy-making, decision-making, and decision-implementation procedures. In his dissertation the trainee should also consider how he would act in the role of political linkage agent to bring about an equitable redistribution of power and effective communication and collaboration between user and political groups within the school system.

5. Criteria for Success in the Role

Four criteria may be listed by which success in the role of political linkage agent may be judged. The first and primary criterion is that there should be an *equitable balance of power* within the system. If power is fairly distributed, there may be minor skirmishes between groups over scattered issues, but there will be no rigidly drawn lines of battle.

The second criterion should be evidence of *collaborative policy formulation*. The user groups and the political subsystems should work together to make decisions on policy, and each group should be reasonably satisfied with its own role. If there are significant dissatisfactions, these may be an indication that power is not yet appropriately distributed.

The third-level criterion is that implementation of policy decisions should result in *genuine adoption of prescribed changes* throughout the system. If all groups are working together in formulating policy, there should be no reason for any one group to resist changes. Therefore, if there is noticeable resistance, we might suspect that policy decisions have not been made in a fully collaborative fashion.

Finally, a most important criterion of success of the PLA is that the school system should be able to meet the above three criteria without further assistance from the PLA. When this occurs, the PLA can move on to another school system.

6. *Evaluation Process*

Evaluation of the effectiveness of a PLA should be based on a survey of the results of a system-wide change recently introduced into the system. A sampling should be made of all individuals affected by the change to assess their views on the following: (a) whether the change was of major or minor significance; (b) whether the change has been beneficial and successful; (c) whether there was adequate preparation before the change was introduced; (d) how much the individual participated in selecting and planning for the change, and (e) whether the individual is satisfied with the role he played in the planning.

The responses given by individuals within each of the subgroups of the system should then be compared with responses from the other groups. From this we can assess whether the change was more appealing to one group than to another, whether each group participated equally and appropriately, and whether each group is satisfied with the role it played in decision-making.

7. *Setting the Role in an Institutional Context*

Installation of the role of political linkage agent within a school system is a particularly difficult problem. Someone trying to be a PLA may be readily accepted by the user groups, but to be effective, the PLA will have to be legitimated by the political subsystem -- the very group whose power he will be seeking to distribute over a broader base. In addition, his role would be compromised if he were required to report to either the school administration or the board of education. Clearly, a good deal of experimentation would be required to determine the optimal institutional arrangements. Independence could be achieved with financial and social support from private sources, foundations, church groups (which often provide much of the support for Saul Alinsky's work), PTA's, neighborhood and community associations and the professional-labor associations of teachers and others (see discussion by Dorros in the Appendix). Each of these arrangements would have its trade-offs so that possibly some combination among them would be optimal.

B. Change-Through-Crisis Model*

Context

Recurring crises are now the norm in most U.S. schools. These crises, however, are not being examined, researched, or utilized to contribute to the

---

*Drafted by Mark Chesler, Arthur Chickering, Per Dalin, Dale Lake, Matthew Miles, Everett Rogers and Lucille Schaible; edited by Roberta McConochie and Mary C. Havelock.

planning and restructuring of the institutions; but are treated as abnormal, aberrant incidents which need to be curtailed quickly so that the status quo may be resumed as expeditiously as possible. One of the reasons that these incidents are not being perceived as a source of growth for the institution is the lack of individuals whose roles would enable them to utilize the opportunities for adaptive growth of the institution and to insure that the institution is in a position to react to crises in such a way that they will contribute to the growth of the individuals within it as well as of the institution itself.

A model of change-through-crisis will be presented here which utilizes disruption in educational systems as an important input variable in creating a self-renewing institution. Special change agent roles will be described which will function in this model to insure that crises will be used constructively to strengthen both system members and system flexibility.

Further insight into this model may be provided by describing the conception of "change" as it is used here. Change is seen as the restructuring of the educational system itself; more than the content of the system must be changed if there is to be a genuine and non-superficial response to crisis. Restructuring in this sense implies that the real power in the educational system may lie outside of one single institution or even a group of institutions that exist along the same dimension in hierarchy. Excluded power forces would be linked to present empowered groups; all groups that have expressed or implicit motives for change would be built into the decision-making processes. One of the advantages in utilizing crises is that the empowered group, finding itself in a vulnerable position, may be brought by the unempowered groups (with the assistance of the change agents) to legitimated accountability to those other groups.

Thus, the general objective of this model is to develop and test models and methods for utilizing crises in educational institutions to produce radical re-design and restructuring of decision-making methods, reward systems, and instructional content, methods and organization.

The targets of this model are high schools, but the model is general enough to permit application to a wider number of institutions.

1. The Roles of the Change Agents

The manner of accomplishing restructuring according to this model necessitates the creation of at least two new roles. The first role is that of an advocator-organizer-agitator (ADORAG), who clarifies and defines the problem -- sometimes by helping it to surface or to escalate. The second role is that of architect-designer, who insures that the crisis be used constructively rather than being reacted to simply for purposes of restoring the status quo.

a. The Advocate-Organizer-Agitator (ADORAG)

Because of his political and ego strength, the ADORAG is relatively invulnerable in the system. He is able to raise the consciousness of his followers and to ride or create a crisis. The ADORAG can translate values into focused action and can escalate frictions to issues of fundamental structural importance. For example, he can translate the issue of the summary expulsion of students to the more important and general issue of due process and civil rights.

b. The Social Architect

The person in this role might take action after the crisis has subsided, or work during it, to create a restructured educational system. He would design new processes to handle value conflicts. The social architect would need "pursuit" skills (to follow through the crisis), would need to maintain his equilibrium in face of the crisis and would need to be creative and adaptive to the special characteristics of the crisis and the system. He would also need to be cosmopolite, aware of alternatives and external resources and posess a sophistication regarding social alternatives and various models of educational practice.

These two roles, however, will not be able to accomplish change alone. Without a support network they are not sufficient to accomplish change. Provisions will be made in this model for providing such a support network and for insuring the integration or linkage of these two individuals with the rest of the support system.

Each of the two main roles may reside within a single person, or possibly in small systems. Most often, however, the roles would be held by several different persons, possibly each with his own support system.

Other important roles, specified but not so well defined in the change-through-crisis model, are the interface with the rest of the system, the executer, legitimator, and supporter. This person, or several persons, insures the power of the first two roles in the system.

2. Preconditions for Selection for Training

Because of a crisis in an educational system, it is assumed that a team of consultants has been called in to diagnose the situation. The primary role of this consultant, or training team, would be to locate persons within the systems in crisis who are already focusing on causes of the crisis and can help redesign the system to better structures. Thus, one of the primary functions of the training team would be to identify and legitimize persons in the conflicted systems who hold the keys to the escalation and resolution of conflict.

Regarding the ADORAG, "naturals" will hopefully become visible to the training team. Oppressed conditions, artificially created in training laboratories, may assist in the identification. Architect-redesigners will also have to be screened on the basis of values and skills. A general rule of thumb will be to select "on the battlefield" as opposed to "in the classroom" or from bull-sessions where rhetoric may predominate.

For the role of interface, the training team may want to take volunteers or informally selected persons and test them under simulated conditions. Other outside support systems and collaborators may suggest themselves; these, however, should always be tested before being put on the firing line. One might check the informal networks for likely prospects or elicit a call to arms and test those who respond.

3. Outputs from Training

a. The ADORAG

The ADORAG who has been identified by the consultant team will already possess some natural skills to perform his role. Hence, training inputs will have to balance the spontaneous natural talents with trained skills which, being less natural, may be more difficult for the person to perform.

Training for the ADORAG should increase his invulnerability in the system and the complexity of his analysis, enabling him to consider many variables simultaneously. His ability to know and recognize the fundamental issues as well as to escalate protests to that level would be enhanced. His capacity to organize his peers will need to be developed, along with discriminatory skills regarding appropriate times to escalate or de-escalate crises. He will need increased skills in bargaining, crowd control, and rhetoric variance. Knowledge of the law and strategies of confrontation and civil disobedience will be extremely helpful. Additionally, he will need to know how to effect quick withdrawals at times, to gather data from his followers, and to move from values to actions.

In order to benefit from the change process, he would need to learn how to work effectively with the social architects, how to collaborate with his earlier enemies, and how to gain a sense of shared consciousness.

b. The Social Architect

As in the case of the ADORAG, the social architect will already possess a number of relevant natural skills, and these should be developed rather than replaced. The pursuit skills, the "vision," and the cosmopoliteness of the social architect would be increased in training. He would need inputs in the areas of value clarification and organization developmental skills. His ability to size up the political and decision-making structures would be increased. Additionally, he would need to know the characteristics of his own educational system and his own "cultural history," as well as characteristics of broader societal systems. The social architect is a link between the executors and will therefore need "diplomatic training" in managing different interest systems.

One additional function of the outside training-consultant team is to insure that the ADORAG and social architect and their supporters function as a team and not just as a collection of various roles. Each role may in itself be a team, but together they must also function as a team.

4. How to Provide Training

The training event will be more a process than a single event, and it is a process which will go on for several years. The estimated time to train the cadres and roles described above is one to two years; the time needed to develop a truly self-renewing system will be three to four years.

As a prelude to the training, there might be a retrieval conference of existing ADORAG's and architect-redesigners. Work conferences with separate but parallel events for the ADORAG's and social architects would be held with an opportunity for mutual confrontation. Materials would be assembled; training designs and strategies would be worked out.

Next, there would be a pilot program or a summer training event for a chosen school district. Teams of advocates and architects would be identified and developed within the system. Emphases would be on cognitive and skill learning and on team building. Recruiting such teams may require financial and academic (in the sense of credit) support from the schools for the students, teachers, and administrators involved.

At this point, the four-year enterprise would actually begin. Three to six "crucial" school districts in one state would be identified in which inside and outside change teams would work on their projects. Opportunities for cross-team communication and support would be provided, and consulting events involving all the participating school districts would be interspersed with team project work during this time.

Intermittent support events for superintendents in the school districts would also be held. And, in the final stages, there would be production of diffusable materials, practices, and models.

Some of the possible products that might be diffused are new decision-making structures and processes, models for alternative future schools, and methods of confrontation and crisis development and use.

All information obtained from a retrieval conference would be distributed to students as well as to the administration. It would be beneficial if networks of national architects were established. Information from such a network pertaining to innovations in education could be distributed to students, parents, and other interest groups, giving these groups some incentive to pressure the system for further change.

VIII
CHANGING
THE LARGER SYSTEM

The task force reports drafted by Benne, et al. and by Millgate and Lippitt are both concerned with improving the effectiveness of the operations of educational agencies other than schools. A brief outline of each report is given in Table VIII.1

TABLE VIII.1
PROGRAMS TO IMPROVE THE EFFECTIVENESS
OF OTHER EDUCATIONAL AGENCIES

REPORT	CLIENT	GOAL OF TRAINING MODEL	CHANGE AGENT ROLE
A. Macrosystems Model -Benne, et al.	Two systems jointly involved in educational change, e.g., USOE and State Departments of Education.	Improve intersystem relationship.	*Interface Agent* 1. Resolve conflicts 2. Set goals 3. Utilize resources 4. Improve on-going relationships
B. "Delivery" Dilemma of State Departments of Education -Millgate & Lippitt	State Department of Education	A conference approach to improve the quality of delivery service by State Departments of Education to Local School Systems.	No change agent role: All personnel in the department work to: 1. Identify quality services 2. Set goal images 3. Diagnose department problems 4. Implement improvement alternatives

Beyond their concern with non-school educational agencies, these two reports have little in common. The model proposed by Benne, et al. has the goal of improving relationships between two systems by means of a change agent who would operate externally to both systems as a permanent linkage agent at the interface. The goal of the Millgate and Lippitt model, on the other hand, is to improve the internal operation of one system, through a program to train all members of the system to be their own change agents.

The model which Benne, et al. designed was prompted by the need to improve the relationship between the USOE and the State Departments of Education in order that they might be more effective in carrying out joint programs. However, the model is equally applicable to any two educational agencies which jointly share the responsibility of carrying out change programs, or to any two systems which must work together. It is felt that the change agent role would most effectively be filled by a team of agents chosen either from within *both* the interacting systems or from outside both systems. The functions of the change agent team would include resolving conflicts and assisting the client systems in setting goals and utilizing resources to meet these goals, but its most important function would be to improve on the ongoing relationship between the client systems.

In order to carry out this role, the team would need training experience in a wide variety of areas, including client relationships, diagnostic skills, process observation and intervention skills, conflict resolution and resource utilization. The trainees would also receive training in team collaboration. The proposed training program would be an in-service process in which the two client systems, the trainee team and a training consultant team would collaborate.

Millgate and Lippitt propose a program to improve the quality of the "delivery" of services by the State Department of Education to local school systems. The program would be initiated with a conference of about two days which would involve all members of the department. The purpose of the conference would be to identify quality services, to derive generalizations about ways in which services are presently being carried out, and to set goal images for future improvement of delivery of services. The conference would conclude with the establishment of inquiry teams to conduct a diagnosis of the system. A follow-up event would be held to derive implications from the diagnostic findings and to choose alternative solutions for try-out. During the implementation stage laboratory sessions for skills development would be held, and finally, at the end of about one year, an evaluation session would be held to decide on future programs.

A. Macrosystems*

Context

The governances of educational macrosystems, e.g. the U.S. Office of Education and the State Departments of Education, often require that these

---

*Drafted by Kenneth Benne, David Bushnell, Norman Hearn, Edwin Hildebrand, Norman Kurland and Robert Neiman; edited by Roberta McConochie and Mary C. Havelock.

systems cooperatively carry out programs. Thus, two or more such systems may find themselves with identical goals, and the systems may all be accountable for success or failure to each other as well as to themselves. In these situations, an effective means of inter-system communication is essential, but the people who now serve in such facilitating roles usually do not have the necessary training, skills, and credentials to adequately carry out their roles. The interface agents that now exist between macrosystems are often self-appointed and are likely to be visibility-seeking or disgruntled members of the staff of one of the macrosystems. Hence, the effects of the change attempts initiated by this type of interface agent are usually episodic and reflect the felt need for implementing new directives and legislation, with little thought of the importance of establishing good on-going relationships between systems. Macrosystems lower in the hierarchy tend to accept unquestioningly the prescriptions and directives of higher agencies which may exacerbate macrosystem relations problems.

The interface between the U.S.O.E. and the State Departments of Education is of particular importance, but the need exists for better relationships between any number of federal agencies which are involved in educational programs. Such agencies as the Office of Management and Budget, the President's Science Advisory Committee, Congressional Appropriation Committees and HEW are often involved in joint programs with the U.S.O.E. or the State Departments of Education.

In this paper we will attempt to generate a macrosystems model which will be equally applicable to any of these interface situations. We will develop a training program for the role of macrosystem interface agent which will speak to some of the difficulties mentioned. The intended beneficiaries are, of course, the client systems involved. In the long run, however, students, parents and local school district personnel would benefit from the improved procedures and more equitable distribution of resources.

1. The Role of Macrosystems Interface Agent

The change agent role developed in this macrosystems model would be filled by a person or persons who function at the interface of two systems for the purpose of improving the quality of the interaction or exchange across system boundaries. Such systems may be at equivalent or at different positions in an educational hierarchy.

The interface agent would seek to help the two systems resolve inter-system conflicts, cooperate in setting goals, utilize resources effectively to achieve these goals, and improve the effectiveness of regular on-going activities and exchanges between the two systems.

Examples of interface positions which now exist are the professional staff of the Department of Education, the Education Commission of the States, state management review teams, and state educational agency consultants to local educational agencies.

2. Preconditions for Selection for Training

If an interface agent were recruited from just one of the two macrosystems involved in an exchange process, the outcome of the interchange could well be biased. Therefore, it would be advisable if key persons from within both systems were "freed up" to function together as a team. Alternatively, change agents could be recruited from outside both systems; such agents would not be subject to the same pressures and expectations as those who come from within the systems. Whether the agents are recruited from inside or outside the systems, however, they should have some intimate knowledge of how one or both systems operate.

The initial selection of the interface agents should be cautious; personality configurations are as important as role responsibilities. Potential agents should have characteristics of trustworthiness and credibility since these are essential to any good working relationship. Beyond this, however, the specification of other desired qualifications would depend on the nature of the macrosystems involved and their unique relationship.

3. Outputs from Training

First of all, the interface agents will have to learn to function together as a team. Members must work out their own inter-relationship and should develop a common image of a shared mission.

Next, trainees should learn how to establish fast working relationships with the client systems.

The trainees should also learn a set of diagnostic skills. First, they must be able to analyze the norms, power structure, and communication network of each of the two client systems. Second, they must be able to recover rapidly and accurately the history of the relationship between the two systems and to use this history constructively to overcome barriers to the successful interactions of the systems. Finally, as well as dealing with the past, the trainees must learn to deal with present hostilities and conflicts between the systems.

Once the past and present capacities and limitations of the client systems have been examined, the agents must know how to establish consensus on working procedures and intended outcomes. Process observation and intervention skills are essential here; the agents must have the ability to stop the interaction at any point and conduct a process evaluation or review.

To effect closure on short- and long-term planning, the helping agents will need the ability to bring work phases to a conclusion, to achieve consensus on what was accomplished and what the next step should be. Agreement must also be achieved on commitments, including the allocation of time and financial resources. Reaching such agreement may require considerable negotiating skills.

Finally, the change agent team needs the ability to recognize and utilize available resources effectively in achieving goals.

4. The Training Program

The development of change agents cannot be accomplished in a single or even a series of workshops. Rather, training of the macrosystems interface agents should be an in-service process combined with working for the macrosystems themselves. Thus, part of the content of the training would be derived from regular on-going work problems.

The training effort would initially be a four-way collaboration, including members of each of the interfacing macrosystems, the interface change agent trainee team, and a training consultant team. Ultimately, however, the training consultants should disengage as the interface team builds its own skills.

The initial training program would be directed toward equipping the helping team to be self-sufficient in dealing with the macrosystems, to gain knowledge about the systems and to plan and direct their own activities. The actual change process would be, in some part, a duplication of this training effort, but it would involve more members of the interface systems, at all levels of personnel, in developing their own skills in the cooperative planning and execution of change processes.

The training and change process would be cyclical: planning, evaluation, action, evaluation, training, evaluation, action, etc. This basic design is adaptable to many types of situations involving cross-system boundaries.

It must be possible to secure or develop resources for change and training. The training design for any particular situation would need to be specifically developed to fit the resources available and to utilize these effectively, but certain general guidelines may be suggested for the types of activities appropriate for the training of interface change agent teams.

First, to increase the ability of the interface agents to function effectively as a team, there would need to be cooperative exercises. Theoretical input regarding small group functioning and emergence of group structure might be helpful. Some sensitivity training would be beneficial in the initial training stages to improve intra-group process as well as being helpful later on during the change effort itself.

Practice should be provided in the area of developing contact skills. These would be put to use at once by the trainees in establishing a relationship with other interface team members. Later, these skills would be used in the actual creation of formal and informal contacts to build fast working relationships within and between systems and teams. At this point, as well as during the entire process, one would try to insure that neither team nor system (particularly the one lower in the hierarchy) is coopted by informal contacts.

To focus on building diagnostic skills, there might be an assessment-simulation game involving each system in appraising and gathering data on the culture of other systems. Initially, the helping team would carry out these exercises to build its own skills. Later, as the team moved into the actual change program, groups of persons from both client systems would be involved and there would be less "simulation" and more real life "sizing up". At this point, some organizational psychology input involving observer checklists for appraising an organization would be helpful.

To aid in the recovery of the interaction history of the two systems, real situation analysis might be employed. Emphasis on identifying stereotypes might benefit the helping team's interactions with members of the macro-systems, as well as its own intra-group interactions.

To facilitate the gathering of data about the client systems, interviewing skills may be of assistance. To illustrate the actual effectiveness of data gathered in this manner, a game or role-playing situation might be devised in which data would be gathered and then "action" would be taken based on the data.

To identify and deal with inter-system conflicts, conflict resolution games and exercises would be played out, first within the helping team and then between members of both macrosystems.

As an aid in achieving consensus on work procedures, simulation and analysis of process intervention could be conducted, first within the helping team and later within and among both systems. "Practice" decision-making, e.g. simulation, games, and negotiating exercises, would contribute to the development of the ability to reach closure on work phases and in ultimately bringing work to a conclusion.

For writing reports, analyzing and criticizing case studies might be constructive.

Finally, training in the skills of critical and constructive evaluation would be essential both for the helping team and for the two macrosystems involved in the change program. This evaluation would pave the way for future interaction both within and between the systems.

5. How to Set the Role in an Institutional Context

It is assumed that one or both sides of an interface will see the need for the linking role. The initiative to create an interface role might come from either system regardless of its relative position in the hierarchy. It is assumed, however, that both systems have a certain openness to change and a readiness to at least talk about it. Any change program must build on, as well as develop, the readiness and receptivity of both systems toward change, thus assuring reciprocity of benefits regardless of which system might have initiated the change.

The possibility of change will, at the early stages in the development of the interface agents, need to be legitimized by both macrosystems. Thus, the improvement desires of key management in both systems might need to be identified, possibly at a meeting involving the interface team and leaders of the macrosystems. At this point, the macrosystems model assumes rationality among members of the two systems; i.e., if there is a conflict of need, or even a disagreement as to the need for change, it can be worked out to the satisfaction of members of both systems. Additionally, the interface agents themselves would need the endorsement of members of both systems if they were to effect the change process.

This model rationally assumes that there need be no crisis, nor an escalation or confrontation, for change to occur. But, although it is assumed that the leadership of the macrosystems will recognize the need for change, proof of this need may have to be demonstrated to the system members by gathering data through questionnaires or other methods, or by confrontation with unhappy members or groups.

Early in the planning and assessment process, the interface agents will want to collect data from both systems regarding perceived strengths and weaknesses of each as well as the perceived history of the interactions between the two systems. This data could provide an orientation for the interface agents as well as suggesting entry strategies to the systems' membership.

Before the training process could be further delineated, the interface-helping team and the client systems would need to collaborate on a cost-benefit analysis: Will this examination and diagnosis be worth the effort and expenditure? Would the present capacities of the interface-helping team be sufficient, or would there need to be a heavy investment in outside resources? The effort required might best be weighed against the capacities of the helping team. A judgment to proceed implies at least the capacity to acquire needed resources. Also, at this point, an explicit decision in favor of change might increase the commitment of both systems to the process.

Subsequent to a decision to proceed, training consultants would collaborate with the interface team to initiate the training process and the helping experience. Training needs would be identified on the basis of diagnoses of the client system.

At this time, working papers would be produced, outlining the characteristics of the client systems and indicating the agreed-upon goals. Members of both systems would be invited to collaborate in deciding on these goals and in revising and changing them as the situation and relationships changed. Collaboration at this point might achieve greater consensus in the long run than would creation of the goals without some participation of persons in both systems.

B. A Proposed Conference Approach to Solve "Delivery" Dilemma of State Departments of Education*

Context

The fundamental task of a State Department of Education is to deliver services to the school systems in that state. At the present time, however, there are decided deficiencies in this delivery system, and these deficiencies can be described in terms of a three-part dilemma.

The first part of the dilemma is that members of the staff of the State Departments of Education generally do not feel any pain about the inadequacy of their delivery of services to the local schools. That is, they may have some degree of sensitivity to the fact that they have potentially valuable facts and materials which are not being conveyed to the schools, but rather than devising new means of transmitting this information, they find it more comfortable to maintain the status quo.

The second part of the dilemma is that these individuals do not make any connection between their sensitivity to the inadequacy of delivery services and their personal sense of impotency about remedying the inadequacies. That is, they do not seem to recognize that by making a change in their own behavior, they would have the power to help to bring about a state of affairs which they realize would be beneficial.

The third part of the dilemma is that the members of the State Departments of Education do not have any shared or interdependent goal images about models or criteria for the delivery of services. That is, even if an individual should want to change his behavior to effect improvements, there is no department policy to guide him in defining what would be an improvement or how to carry it out.

1. Proposed Approach to Solve Dilemma

Rather than proposing the creation of a new role of change agent to stimulate better delivery of services to local schools, we feel that this dilemma can best be solved by a program designed to improve the internal operation of the State Departments of Education. In this paper, the outline of such a program will be developed. This can be viewed as a training program which defines and improves the functioning of each role within the system rather than a training program for a new role.

The program would be initiated by the Superintendent or Commissioner of Education, who would propose a professional development conference which would include the whole department of education. The content of the

*Drafted by Irving Millgate and Ronald Lippitt; edited by Mary C. Havelock.

conference would be designed to address in detail each part of the dilemma described above. Participants would first consider different types of delivery services for the purpose of distinguishing services of good quality from those of poor quality. They would then derive from this a goal image of how to improve the quality of their own services. Once the goals have been established, individuals will be able to plan how their own behavior can be altered to contribute to goal achievement.

This conference would be the opening event of a one-year program which would ultimately result in implementation of behaviors and goals. Following the conference, back-home continuity would be provided by a commitment to applying, testing and developing in-service models formulated at the conference. There would be a continuous sharing of utilization on a voluntary basis at different levels of involvement and commitment. During the year, additional events should be scheduled for follow-up, evaluation, and skills development.

2. The Training Program

The opening conference should be planned to cover one evening and the two following days. At the start of the conference, participants should be divided into small groups according to a pre-drawn plan, with a table provided for each group of about eight members. Membership in each group should be heterogeneous and should represent cross-status levels. No one should report to anyone else at the table and everyone should be a peer to everyone else.

On the first night of the conference, all participants should view a film that compares two different approaches of State Department staff trying to deliver services to local schools.

Each table should then be provided with a set of ten generalizations, taken from research, on relationships between the types of services rendered by the State Department of Education and the quality of educational performance of the school staff serviced.

The remainder of the evening should be spent in an open-ended session in which each group questions the validity of the research generalizations and determines under what circumstances each of the generalizations is true.

The session on the following day should be conducted in the same small group formation, and no breaks should be allowed during the day. Coffee could be available at all times, and a buffet lunch served from 11:30-1:30 on portable trays. The day-long session should be scheduled to include the following activities to be performed by each group:

a. From the generalizations which they examined on the previous evening, participants should be asked to derive as many implication statements as they can about ways of improving quality of service.

b. Each table should be instructed to take a group fantasy trip through a State Department of Education of a mythical state, one year from the present. Each participant can choose to observe any department in the mythical Department of Education and note any change which makes him happy.

c. Each participant should jot down his thoughts on the above for ten minutes. The group members should then share these thoughts and identify the most exciting goal images. The two most important goal images should then be selected.

d. The groups should brainstorm on these selected goals, thinking of all the possible things people could do in the present to move toward such goals. (No ideas should be called "crazy"--everything is acceptable.)

e. The groups should then repeat items (b), (c) and (d), but this time, they should consider their own Department of Education in particular, rather than the general or mythical situation.

f. Participants should be asked to consider again the generalizations that they felt were true about other settings. They should now check the ones which they think are also generalizable to themselves. This should be done individually to provide maximum transition to self in this exercise.

g. Each group should make additional generalizations (like the ones they examined the previous evening) about what they do in the delivery of services to school systems and what effects this has.

At the end of the day, each group should have arrived at two primary goal images for their own department and a set of generalizations about the quality of services which they deliver to local schools. These findings should be handed in to the conference leaders who will collate and combine findings from all groups during the evening.

On the final morning of the conference, each group should receive a copy of the composite group findings from the previous day. The groups should then consider what additional things they need to know about themselves to improve the quality of their services and to meet the specified goals. They should then discuss how to go about getting this additional data; specific sets of needed fact-finding activities should be grouped together so that about 10-20 general areas of needed inquiry activities will result.

There should be a break for lunch at this point, during which time the conference leaders should collate the results of the morning meeting. They should arrive at a final list of about 20 areas of needed inquiry, and, after the lunch break describe this list to the conference as a whole.

Each participant should then sign up for the inquiry team which appears to be most appropriate to his skills and interest. The resulting teams should then meet during the remainder of the afternoon to consult about plans for the inquiry it will conduct, and the conference should then be adjourned.

A follow-up meeting of one-half day should be held about a month later. At this meeting, the progress of the inquiry teams should be reported. It should be determined that all areas of inquiry are being adequately covered and that there is no overlap between teams. Any indicated adjustments in activities of teams or individuals should be made at this time.

About a month later a derivation session of one day should be held. At this meeting the findings of the inquiry teams will be reported. From these findings implications will be derived about ways in which delivery of service may be improved. The best alternatives should be chosen and a decision should be made to implement try-outs of these.

Following this meeting, details of the implementation strategies should be planned by the individuals involved in each of the change alternatives to be implemented. These groups of individuals will work together as change teams throughout the remainder of the year. Scheduling of necessary training events and activities will depend on the nature of the change alternatives which have been selected for implementation, and different events will be scheduled by each change team. There will, however, be some overlap in indicated activities and in personnel involved in the different change programs, and change strategies for the various programs should be compared so that joint activities may be scheduled when possible. For instance, it is most likely that skills training will be indicated for each change team and a confrontation laboratory for skills development could be held for all members of the department.

In addition to holding joint training sessions where appropriate, communication among change teams at frequent intervals should be encouraged. Meetings might be held each month in which representatives from each change team could meet together to discuss progress, coordinate the programs, and help each other in future planning.

At the end of the year, an evaluation conference should be held which would involve all members of the department. Evaluation of each implemented change should be made on the basis of: 1) level of satisfaction of the involved State Department personnel with their roles and contributions; 2) the effect of the change on the local school system; and 3) the degree to which the change has measured up to the goal image which was agreed upon at the start-up conference. A decision should be made in each case as to whether any alterations should be made in the implemented change. Finally, plans for implementation of future change alternatives should be made.

IX

SAMPLE MODEL OF A FULLY DEVELOPED TRAINING DESIGN

In Chapter IV we presented a framework for designing training programs regardless of the type or level of change process. Chapters V through VIII of Part Two included outlines of training program alternatives. In this last chapter, we would like to detail a training design which follows the framework of Chapter IV fairly closely. This design was prepared initially in June 1970, at the specific request of the National Center for Educational Communication as a planning document for their pilot program to train and install a small number of state education agency consultants as full-time professional change agents. The program was conceived as a 10-day training sequence distributed over a one-year period with intervening reading and writing assignments and several types of on-the-job practice. It is intended to be used in conjunction with *A GUIDE TO INNOVATION IN EDUCATION*. The program is systematic and intensive, calling for a high investment of intellect and behavior of trainers and trainees. However, the end result would be a solid sense of accomplishment and a set of action skills for educators useful at every career stage. *Every* educator might eventually possess the skills described here. However, this program singles out particular individuals in a strategic location, the state education agency, as the "change agents" who will become, over time, a core training staff for the agency and for the state system as a whole. In this sense, therefore, the proposed program is not for the training of change "agents" as much as it is for the training of *trainers* in change planning and managing skills.

The program description is outlined as follows:

1. The Role
   a. Title
   b. Definition and General Description
   c. Rationale
   d. Limiting Assumptions

2. Trainee Candidate Qualifications for Participation

3. Anticipated Outcomes of Training
   a. Attitudes
   b. Knowledge
   c. Skills

4. The Training Procedure, including:
   a. Schedule
   b. Trainer and Trainee Preparation
   c. Readings
   d. Outline Descriptions of Training Units

5. Guidelines for Installation of Trainees in State Agency Positions

6. Suggested *Criteria* for Evaluating
   a. Training Transfer Effectiveness
   b. Role Installation Effectiveness
   c. Long-Term Benefit to Education

7. Suggested Alternative *Procedures* for Evaluating Training

8. Suggested Procedures for the *Feedback* and Utilization of Evaluative Data, so that the program can be systematically redesigned and improved from year to year.

1. The Role

a. Title

Any of the following set of combinations should be reasonably descriptive while avoiding the "change agent" stigma:

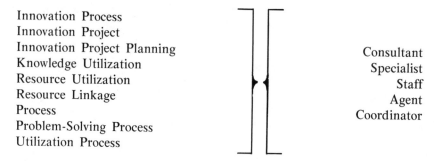

Innovation Process
Innovation Project
Innovation Project Planning
Knowledge Utilization
Resource Utilization
Resource Linkage
Process
Problem-Solving Process
Utilization Process

Consultant
Specialist
Staff
Agent
Coordinator

The descriptive term "change agent" has wide currency, but is probably offensive to a number of educators because it implies a "know-it-all" expert who pushes change for the sake of change. Such connotations are misleading and destructive for the man who is trying to establish a new position.

b. Definition

The training program suggested below presupposes the need for at least one individual in each state education agency who (1) understands the process of educational *innovation through effective and collaborative utilization of resources*, and (2) is able to *transfer* this understanding to others. This individual should be an expert who imparts specifically useful understandings and skills relevant to the process of innovation in all its dimensions. More specifically, he should impart understanding and skills relevant to:

1. building and maintaining collaborative helping relationships
2. sensing and diagnosing needs and defining objectives relevant to needs
3. identifying, relating to, and linking relevant resource persons and systems
4. solution finding and choosing
5. gaining acceptance for well-conceived innovations by individuals and groups
6. generating a continuing problem-solving and self-renewing capacity

He should be seen by the staff of the state agency as their *key general resource linker* with respect to these processes.

In fulfilling the role of general process consultant, this person should be able to assume some or all of the following duties:

1. Advisor (and some-time speech writer) to state superintendent and his staff on the change-innovation process
2. Initiator and some-time advocate of innovative projects within the state agency
3. Overseer-monitor of statewide change-innovation efforts
4. Trainer of state personnel in change-innovation process
5. Linker of state agency to outside expertise on change-innovation process
6. Chief librarian and resource locator for state agency on all aspects and approaches to planned change nationally
7. Consultant to state agency consultants

8. Consultant and regular field visitor to regional education resource centers within the state
9. Prime human resource on information resources
10. Spokesman (and some-time speaker) for innovation in education throughout the state

c. Rationale

Current and projected national policy in education points to a greater role for the states in the dispersement of federal education funds and the management and support of education generally. In accord with this policy emphasis, the states have been asked to assume a much greater role in the design, planning, and implementation of *new* programs, *new* projects, *new* types of training, *new* curricula, and *new* management practices. In short, they have been asked to be the leaders and coordinators of innovation across the entire front of educational change.

For most state education agencies, assuming this task is a major innovation in itself. They are not equipped by staff, training, orientation, or image to be statewide innovation leaders. This means that there has been and will continue to be great stress on existing roles in the state agency from top to bottom. People who have been working hard and conscientiously trying to do a good job for their constituents within a traditionally defined role and set of expectations are now being asked to play an entirely new role without the training or experience required. In many cases, they do not even have an appreciation that such a shift in orientation is either necessary or desirable because they have not been given adequate background on the need and the potential benefits which dictate such changes.

At the same time, to meet this challenge the state agency must be able to change its image of caretaker and bureaucratic gatekeeper and create a new image as a helpful and progressive force on the education scene.

If the state agencies can make this transition in image and in fact, they will usher in a new era of educational reform in the United States. But the transition will not take place unless the federal government aids the state agencies by providing clear guidelines for reorganization, and adequate training and support for new functions and roles. It must move to relieve the stress and the sting of changing.

This training program is designed in recognition of the fact that there is no practical way to give all staff of state education agencies the requisite training for a new agency role within the immediate future. However, we do see the possibility that a few individuals can receive a special type of intensive training in change-and-innovation planning and management so that they can become effective consultants and trainers to the rest of the agency.

d. Limiting Assumptions

These guidelines recognize that training programs, however ambitious in their ultimate aims, must begin with existing realities if they are to be realized. We therefore make the following assumptions about the existing state of affairs:

(1) PREEXISTING ROLES IN THE STATE EDUCATION AGENCIES

This program does not ask for a complete restructuring of the change agency as a precondition. It assumes that most agencies will retain their existing set of roles and functions in the immediate future with the sole exception that at least two individuals (the trainees) are sanctioned to receive training for the full-year course with the necessary freedom and release time to read and practice on-the-job in their home setting.

(2) AVAILABLE MANPOWER

We *do not* assume that all state agencies will be able to supply the training workshops with outstanding scholars who have extensive backgrounds in the social sciences. The program takes a realistic view of the existing manpower pool and asks only for college educated and reasonably experienced staff members who have the respect of their colleagues and who are motivated to take on the training with its implications for new role development.

(3) FUNDING

The program assumes fairly stringent constraints on federal funding for the next two to three years. Therefore, we propose a minimum program of one-year training projects involving approximately two weeks total off-site training for only two to three individuals in each agency. This type of program is currently fundable on a pilot basis. Presumably, on a longer time perspective, and after evidence of program success, more ambitious training projects will be contemplated.

2. Minimum Qualifications for Candidates to the Training Program

Experience:

Candidates should be professionally mature. Colleagues should regard them as "experienced" and "capable," preferably in a variety of roles. Some service as supervisor and consultant at some level in education should be required, but not necessarily as a staff member of a state education agency.

Age:

Candidates should be in mid-career (approximately 35-55 years). They should have at least a decade of service remaining before retirement, and at least five years previous experience post-university.

Education:

Bachelors degree and preferably masters or doctorate. The program is intellectually demanding, requiring considerable reading and some writing ability.

Specialization:

It is most important that the candidate have a strong sense of confidence and competence as an educator, but this does not mean being a specialist and expert in a given area. On the contrary, he should see himself as a generalist. Career commitment to a particular subject matter area such as "reading" or "social studies" curriculum is not desirable. On the other hand, specialties which cut across a range of educational concerns (e.g., administration) or have direct relevance to training and knowledge utilization (e.g., expertise in utilization of audio-visual equipment or information systems) are probably highly desirable.

Attitudes and Values:

1. Candidates should be committed to the belief that significant improvements can be made in education by a more effective utilization of resources and more adequate appreciation of democratic problem-solving procedures.

2. They should additionally believe that new roles can be developed within the state agency to facilitate resource utilization and problem-solving.

3. They should additionally believe that specific types of training, suggested in these guidelines, are a necessary part of such role development.

4. They should be interested in and willing to assume such roles during and after training.

5. They probably should *not* be a zealot for particular educational causes, philosophies, or products.

Knowledge:

1. Candidates should have a broad awareness of educational needs and problems.
2. They should have a basic understanding of scientific method and an awareness of the range of potential strategies and procedures for scientific evaluation of education projects.
3. They should have an understanding of the contents of these guidelines and a recognition of the rationale for the program they are about to enter.

Skills:

1. Candidates should be able to read and comprehend social science literature. (This does not mean that a background in social science is necessary, only that there be a reasonable tolerance and facility for reading semi-technical literature in fields outside one's own sphere of specialization.)
2. They should be able to contribute to and participate actively in small group interaction.
3. They should be able to compose and write for general audiences.
4. They should have some ability to talk and make presentations and demonstrations before groups.
5. They should be able to interact with superiors without undue inhibition.
6. They should show some evidence of leadership ability.
7. In no case should they be coming to the program because of failure to perform in other assigned roles in the state education agency.

Commitment by the Individual

Trainees should certify in writing that they will be willing and able to undertake the course and continue in it through the entire year of the training program.

Additionally, trainees should indicate in writing that they have read the guidelines for the program and understand and accept their implications. Specifically, they should signify that they meet the prerequisites for candidacy outlined above.

Commitment by the Employing State Agency

The state superintendent should be committed in writing to support the development of the new role by providing:

a. necessary release time for training, including paid time for reading and writing assignments performed on the job

b. necessary freedom from traditional routine duties or other prior role encumbrances to allow the full development of the new position

c. official approval and public announcement of official sanction for the new role. It is the responsibility of the state superintendent to inform all the key individuals who will relate to the candidates in their new role either as peers or superiors

d. appropriate support staff, materials, and space to allow development of the role

3. Anticipated Outcomes of Training

One year from the beginning of training, provided that the candidate has met the entry criteria and followed the program diligently and sincerely with maximum personal investments, he should possess a coherent and inter-related set of attitudes, understandings, and skills to fulfill the role requirements specified in section #1 above.

a. Attitude and Value Outcomes

It may seem inappropriate to suggest that a training program should generate any special set of values and attitudes. We are certainly not proposing an indoctrination or brain-washing program. Nevertheless, we do expect that trainees will develop or strengthen certain attitudes or orientations during training, because such changes are vitally important in maintaining the individual's motivation to pursue an active career as a change agent.

1. First of all, the graduating trainee must feel that the training has been worthwhile for himself and for his agency. This attitude should become stronger as he proceeds through phases of training and practice and comes to perceive and experience the role in its total dimensions.

2. The trainee should also strengthen his initial belief that significant positive changes can be wrought in U.S. education through the more effective utilization of existing and emerging resources. He should not be a blue-sky optimist but he must have a considerable degree of conviction that progress is possible.

3. He should believe that positive change can be accelerated by the systematic application of what we now know about the *process* of change.

4. He should become more convinced that the particular type of process

trainer-consultant envisaged in this training program can make a significant positive contribution to educational change.

5. He should have a growing conviction and *confidence in himself that he is someone who can fill this role.* This is perhaps the key attitude we would wish to inspire in the trainee because it will constitute the motivational underpinning of a successful new career as a state agency change agent.

There are, in addition, a few values implicitly or explicitly contained in the training content of a program designed around the concept of collaborative problem-solving.

6. First of all, collaborative problem-solving requires that change agents respect the integrity and good intentions of the clients with whom they work. There are sound reasons for such an orientation from a technical standpoint; generally speaking, we must work with existing systems and we must take people as they are if we want to achieve measurable improvements in education. More importantly, it is not morally acceptable in a free and democratic society to proceed in a way which bypasses, exploits, destroys, or undermines the integrity of other human beings. In the course of training we expect this point to be brought home a number of times and, by the end of training, we would hope that trainees would have a much stronger appreciation and acceptance of other people and groups, including those who stand in the way of innovations.

7. A corollary of the above is the recognition that problem-solving is an interdependent process which succeeds only when the system as a whole benefits from the outcome.

8. By the conclusion of training, the trainee should also have a much stronger conviction that users can help themselves through an optimum utilization of resources. This attitude should develop because the program focuses on resource utilization strategies and provides the trainee with a variety of opportunities to learn, explore, and practice alternative strategies, applying them synergistically to specific problem situations.

9. Finally, the trainee graduate should have a strong concern for helping without hurting, for helping with minimum jeopardy to the long-or short-term needs of society as a whole and of the individuals who make it up.

b. Knowledge Outcomes

The program calls for a large number of cognitive inputs to trainees in the form of readings, demonstrations, lectures, and discussions. Each of these inputs is designed to fit together and to relate specifically to the behavioral skill training and practice so that the trainee develops a sophisiticated and rounded conception of the role. Intellectual inputs are especially important for *two* reasons. First, they reinforce behavioral learnings, putting them in a coherent framework. Second, they enable the trainee to become a trainer in his home setting, to articulate and impart to others an understanding of the change process. As noted in the role rationale (section #1), the program must be seen as *training for trainers* if it is to be truly cost-effective. This means that trainees must be able to demonstrate that they can *tell others* in their agency what they know about each of the following topics in a reasonably clear and concise manner.

1. General understanding of the existing national system of educational innovation in the U.S., including subsystems of planning, research, development, training, and dissemination.
2. An understanding of the major alternative models of the change process, summarized by Havelock in PLANNING FOR INNOVATION, Chapter 11.
3. An understanding of alternative models and conceptions of specialized roles in the change process.
4. A detailed understanding of the specific role model envisaged in these guidelines, including rationale, anticipated outcomes, and installation problems.
5. An understanding of key segments of the state education agency with which the trainee will be working, their functions, reward systems, perspectives on education and educational needs within the state, and attitudes and orientations to educational innovation. This understanding will be accrued largely through on-the-job interviewing and consulting activities of the training program.
6. A detailed understanding of the points of view, function, skills, and knowledge of the particular individuals within the agency with whom the trainee works most closely (*hereafter referred to in these guidelines as the ROLE SET of the trainee*). This understanding should include a clear and accurate understanding of how these individuals see the trainee and his role.
7-12. A detailed and sophisticated understanding of the six stages of problem-solving, identified in section #1 as the defining skills of the role, and described by Havelock in A GUIDE TO INNOVATION IN EDUCATION as the basic elements in the change process (building relationships, diagnosis, resource acquisition, solution choosing, gaining acceptance, and self-renewal).

c. Skills Outcomes

The program puts special emphasis on the development of a specific set of skills, coherently related to the knowledge inputs and to the overall role conception. Additionally, these should be skills which will be seen as relevant and useful to others in the state agency.

The core set of skills which should be learned in this program are those identified in section #1 of this training design and in GUIDE TO INNOVATION as "Stages I through VI". A successful graduate of this program should know how to:

1. Build helping *relationships* with a variety of clients and client systems.
2. *Diagnose* client needs including the identification of weaknesses and strengths and basic systemic features, formulation of needs as problems, and statement of change project objectives.
3. *Acquire resources* relevant to diagnosis, including print, persons, and products as required from internal and external sources.
4. Generate a *range of solution ideas* and *choose among them* collaboratively with the client, evaluating criteria of benefit, workability, and acceptability.
5. Develop strategies and programs to gain *acceptance* of the chosen solutions by the client system as a whole.
6. Design and install mechanisms which assure the client of a continuing capability to innovate, adopt, and adapt (self-renewal) with respect to this and other innovations.
7-12. Of equal importance to the above six skills is a corresponding set of *training* skills to impart these skills to others and to teach clients to be their own problem-solvers.
13-18. Additionally, for each of these same set of problem-solving skills the trainee-graduate should know *how to gain further training* for himself and others. In other words, he should be a resource expert on each of the six stages of problem-solving.
19. By the end of training, the graduate should be on his way to becoming an *articulate spokesman* for the planned change process generally and, specifically, for the role of the state agency within it.
20 The graduate should have the ability to *develop evaluative criteria and to design evaluations* for the change projects in which he is involved. We do not see him as an expert evaluator or researcher, but he should have enough knowledge and skill in this area to work effectively and collaboratively with more expert evaluators within the state education agency and outside. He should have the ability to call upon individuals with requisite skills in these areas when necessary.

Long-Term Outcomes

The program graduate, with all the skills, knowledge, and attitudes identified above, is not the ultimate desired output of this program. Rather, he is a means to an end: increased innovative problem-solving in our nation's schools. Beyond training there is, first of all, the problem of installation of the new role in the state agency, and beyond installation is the reorientation and retooling of the state agency to fill the role of innovative leader and coordinator for the state.

Finally, beyond that reorientation should come the benefits for the schools from a state system which is truly able to provide useful, beneficial, and timely innovations and innovative programs.

4. The Training Procedure

The details of a prototype training design are spelled out in the pages which follow. The design includes:

a. A schedule covering one year for three workshops and in-between planning and in-service activities.
b. Reading list for program as a whole.
c. Trainer and trainee preparations.
d. Trainee notebook.
e. Outline descriptions of Units #1 - 9.
f. Outline of features to incorporate in a case simulation exercise.
g. Outline descriptions of Units #10 - 12.

In recognition of the special constraints of various training situations and trainers, we have tried to include "adaptation" suggestions at several points in the outline.

Schedule of Training Workshop Series
With Outline of Contents

2 Months **Planning Phase**

Trainer Team Building
Trainer Planning Meeting
Trainee Recruitment and Selection (preferably in pairs)
Reading Mail-Out (one month prior to first event)
Trainee Notebook and Materials Preparation and
Acquisition

4 Days **First Workshop**

Unit #1 - ½ Day: What is Planned Change?
Three Perspectives
Unit #2 - ½ Day: Who is a Change Agent?
Why is it Important to Develop Such
a Role?
Unit #3 - ½ Day: Who is the Client?
Unit #4 - ½ Day: Relationships
Unit #5 - ½ Day: Non-directive Consultation
Unit #6 - ½ Day: Diagnosis
Unit #7 - ⅔ Day: Working with the Role Set
⅓ Day: Instructions for back home On-the-
Job: Practice, Data Gathering, and
Role Development; Reading Assign-
ments for Second Workshop

3 Months **On-the-Job**

Log Taking
Non-Directive Counseling
Establishing Role-Set Relationships
Defining Own Role
Collecting Diagnostic Data and Relationships for Case
Building
Reading on Resource Acquisition and on Solution
Choosing for Second Workshop

Trainer Planning for Second Workshop
Post Mortem on First Workshop: What should we do

differently next time?
Consultation Visits with Trainees and Log Analysis
Design Case Simulation Exercise

3.½ Days　　**Second Workshop**

⅓ Day: Review of Diagnostic Activities
⅓ Day: Review of Role Development Activities
⅓ Day: Counseling and Conflict Resolution
　　　　Skill Practice
Unit #8 - ½ Day: Resource Acquisition
Unit #9 - ½ Day: Solution Choosing
1 Day: Complete Case Simulation Exercise
¼ Day: Case Building and Recording
¼ Day: Instructions and Discussion of
　　　　On-the-Job Practice, Using Pairs,
　　　　Design and Planning of an In-State
　　　　Workshop Series

6 Months　　**On-the-Job**

Log Taking
Case Development - (following STAGES I through IV of
　GUIDE)
Reading on Dissemination, Evaluation, Self-Renewal
Continued On-the-Job Practice of Change Agent Skills
In-State Workshop Series Planning

2-½ Days　　**Third Workshop**

½ Day: Review and Critique of Cases
Unit #10 - ½ Day: Gaining Acceptance
Unit #11 - ½ Day: Generating Self-Renewal
Unit #12 - ½ Day: Evaluation Process
¼ Day: Evaluation of the Workshop Training
　　　　Experience
¼ Day: Plans for Continued Training of
　　　　Self and Others;
　　　　Plans for Continued Role Development;
　　　　Plans for Continued Building of a
　　　　Self-Renewal Capacity for the State.

Adaptation of the Schedule

The schedule as presented is intended for a one-year sequence in which there are funds for two weeks of training and adequate travel money for three separate sessions. This is the optimum program, given these constraints. For some trainers, three sessions may not be possible. If it is practical to hold only two sessions, the second and third workshops may be combined and presented four to five months after the first. Unit #8 could be included in the first workshop.

The intervening periods are critical for implanting and integrating the training experience with the work experience. However, if only *one* two-week block of time is available, trainers should include at least a two-day component of very intensive and realistic simulated work experience.

In any adaptation of the schedule it is important to note that skill practice and case analysis exercises in Workshops #2 and #3 depend on inputs gathered by trainees in on-the-job log-taking and case-building activities.

Adaptation of the Content Sequence

If a one-week course is all that is possible, it is preferable to miniaturize *all* units identified here. Such a course, however, should be seen only as an introduction and not as a complete training to qualify for the role. If only a 2-3 day course is possible, it is advisable to limit the content to Units #1 and #2, with at least one full day for a complete simulation of the problem-solving "STAGES" described in the GUIDE.

Adaptation of the Pairing Principle

Pairs trained together provide critical mutual support for new behaviors when they return to their home setting. This is especially important in establishing a new role. However, if it is not possible to provide training in pairs, there should be some alternative which partially achieves the same end; e.g., creating partnerships for adjoining states, identifying a knowledgeable and supportive change agent within the state and in easy access to the trainee to serve as periodic consultant, advisor, and commiserator.

Basic Reading List

Essential	Why
Havelock, THE CHANGE AGENT'S GUIDE TO INNOVATION IN EDUCATION	The GUIDE is a step-by-step field manual on collaborative problem-solving, for use in conjunction with workshop series and as a continuing reference in the management of innovation projects.
This training design (i.e. chapter IX of this volume)	All trainees should understand the rationale for the training program and should see themselves as future trainers of other change agents.
Bennis, Benne and Chin, THE PLANNING OF CHANGE (1969 edition)	The only comprehensive set of readings on planned change. Several selections will be used in conjunction with proposed workshop series.
Havelock, DISSEMINATION AND TRANSLATION ROLES (Paper available as reprint from author or from sources identified in GUIDE.)	Provides a comprehensive overview of roles related to the change process and describes some of the key issues which change agents will confront.

Desirable	
Havelock, PLANNING FOR INNOVATION	A comprehensive and systematic review of the literature on change and knowledge utilization; it would be a very useful reference on many aspects of the process. Summary chapter provides a good overview of models of change and major factors in successful innovation programs.
Lippit, et al., THE DYNAMICS OF PLANNED CHANGE	The first manual for change agents, and the cornerstone work for planned change as a discipline and a coherent set of skills; readable and relevant for working with all types of client systems from persons to communities.
Miles, INNOVATION IN EDUCATION	The largest and most wide-ranging collection of readings on the subject. Chapters by Miles (Introduction, closing, and chapter on "Temporary Systems") are especially valuable.
Rogers and Svenning, MANAGING CHANGE	A concise overview of research on change from the leading authority on the diffusion of innovations.
Havelock, TRAINING FOR CHANGE AGENTS (this volume)	Provides a conceptual framework and context for the role and for training for the role and associated issues of installation, evaluation, etc.
Rogers and Shoemaker, THE COMMUNICATION OF INNOVATIONS	The most authoritative review of research on this topic.
Eidell and Kitchel (Eds.) KNOWLEDGE PRODUCTION AND UTILIZATION IN EDUCATIONAL ADMINISTRATION	A set of six thoughtful and well-documented analyses of topics relevant to change and change agent role development.
Trainers should also call for an ERIC search and printout of studies pertinent to state department structure, function, change, role in U.S. education, relationships to other organizations etc.	(a) Trainers and trainees should practice using information resource systems. (b) These abstracts provide leads and ideas for demonstration skits and simulated case materials at a number of points in the workshop series, in addition to specific base for Units #8 and #9.

Trainers may want to refer to recent annotated bibliographies on change in education, e.g., THE CHANGE PROCESS IN EDUCATION, ERIC Clearinghouse on Vocational and Technical Education, The Center for Vocational and Technical Education, Ohio State University, Columbus, Ohio, or listing by Havelock, et al. incorporated in A CHANGE AGENT'S GUIDE TO INNOVATION IN EDUCATION as "Appendix C".

Trainer Preparations for Workshop Series

1. Should be thoroughly familiar with all reading assignments given to trainees throughout the series.

2. Should meet as a team (preferably three-man team; minimum two-man team):

   to discuss guidelines point-by-point, and make appropriate adaptations;
   to divide up formal presentations;
   to discuss implications of research on state education departments;
   to design skill practice sessions, including skits;
   to practice skit demonstrations with each other;
   to schedule the series.

   It is probably desirable for the trainers to generate one or two real case examples of innovation initiated by state agency change agents following the model used in the GUIDE. They should be written up for distribution to all trainees so they can be used along with the GUIDE as discussion starters and simulation bases.

3. Should arrange for selection and recruitment of trainees *in pairs* or co-located teams and according to specified criteria.

   All prospective trainees should be informed of entry conditions and should certify in writing that they meet them.

4. Should arrange for trainees to receive necessary advance materials and readings.

5. Should arrange for necessary conference supplies, including:

   newsprint pads and markers;
   name tags;
   materials packet for trainers;
   loose-leaf notebook* for each trainee, to include:
   a. tests
   b. log formats
   c. workshop rating forms
   d. case outlines
   e. series schedule
   f. training guidelines

---

*See separate page for complete description of notebook.

Trainee Preparation for First Workshop

1. Readings	Rationale
Havelock, Roles Paper (PLAN-NING FOR INNOVATION, Ch. 7)	The range of roles involved in planned change: problems.
Rogers and Svenning, MAN-AGING CHANGE	Exposure to quantitative literature on change.
Havelock, THE CHANGE AGENT'S GUIDE TO INNO-VATION, Introduction and Case Studies.	Alternative change agent roles for self and others; images of change agent.
Havelock, PLANNING FOR INNOVATION, Chapter 11 〔 Bennis, Benne and Chin, THE PLANNING OF CHANGE pp. 28-59	Two overviews of models of the change process.
Havelock, TRAINING FOR CHANGE AGENTS (this volume), Chapters I, II, and IV-A.	Overview of knowledge about change process in context of change agent training and images of range of roles with relevant knowledge, skills, attitudes and values.

2. Make at least one face-to-face contact with trainee-partner.

3. Describe (on paper) role of state agency in educational change.

4. Describe (on paper) one example (success *or* failure) of a change in education in your state in which the state agency or state agency personnel had major involvement:

> Who was the change agent?
> Who was the client system?
> What change was contemplated?
> What diagnostic efforts were made (if any)?
> What resource acquisition efforts were made?
> Were alternative changes considered?
> What strategy was used to gain acceptance?
> Which perspective on change (P-S, S-1, R&D) is most relevant to this case?
> What change agent roles are visible to you in your case?
> (e.g., Havelock roles taxonomy, three role alternatives in GUIDE, etc.)

Trainee Notebook

Each trainee should have a loose-leaf notebook to include essential reference materials, preferably in outline form. All written exercises which are done individually should be seen as pieces of the trainee's permanent and growing working file on the role.

The notebooks should be multi-purpose:

1. Helping the trainee keep track of the training program and the role concept.
2. Helping him keep track of his progress in the training program, and in his emerging role in the state education agency.
3. Giving him a ready reference and *work-book* for case recording and work logging.
4. Providing a written record of the role which can be used for *evaluation* by self and others.
5. Providing a role diagnostic file to help consultants and trainers who make consultation visits to the trainee.

Therefore, they should include:

1. Statement of training program rationale and guidelines.
2. List of alternative role models and strategies.
3. List of key readings and materials.
4. The trainee's log and log blanks (in the format determined by trainers and trainees).
5. Workshop Unit written exercises with the trainee's own responses. (These should represent a summary of the training program in his own words.)
6. Case analyses and case analysis blanks (following Havelock's "SIX STAGES" or some adaptation as developed by trainers and trainees).
7. Some device for recording and counting the number of times the notebook or pages within it are used as a reference by the trainee in his work.

Adaptations of the Notebook Concept

It is not essential that the above notebook design be realized in detail, but it is important that trainees have a notebook which contains essential resource information on their role and their notes on their progress on a day-to-day basis. The notebook is a key link between training and real-life experience in the new role.

Unit Design

With the exception of Unit #7, each unit is described as a ½ day segment (4 hours). Unit #7 is a ⅔ days segment (6½ hours). Each unit includes some separate periods for:

1. Reading: (For most units, background readings are assumed. For units to be fully effective, they probably should be accompanied by at least four hours of background reading.)
2. Lecture or other formal presentation. (Large Group-"L.G.")
3. Questions by all participants on reading and lectures.
4. Small Group discussions ("S.G." - 6 to 8 persons), usually with news-print summarizing.
5. Large Group ("L.G." - all trainees) sharing of small group summaries.
6. Behavior skill practice exercises (role playing, simulation, etc.). (For units to be effective, they probably should be followed by at least four hours of concentrated structured practice *on-the-job* in addition to the above.)
7. Individual written exercises (to be incorporated in the Trainee Note-book). These exercises serve as a self-test for the trainee and a written record in his own words of the workshop experience.

Units are supplemented with review periods, case analyses, and simulation sessions which integrate learnings from all units.

Adaptation of the Units

It is expected that trainers will want to tailor the units to fit their own program requirements, emphases, and limitations.   Any unit can be expanded easily with more readings and more skill practice using case materials from the trainees' experience. If cutting is required, however, each unit should minimally retain at least one reading, one reading discussion, and one skill practice exercise.   If the individual written exercises are abbreviated or eliminated, the experience will probably leave its mark on fewer trainees.   This may be allowable where evaluation and cost-effectiveness of the training are not critical issues, but the exercises should not be cut simply because it is too much like "going back to school." Trainees should know that they are there to learn and to demonstrate in word and behavior to themselves and others the results of their learning experiences.

The behavioral skill practice exercises have not been spelled out in detail; the trainers must think through each exercise, add to them, alter them creatively from their own experience and from material and ideas generated in the flow of the training events.

Unit #1
What is Planned Change?

Read prior to Unit #1 {

(3 hrs.)   Havelock: PLANNING FOR INNOVATION, Chapter 11

(2 hrs.) {

Benne, Bennis and Chin: "Planned Change in America" in Bennis, Benne and Chin, THE PLANNING OF CHANGE, Chapter 1.2

Chin and Benne: "General Strategies for Effecting Changes in Human Systems" in Bennis, Benne and Chin, Chapter 1.3

(3 hrs.)   Miles: "Educational Innovation: the Nature of the Problem" in Miles, INNOVATION IN EDUCATION, Chapter 1

½ hr. Lecture   With Questions:

Orientation: Why the program was created and funded; overview of the course; the intermediate and ultimate goals; the knowledge gap and the macrosystem needs.

1 hr. Lecture   With Questions:

Differing orientations to planned change - an overview of models, perspective, theory and research.

(Benne, Bennis, Chin, Havelock, Miles, E. Rogers, G. Watson would all serve well as possible keynoters here.)

Should cover roughly the same ground as the readings and should make references to the readings where possible.

1-½ hrs. S.G.*   Discussion:

Which model or combination of models is most

---

*"S.G." = Small groups, 6-8 persons.

relevant to:
a. The state education agency (SEA)
b. The local education agency (LEA)
c. The nation as a whole?

½ hr. L.G.*   Discussion:

Sharing S.G. conclusions.

½ hr. Individual   Written Exercise:

What is the best model for SEA and why?

What components of other models are also relevant?

---

*"L.G." = Large group; all trainees.

Unit #2

Who is a Change Agent?
Why is the Development of Such a Role Important?

1 hr. S.G.

Discussion:

What is a Change Agent in a SEA?
(Posting of points on newsprint.)

Questions to raise after two pages of newsprint have been filled:
    a. Are there alternative role models?
    b. Does anyone think he is a C-A* now?
    c. How do readings apply?

½ hr. Individual

Reading:
This Training Design (i.e. Chapter IX of this volume)

½ hr. L.G.

Discussion:

Of *Design* and comparison to postings.

(Members should be given an opportunity to reject or qualify some of the program objectives.)

½ hr. L.G.

Discussion, led by trainer:

What types of C-A's were represented in GUIDE cases?

1 hr. S.G.

Discussion:

Role types represented in on-the-job cases brought to the workshop by the trainees.

½ hr. Individual

Written Exercise:

1. What change agent role types have you observed

---

*"C-A" = Change Agent

in your SEA?

2. What C-A roles have you played in the past?

3. What role do you expect to play after training? Why is this role needed? Why do you think you would be an appropriate person for it?

Unit #3
Who is the Client?

Read Evening prior to Unit #3	(2-3 hrs.)	Havelock: PLANNING FOR INNOVATION, Chapters 2 and 3. Some additional readings on the nature of social systems, school systems, and educational systems (micro and macro).

½ hr. Individual   Read at beginning of the Unit:

Havelock: GUIDE TO INNOVATION, STAGE 1-A

Bennis, Benne and Chin: p. 595, Benne: "Some Ethical Problems."

1 hr. S.G.   Discussion (with Posting case-by-case):

Who was the client in each of the four cases described in the GUIDE?

½ hr. L.G.   Discussion:

Sharing of newsprint summaries with observations from the trainer which lead to the lecture segment following.

½ hr. Lecture   With Questions:

Covering the following points:

1. The question "Who is the Client?" is more complex than it looks.

2. The change agent must try to answer it satisfactorily at least to himself (he should be clear who he is working with and why).

3. Human and social systems are interrelated.

4. Defining the "Client" too narrowly leads to practical difficulties, e.g., the "client" may not truly represent the people he thinks he represents, overestimating the degree of inter-dependence in his system.

5. Defining the "client" too narrowly leads to moral and ethical difficulties, e.g., we may be "helping" one man but inadvertently hurting or ignoring the needs of others by so doing.

6. The ultimate consumer of our change efforts has to be a part of our thinking at some point, i.e., society as a whole, community, students as a whole, special segments of the student population (poor, black, gifted, handicapped, adult, etc.); and each of these has to be considered on a time dimension (now, near future, far future).

This point leads into the discussion segment following:

½ hr. S.G.   Discussion:

(With Posting):
Who is our ultimate client?

½ hr. L.G.   Discussion:

Sharing and discussion of priorties (i.e., which client or which segment of the client population is my *first* concern, my *next* concern, etc.).

½ hr. Individual   Written Exercise:

Who is my ultimate client? Why?

Who is my immediate client?

How do I define who my client is?

Unit #4

Defining, Understanding and Building Relationships

Read prior to Unit #4 } (1 hr.) {

Carl Rogers: "The Characteristics of a Helping Relationship" in Bennis, Benne and Chin, THE PLANNING OF CHANGE, Chapter 4.1

Argyris: "Explorations in Consulting-Client Relationships," especially section on marginality, in Bennis, Benne and Chin, Chapter 8.5

½ hr. Individual   Reading:

Havelock, GUIDE TO INNOVATION, STAGE I-B through F.

C. Rogers (in Bennis, Benne and Chin), pp. 162-166.

1 hr S.G.   Discussion:

What sort of relationship did each of the GUIDE change agents have with his client?

To what extent did they meet the nine criteria in the GUIDE?

1 hr. L.G.   Discussion:

Trainers illustrate "relationship" issues by using their own relationship to trainees as a case in point. They should allow maximum group "kibbitzing" and editing on this.

1. Definition: major characteristics.

2. Characterized on nine criteria in GUIDE.

3. Conditions suggested by Carl Rogers, pp. 162-166.

4. What can we do to improve this relationship?

½ hr. S.G.   Discussion:

1. How do we size up our relationships with our trainee-partners on various criteria at this point? (All partners should be in separate groups.)

2. What can we do to improve these relationships?

½ hr. Dyads   With Partners:

Sharing of diagnosis of relationship and of group ideas on how to make it better; decisions on specific commitments in this direction.

½ hr. Individual   Written Exercise:

Describe your relationship to SEA using the nine criteria in the GUIDE and indicating specific steps that could be taken toward improving it.

Unit #5

Non-Directive Consultation

Rationale for Unit #5:

The rationale for this unit is the need to provide trainees with helping skills which can be used at the very beginning of a relationship, and which will simultaneously build the relationship, generate diagnostic data, and give feedback to the client in the form of a reflection of his own problem definition. A very rudimentary form of non-directive counseling should do this without excessively threatening the client, without intruding too far into his life space, and without undermining his initiative for self help. It is a fundamental first step helping skill. Training in this skill should inhibit a natural tendency of change agents to rush in with "solutions" prior to gaining a real understanding of the client's needs and prior to building a trusting relationship.

Read prior to Unit #5 { (1 hr.) {

Charles Ferguson: "Concerning the Nature of Human Systems and the Consultant's Role" in Bennis, Benne and Chin, THE PLANNING OF CHANGE, Chapter 8.3

Gerald Caplan: "Types of Mental Health Consultation" in Bennis, Benne and Chin, Chapter 8.4

Carl Rogers: one of his papers on this subject should be used.

½ hr. Individual   Reading:

> 10 - 20 page description of the technique and rationale of non-directive consultation. (Trainers would have to find or assemble this from C. Rogers and other sources.)

½ hr. L.G.   Discussion of Readings:

> Posting by trainer of main points about technique of non-directive consultation.

½ hr. L.G.

Demonstration:

> By trainer of non-directive consultation with critique by group.

1-½ hrs. Triads

Role-Playing:

> Rotating into roles of client, consultant, and observer, with each trainee using a live problem from the SEA when he sits in the "client" role.

½ hr. L.G.

Discussion:

> Reporting difficulties encountered in role of consultant and client; suggestions on how these difficulties can be overcome.

½ hr. Individual

Written Exercise:

> Describe the technique of non-directive counseling, indicating:
>
> 1. specific groups or individuals who would be potential clients for this type of help in your own setting;
>
> 2. problems you will need to be aware of in yourself in trying out this technique.

Unit #6

Diagnosis

Read prior
to Unit #6 } (1-½ hrs.) {

James V. Clark: "A Healthy Organization" in Bennis, Benne and Chin, THE PLANNING OF CHANGE, Chapter 6.2

Lorsch and Lawrence: "The Diagnosis of Organizational Problems" in Bennis, Benne and Chin, Chapter 8.7

Daniel E. Griffiths: "Administrative Theory and Change in Organizations" in Miles, INNOVATION IN EDUCATION, Chapter 18

Havelock: GUIDE TO INNOVATION, STAGE II

½ hr. L.G.

Demonstration:

Trainer demonstration of diagnostic interview with one of the trainees role-playing one of his own clients.

½ hr. L.G.

Discussion:

Discussion led by trainer: making a diagnostic inventory. (Use a sheet of newsprint for each of the major questions "a" through "e" identified in the GUIDE, STAGE II. Similarities between diagnostic interviewing and non-directive counseling (Unit #5) should be noted.)

Critique by L.G. of trainer's technique of interviewing.

1 hr. Dyads

With Partners:

Each interviews the other on his case, each in turn role-playing his clients.

½ hr. Individual   Written Exercise:

Complete a diagnostic inventory on the other man's case.

¼ hr. Individual   Reading:

Havelock: GUIDE, STAGE III (Techniques of Acquiring Diagnostic Information)

½ hr. S.G.   Discussion:

Diagnostic methods used in cases from on-the-job experience. Advantages and pitfalls of these methods as they experienced them.

¼ hr. L.G.   Lecture:

The diagnostic process as a catalyst for solution finding by the client. Diagnostic data (e.g., survey feedback) as a catalyst for solution finding by the client.

½ hr. S.G.   Discussion:

When you were role-playing your client, how much did you think you were being helped by the diagnostic interviewer? Was he being a good non-directive consultant? (See again Unit #5)

There should also be something on generating statements of objectives based on diagnosis by client and consultant.

Unit #7

Working with the Role Set*

Read prior
to Unit #7 } (1 hr.) {

Robert K. Merton: SOCIAL THEORY AND SOCIAL STRUCTURE, pp. 368-384; or some brief summary exposition on role theory

Sam Sieber: "Organizational Influences on Innovative Roles" in Eidell and Kitchel, KNOWLEDGE PRODUCTION AND UTILIZATION IN EDUCATIONAL ADMINISTRATION

1-½ hrs. S.G.   Discussion:

Who is the role set? Discuss and post on newsprint:

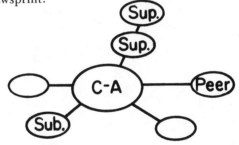

Problems in dealing with each of these role set members as we see it - Discuss and Post.

Rank order degree of anticipated difficulty in working with each member of the role set.

Problems in dealing with us as *they* might see it.

½ hr. L.G.   Discussion:

Sharing S.G. discussion, comparing newsprint diagrams.

---

*"Role Set" = The set of positions in the organization with which the new role must be related and integrated.

½ hr. L.G.   Demonstration:

Role-play demonstration skit - conflict - fail.
(Trainers will have to design this in advance.)

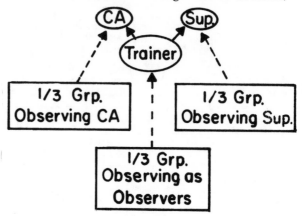

Discussion:

What was CA trying to do?
What was Sup. trying to do?
What was going on between them?

1-½ hrs. Triads   Role-playing:
(½ hr. each)

All participants take all roles in rotation.

½ hr. Individual   Reading:

Handout on Misunderstandings and Conflicts
(See attachment following this Unit) plus something from Carl Rogers.

½ hr. L.G.   Role-playing:

Handling misunderstandings in interpersonal
conflict situations (Carl Rogers' Echolalia
Exercise: CREE).

Demonstration Skit:

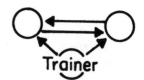

1-½ hrs.
NEW TRIADS

CREE Practice:

Rotate using the three most problematic relationships in the CA role set as defined at beginning of the unit.

CENTER FOR RESEARCH ON UTILIZATION OF SCIENTIFIC KNOWLEDGE

Handling Misunderstandings and Conflict

Dealing With Breakdowns in Communication*

Real communication is very hard to achieve. We tend to judge, to evaluate, to approve or disapprove before we really understand what the other person is saying--before we understand the frame of reference from which he is talking. This tendency of most humans to react first by forming an evaluation of what has just been said, to evaluate it from our own point of view, is a major barrier to mutual interpersonal communication.

Progress toward understanding can be made when this evaluative tendency is avoided--when we listen with understanding--when we are actively listening to what is being said. What does this mean? It means to see the expressed idea and attitudes from the other person's point of view, to sense how it feels to him, to achieve his frame of reference in regard to the thing he is talking about.

This sounds simple, but it is not.

To test the quality of your understanding, try the following. If you see two people talking past each other, if you find yourself in an argument with your friend, with your wife, or within a small group, just stop the discussion for a moment, and for an experiment, institute this rule of Carl Rogers: "Each person can speak up for himself only *after* he has first restated the ideas and feelings of the previous speaker accurately--and to the speaker's satisfaction."

This would mean that before presenting your own point of view, it would be necessary for you to really achieve the other speaker's frame of reference--to understand his thoughts and feelings so well that you could summarize them for him. This is a very effective process for improving communications and relationships with others. It is much more difficult to do behaviorally then you would suspect.

What will happen if you try to do this during an argument?

You will find that your own next comments will have to be drastically

---

*The approach proposed here for dealing with misunderstandings was first stated by Carl Rogers in 1951. See Carl Rogers: *On Becoming a Person*. Boston: Houghton Mifflin Co., 1961, Chapter 17. This abstract, elaboration, and extension of these ideas on handling conflict was prepared by Floyd Mann of the Center for Research on Utilization of Scientific Knowledge at The University of Michigan.

revised. You will find the emotion going out of the discussion, the differences being reduced. There is a decrease in defensiveness, in exaggerated statements, in evaluative and critical behavior. Attitudes become more positive and problem solving. The differences which remain are of a rational and understandable sort--or are real differences in basic values.

What are the risks? The obstacles? What are the difficulties that keep this bit of knowledge from being utilized?

Try this and you risk being influenced by the other person. You might see it his way--have to change your position. There is the risk of change. In this sense, listening can be dangerous--and courage is required.

There is a second obstacle. It is just when emotions are strongest that it is most difficult to achieve the frame of reference of the other person or group. A third party, who is able to lay aside his own feelings and evaluations, can assist greatly by listening with understanding to each person or group and clarifying the views and attitudes each holds. A third party catalyst may, incidentally, have great difficulty in intervening and proposing the use of this approach. Any intervention into a heated discussion can be interpreted by one party or the other to the dispute as someone taking the other person's side. This is especially true if the third party asks you to try and state the other person's ideas and feelings when you have not really been listening, but thinking what you should say next when he pauses to take a breath.

Another difficulty stems from our notions as to what it is proper to ask a person to do in a discussion. It seems quite within good taste to ask a person to restate how he sees the situation. But to ask him to restate the other man's position is not consistent with our common sense ways of handling differences. The one who would change the pattern--try to break out of the vicious circle of increasingly greater misunderstanding--must have enough confidence in himself to be able to propose something different. He will have to have an appreciation of how to go from dealing with misunderstandings to handling conflict and using differences--of how differences can be used to find more elegant solutions to problems. Equally useful will be an awareness that thesis, antithesis, synthesis is a potential outcome from a developmental discussion of differences. Discussions in which one person loses and the other wins seldom solve anything permanently. When a person senses a win-lose situation developing, it should be interpreted as a clue to the need for a new approach, a search for alternate solutions, to be sure that there is not another answer to the problem.

The greatest difficulty of all of course is to learn to use the rule when you yourself are in an increasingly heated verbal exchange. Not to be dependent on a third person to intervene when you create or are a party to a growing misunderstanding is real evidence of understanding the approach proposed here. The full value of this rule is available to us only when each of us can note that we are getting increasingly irritated, angry, and unable to communicate effectively--when we can use these signals to identify the situation in which we are personally involved and even trapped in which the rule might be employed--*if* we could retrieve the rule from our memory, and *if* we could behaviorally use it in an effective manner.

On Handling Conflict

What should a person do if after carefully checking his understanding of the other person's ideas and feelings, he finds the differences are real--they stem from different value assumptions and premises? There is no longer any misunderstanding, each person understands the other's position and believes the other's value premises are inappropriate.

A first step might be to check to see if this is a difference that has to be worked through. Is the difference important enough to be sharpened further and a search for a solution undertaken jointly? Is there real interdependence between the persons who no longer are misunderstanding each other but have found there is truly a conflict? If the two parties do have to work together--if the differences in positions taken appear to jeopardize the attainment of an important common purpose--and if there is time to begin to recognize the meaning of these differences--then one or both of the parties need to move ahead toward the positive confrontation and resolution of these differences.

A useful step at this point is often to be sure once again that you understand the other man's position and that the other person understands the difference between the values you hold and those he holds with regard to the issue at hand. This may be done by asking the other person if you really understand his position in a very directive manner--even using leading questions that imply that you do not believe that he would want to hold that position if he fully understood the value implications of it, and accepted the common goals toward which you are both working. If this step indicates goals are not common and shared, this needs to be clarified. There may have simply been a misunderstanding about what the common purpose was in this instance. If after this has been done the differences still remain, it is then essential to check out the values that are held in common. Often it is helpful to move up the hierarchy of values which might be shared to find overarching values which are subscribed to jointly. Once these have been identified and common goals have been restated, the present differences need to be reviewed in terms of these newly stated facts. Differences with regard to the immediate problem are often resolved by this process.

If they are not, then both parties might agree to a problem-solving approach--using another value which they might hold in common--and to adopt one or the other's recommended course of action for the time being. This should be done with the explicit understanding that they will later review carefully the outcome and decide what actual experience has indicated about their different approaches and value premises. They could even use the orderly, systematic collection of data and analysis to test what is the best position or the better way of proceeding.

Practice and Repractice

It is essential not only to be aware of these ideas about how one might deal with breakdowns in communication and move on to the positive confrontation of differences, but to be able to recognize when these ideas are relevant and might be used, and more importantly to be able to put these ideas into action behaviorally. Cognitive awareness alone is not enough; the behavioral skills necessary to adopt, adapt, and utilize this approach are also essential. Skills as complex as these, requiring dropping old habit patterns of handling conflict which were supported perhaps with deep inclinations to move away from rather than face up to confrontations, can only be changed through practice and repractice. Often a tangential requirement is being able to handle another's expressions of hostility and distrust.

This approach is not easy to incorporate into a person's intellectual and behavioral everyday ways of living with others. But it can be learned--and shared with others. It is not a panacea, but it is an approach that leads steadily and rapidly toward better interpersonal relations. It is relevant to a good deal of what is necessary for self government. The other man's point of view is valued. His ideas and feelings--and probably yours in return--are treated with human dignity.

The Action Steps

Now what do you really have to remember to do?

1. Watch for breakdowns in communications between others or between yourself and others.
2. Intervene to suggest the use of the rule to ensure understanding of the other person's ideas and feelings.
3. Stress the restatement of both ideas and feelings to the satisfaction of the participants to the conflict.
4. If misunderstandings have been resolved, but differences still remain, have participants check to see what other values or goals they hold in common.
5. Relate the present differences in value assumptions to these larger, broader goals, values, and reasons for interdependence.
6. If differences are still unresolved, suggest selection of one alternative course of action, but build in commitment to subsequent review and evaluation.

Floyd Mann, C R U S K, Institute for Social Research, The University of Michigan

Unit #8

Resource Acquisition

Read prior to Unit #8 { (2 hrs.) { Havelock: PLANNING FOR INNOVATION, Chapter 8.

Havelock: GUIDE TO INNOVATION, STAGE III

1 hr. S.G.   Discussion:

Each man in turn names a recent information acquisition effort. With group asking him questions he should list:

1. Purpose of effort.
2. His initial awareness level.
3. Homing-in strategy.

½ hr. L.G.   Sharing:

1. What was the range of (number of different) purposes represented in the S.G. discussions.

2. What was the range of homing-in strategies, e.g.:   Use of information systems
                Use of consultants
                Data Collection
                People-to-print
                Print-to-people
                Site visiting

3. Communication media used: written, phone, face-to-face.

½ hr. L.G.   Lecture:

How to use ERIC system (probably using an outside resource person from USOE, Washington or an ERIC Center).

½ hr. Individual Exercise:

Scanning and reading of ERIC printouts of research on SEA (previously made available by trainers).

½ hr. Individual Exercise:

Follow-up of any sort (people-print-product) on one of the references.

½ hr. S.G. Discussion:

Discussion of problems in using printout, purposes of trainees in searching, further homing-in possibilities.

½ hr. Individual Written Exercise:

Describe your resource acquisition effort which you shared with small groups at the beginning of the Unit in terms of STAGE III: What would you do differently or additionally now?

Unit #9

Solution Choosing

Read prior
to Unit #9 { (1½ hrs) {

Havelock, GUIDE TO INNOVATION, STAGE IV

Lippitt, Fox and Schindler-Rainman, HUMANIZING SCHOOL AND COMMUNITY: IMAGES OF POTENTIALITY

Charles Jung and Ronald Lippitt, "The Study of Change as a Concept," THEORY INTO PRACTICE Vol. V. No. 1. Feb. 1966

½ hr. L.G.

Lecture:

Using ERIC, search findings for a diagnosed problem; in advance of session prepare a handout sheet with several summary findings generated by search. Trainer demonstrates the techniques described in GUIDE, STAGE IV, for deriving implications and generating a range of solution ideas.

¾ hr. S.G.

Discussion:

Groups are given a diagnosed problem and summary statements retrieved from a search of ERIC on this problem. They are to follow the techniques described in GUIDE, STAGE IV, for deriving implications:
1. Summarize
2. State implications for action

¾ hr. S.G.

Discussion:

Using above implications, group should generate a range of solution ideas. They should use the brainstorming strategy and should post their synthesis and summary of ideas on newsprint.

½ hr. L.G.   Sharing:

The newsprint summaries of each group showing the range of solution ideas generated should be compared. The most commonly generated ideas should be selected for further examination in small groups.

1 hr. S.G.   Discussion:

Each of the selected solution ideas should be examined to determine its feasibility on the basis of:
1. Potential benefit
2. Workability
3. Diffusibility

½ hr. Individual   Written Exercise:

Select the solution idea from S.G. discussion which is most relevant to a problem in your own agency and describe how it might be adapted to your own needs.

Case Simulation Exercise

Possible Features to Include:

1. Divide group into teams, but let them organize their team effort as they see fit.
2. For each team, provide a real-life client team (could be students or others role-playing clients or could be actual school building teams from a school district located in the vicinity of the workshop site).
3. Ask teams to go through all stages of a project from relationship building to solution choice, putting their process on newsprint.
4. Provide budget for phoning to resource persons and information centers.
5. Provide some sort of information library or resource center at the workshop site.
6. Provide an ERIC printout on areas relevant to the problem or preferably an ERIC terminal.
7. Each team should review its total process stage-by-stage to the L.G.
8. Allow a post-mortem period for evaluation by "client teams" of quality of "help" they received.
9. Arrange for trainers to lead a L.G. discussion comparing the quality of team efforts for each stage.
10. Possibly provide some sort of mock prize to the best group.

Individual written exercise at close of day (½ to 1 hr.)

"Review your group's simulation activity step-by-step."
"What would you do differently or additionally if you were to do it again?"

Unit #10

Gaining Acceptance

Read prior
to Unit #10 (1½ hrs.)

Havelock: GUIDE TO INNOVATION, STAGE V

Rogers and Svenning: MANAGING CHANGE
or
Thomas E. Woods: THE ADMINISTRATION OF EDUCATIONAL INNOVATION

1 hr. S.G.

Discussion:

Each man in turn describes his on-the-job case in terms of:
1. Did he identify and utilize the key people in the group?
2. Did he identify individual phases of adoption?
3. Did he coordinate his activities with the adoption phases of individuals?
4. Describe current adoption status of case.

½ hr. L.G.

Discussion:

Posting of major points and problems arising in S.G. discussion.

¼ hr. L.G.

Lecture:

The complexity of communication strategy in gaining acceptance: what medium for what audience at what stage and for what effect.

1 hr. S.G.

Simulation Game:

"CHANGE AGENT" developed by Everett Rogers, Michigan State University.

Game illustrates major points in a successful innovation diffusion strategy in a community.

½ hr. Individual   Written Exercise:

1. How could your communication strategy have been altered to produce better results in your on-the-job case?
2. What strategy will you employ when you return to the job?

½ hr. S.G.   Discussion:

Group critiques proposed strategies of each man in terms of its flexibility, feasibility and effectiveness as might be predicted from research on diffusion.

¼ hr. Individual   Written Exercise:

Should your case program be changed in any of the following ways:
1. Readapt the innovation
2. Shift gears
3. Change implementation strategy?

Unit #11

Generating Self-Renewal

Read prior to Unit #11	(1 hr.)	Havelock: GUIDE TO INNOVATION, STAGE VI Lippitt, Watson and Westley: THE DYNAMICS OF PLANNED CHANGE, Chapter 9 "The Transfer and Stabilization of Change"

½ hr. L.G.   Lecture:

What characterizes a self-renewing system.

1 hr. S.G.   Discussion:

Each man should consider whether his agency has features characterizing a self-renewing system:
1. A positive attitude towards innovation
2. An external orientation
3. A future orientation

1 hr. L.G.   Film:

"The Foreigners"(Developed by Peace Corps and illustrates dilemmas of the outside change agent trying to generate self-help on both micro-technical and macro-political levels)

½ hr. S.G.   Discussion:

How effective each man has been in helping to generate self-renewal in his agency. How do these experiences compare with those of the people in the film?

½ hr. S.G.   Discussion:

Developing plans for return to the job: how to begin to train other members of the agency in skills the trainee has learned during this training program.

½ hr. Individual   Written Exercise:

> Describe the steps you would like to take in your
> agency to help it develop a self-renewal capacity.

Unit #12

Evaluation Process

Read prior to Unit #12 } (1-½ hrs.) {

Havelock: TRAINING FOR CHANGE AGENTS, Chapters II and IV

Havelock: WORKBOOK OF CHECKLISTS to accompany GUIDE TO INNOVATION

Lippitt, Watson and Westley: DYNAMICS OF PLANNED CHANGE, pp. 263-273

Miles: "Educational Innovation: the Nature of the Problem" in Miles, INNOVATION IN EDUCATION, Chapter 1 (Assigned for Unit #1 but would be worth reviewing again here)

½ hr. L.G. Lecture:

To be conducted by Training Evaluation Staff, on the design, philosophy and methodology of evaluation.

½ hr. L.G. Directed Discussion and Posting:

What are the outcomes we hope for:
1. For ourselves as change agents?
2. For the agency in which we work?
3. For our agency's clients?

1 hr. L.G. Discussion:

What sorts of things can we identify as evidence of progress in each of the above outcome areas?

1 hr. S.G. Discussion:

Carrying on the topic of the large group discussion, consider:
1. What have we used so far as evidence of progress toward desired outcomes?

2. Have we recorded this evidence?
   If so, how have we recorded it?
3. Have we used this evidence to improve our performance?
4. Have we used it to improve the performance of others?

½ hr. Individual

Written Exercise:

1. Construct a personal daily/monthly progress check list.
2. Design a project progress check list; compare this with Havelock's Checklist #1.

½ hr. S.G.

Discussion:

Share and critique individual check lists.

Table IX.1 presents a general outline of the relationship between the scheduled series of training experiences and the anticipated outcomes of the training program which were listed above in Section 3.   It should be remembered that although one workshop unit may have direct relevance for one or more anticipated outcomes, the training events build on each other. Thus, in the later stages of training, a particular unit may call into play all the knowledge and skills learned to date and may help to generate all of the desired attitudinal outcomes.   Not listed in the table is a relevant input producing skill number 19, which specifies that: "By the end of training, the graduate should be on his way to becoming an *artiuclate spokesman* for the planned change process generally and, specifically, for the role of the state agency within it."   This skill, should, as indicated, be a product of the entire training sequence.

TABLE IX.1
RELATIONSHIP BETWEEN TRAINING EVENTS
AND ANTICIPATED OUTCOMES

Training Activity	Attitudes*	Knowledge*	Skills*
Trainee pre-workshop preparation	To provide an introduction to all aspects of training program.		
Trainee Notebook	To provide a record, reinforcement and review of training workshop and on-the-job experiences.		
FIRST WORKSHOP Unit #1: Planned Change Perspectives	1. See training as worthwhile 2. Optimism about change potential 3. Belief in change *process*	1. U.S. educational system and sub-system 2. Planned change models 5. State education agency	
Unit #2: Who is a Change agent? Why is role important?	4. Value of role 5. Self-confidence in role	3. Roles in change process 4. This role model 5. State ed. agency	
Unit #3: Who is the client?	6. Respect for client integrity	5. State ed. agency	
Unit #4: Relationships	6. Respect for client integrity	7. Stage I: Relationships	

*Numbers of items refer to numbered lists of anticipated outcomes of attitudes, knowledge and skills in section 3 above.

Training Activity	Attitudes*	Knowledge*	Skills*
Unit #5: Non-directive consultation	6. Respect for client integrity 9. Help without hurting	7. Stage I: relationships	1. Building helping relationships
Unit #6: Diagnosis	7. Collaboration 8. Client self-help	8. Stage II: Diagnosis	2. Diagnosis
Unit #7: Role Set	6. Respect for client integrity 7. Collaboration 8. Client self-help 9. Help without hurting	6. Role Set	1. Building helping relationships
ON THE JOB	Reinforcement and practice of all learning to date. Readings introduction to second workshop.		
SECOND WORKSHOP Review: Diagnosis, role development, counseling and conflict resolution	Review of on-the-job experience and all learning to date.		
Unit #8: Resource Acquisition		9. Stage III: Resource acquisition	3. Acquire resources
Unit #9: Solution Choosing	7. Collaboration	10. Stage IV: Solution choosing	4. Generating and choosing solutions
Case Simulation and case building	5. Self-confidence in role 7. Collaboration	7. Stage I: Relationships 8. Stage II: Diagnosis 9. Stage III: Resource acquisition 10. Stage IV: Solution choosing	1. Build relationship 2. Diagnosis 3. Acquire Resources 4. Generate and choose solutions
ON THE JOB	Reinforcement and practice of all learning to date. Readings introduction to third workshop.		

*Numbers of items refer to numbered lists of anticipated outcomes of attitudes, knowledge and skills in section 3 above.

Training Activity	Attitudes*	Knowledge*	Skills*
THIRD WORKSHOP			
Case review	Review of on-the-job experience and all learning to date.		
Unit #10: Gaining Acceptance		11. Stage V: Gaining acceptance	5. Strategies to gain acceptance
Unit #11: Generating Self-Renewal	8. Client self-help	12. Stage VI: Self-renewal	6. Design and install self-renewal mechanisms.
Unit #12: Evaluation Process			20. Evaluation
Workshop Evaluation	Review, reinforcement and evaluation of all learning to date.		
Plans for continued training of self and others: 1. Continued role development	4. Value of role 5. Self-confidence in role		13-18. For numbers 1-6 know how to gain further training for self and others
2. Continued building of a self-renewal capacity for the state.	7. Collaboration 8. Client self-help		7-12. For numbers 1-6 impart training skills to others. 13-18. For numbers 1-6 know how to gain further training for self and others.

*Numbers of items refer to numbered lists of anticipated outcomes of attitudes, knowledge and skills in section 3 above.

5. Guidelines for Installation of Trainees in State Agency Positions

When we are building a new role, there are many additional factors which have to be accounted for beyond those normally considered in training for existing and traditional roles. Most of these conditions pertain to all roles in society. We take them for granted for existing roles because they evolved over years and even centuries. For the role of teacher, our cumulative role development experience goes back at least 5,000 years; for doctors at least 3,000, for lawyers at least 2,000 years, and so forth. Even the rather specialized role of educational research has a history of at least 70 years. Now we are asking just one year for a new and largely unique role in the state agency. This means we have to think through and plan for the installation with considerable care. At least five conditions must be met for the new role holder. He must have:

1. *Identity:* i.e., a clear sense of what the role is in theory and fact and a realization that it is recognized by others as such.

2. *Security:* i.e., the knowledge that the role will still be there with the same definition tomorrow and maybe even the day after that.

3. Defined *limitation* on responsibility and function: i.e., he should not have to be all things to all men at all times in all places.

4. *Freedom* and flexibility in redefining the role and its limits and exploring its potential.

5. *Reward* for performing in the role:
   a. from pride in personal success and achievement
   b. from a salary commensurate with risk, skill, and commitment of the role holder
   c. from the recognition of colleagues, superiors and subordinates as being a key man on the state team.

a. The Contract

The training program provides a number of inputs relevant to *identity* (1) and *delimitation* (3) and indirectly for *freedom* (4) by showing the trainee a number of alternative strategies and role models and for *reward* (5) by increasing his chances of success. However, the state agency must be committed by written contract to provide job security and adequate salary for at least one year following training, and to guarantee freedom to the trainee within the limits defined in the program guidelines. Above all, the state superintendent and any supervisors who would stand in direct line authority to the new role must know the conditions of the contract and must assent to them. These are the minimum conditions for the viability of a new role and the prime guarantor that the agency will not exploit the trainee and negate the federal intent in designing the program.

b. Preparing the Role Holder

The training, itself, incorporates or anticipates most of the preparations needed by a successful role holder. Of particular importance is the inclusion of procedures and practice in self-training and retraining, role problem diagnosis, and resource acquisition skills relevant to self-renewal. In addition, the program should supply the trainee with readings and reference materials including the GUIDE which should be retained by him and used on a day-to-day basis as an aid in fulfilling the role requirements.

c. Preparing the Role Set

This program takes special note of the key individuals in the state agency who will be relating to the trainee in his new role. Collectively we designate these individuals as the "role set." One entire unit of training in the first workshop is devoted to understanding and effectively relating to the role set, but attention should also be given to preparing the members of the role set, themselves, for relating to the role holder. At a minimum this means informing them of the new role, the reasons for it, and its implications for their work. Some of this informing should be done by the trainee, himself, but his way should be cleared and sanctioned officially from the top.

Members of the role set should be led to expect benefits to themselves from the trainee's experience including consulting, information sessions on what the trainee is learning, and possibly even some skill practice exercises and demonstrations similar to those the trainee is receiving. The role set should be seen as one primary client system for the trainee as he begins to experience the new role.

d. Building a Role Maintenance Team

A role becomes viable and stable as it begins to receive recognition, acceptance, and support from the role set, from the clients it serves, and from the system in which it is embedded, and particularly from the leadership of that system. As part of the articulation of this recognition, the trainer and a committee of relevant peers and superiors should be formed to meet periodically to review the progress of the role's development (not the training) and to consider ways to strengthen it.

e. Role Monitoring and Adjustment Mechanism

To aid the role holder and the role maintenance team in judging progress, some procedure should be set up for collecting information at regular intervals. Such information may merely be in the form of checklists by the role holder concerning work started and completed, activities engaged in, and difficulties encountered, or it may be elicited from clients or the role set. However, the prime purpose of such data collection is feedback to the role holder and his team so that they can adjust accordingly. Hence, it fits in the category of "formative" as distinct from "summative" evaluation. Ideally this monitoring should be *continuously* formative, becoming an integral part of the role configuration, itself.

f. Role Partnerships

It is most important that individuals adopting a new set of behavior receive social support from continuous fellowship with others in the same circumstances. Therefore, training should be given to pairs who come from the same agency and will have the opportunity to compare notes regularly on how they are doing and problems they are encountering. This is a critical aspect of installation and maintenance after training.

g. A Role Reference Group

Long-term maintenance of a new role with a special set of skills calls for the building of a national reference group composed of other program graduates filling similar positions in other agencies. Newsletters, periodic reunions, and a professional association are a few of the formal mechanisms by which reference group identity can be established.

6. Suggested Criteria for Evaluation

In evaluating a program of this sort, there are three levels of outcome analysis. First, did the training get across to the trainee? Second, was the trainee able to assume the role for which the training was designed and to operate successfully in the role over a period of time? Finally, did the entire program, successful training, and successful installation, produce any measurable benefit in the field of education? The first question is probably the simplest, most immediately measurable and most conducive to quantitative measurement. It is also perhaps the most trivial as far as the policy maker is concerned. The second question calls for a somewhat longer time-frame and measurement in a more complex field context. The third question requires a still longer time-frame in a much larger and more complex field context, least amenable to direct quantitative measure. Yet this third question is the decisive one, speaking to the true pay-off of the entire effort and the validity of the original conception.

It is important to realize, however, that all three levels must be answered if we are to attribute benefits to the training program. The following diagram may help to demonstrate this chain of causation (the control groups identified in the diagram are theoretical and illustrative, only, and not intended as requirements of an evaluation design). Because the diagram separates training from installation, it introduces the possibility that the role could (at least logically) be developed without training.

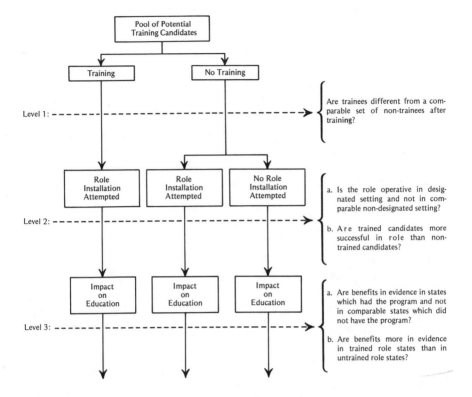

If the answers to all these questions are affirmative, then it is a reasonable inference that the training program had some positive impact on education.

a. *Training Transfer Effectiveness Criteria*

In theory at least, the ideal training program is self-evaluating, i.e., it incorporates exercises which provide public evidence to the trainee and others that he has received and incorporated the inputs of the program. Hence, the criteria for evaluation theoretically should match the inputs described in section #4, item by item and unit by unit. If the program is designed properly, these inputs should also match the "anticipated outcomes" point for point, just as the anticipated outcomes match the role description, itself (section #1).

Therefore, section #3 should provide a good list from which to begin formulating specific performance criteria. Forty-one "outcomes" are listed (9 attitudes and values; 12 knowledge; 20 skills); each one could stand as a criterion for evaluation. In formulating criteria, however, certain guidelines should apply even if all anticipated outcomes cannot be measured:

(1) Criteria should match inputs (and it should be determined that inputs were actually made by the trainers).
(2) Separate attitudinal, knowledge, and skill criteria should be distinguished.
(3) Criteria should be centrally relevant to the intended role description and rationale.
(4) Ability to transfer training to others should be given special weight because it is central to the role conception and rationale.
(5) Ability to synthesize and integrate separate learnings in the performance of on-the-job or simulated tasks or problems should be included.

b. Role Installation Effectiveness Criteria

The minimum criterion of installation is that the trainee occupies a designated role position in the state educational agency at the end of the training program, a role position which corresponds in some way with the type of role for which training was provided. The longer the time span and the more points of correspondence, the more effective the installation has been. The same 41 "outcomes" apply here, now seen explicitly in the on-the-job context.

Of special relevance for installation are the ten categories of "duties" listed in section #1. Does the trainee, in fact (1) advise the superintendent, (2) initiate projects, (3) monitor statewide innovation, (4) train SEA staff, (5) link to outside experts in change, (6) serve as chief resource locator on planned change process, (7) serve as consultant to consultants, (8) visit and consult regional resource centers, (9) serve as information resource specialist, and (10) act as spokesman for educational innovation? Moreover, in each of these duties does he incorporate specific inputs from the training including the 41 items identified as "outcomes?"

It should be evident from this discussion that the completely successful role holder displays himself in an extraordinary array of activities. Any set of these can be taken as a criterion. Program evaluators should therefore be cautioned to cast a wide net if they want to make a fair evaluation.

c. Producing Desirable Change (Benefit)

The effectiveness of the change agent must ultimately be measured in terms of benefits to school systems and to the people who inhabit them and the ratio of these benefits to costs incurred: human, material, financial. The primary clue to the assessment of such benefits in the short run comes from the actual projects in which the trainee involves himself in the first year or two of occupying the new role position. It is difficult to state in advance the particular types of benefits that could be expected. Again the evaluator should cast a wide net because the benefits will often be unintended or "not counted" even by the trainee, himself. Probing inquiry is likely to uncover minusses *and* plusses that the policy maker should be informed about.

As a general rule and guideline in setting criteria, however, any time a change takes place at any level in the system from state to local and such change results in time or money saved, effort reduced, relevant skills upgraded, feeling of well being enhanced, or feeling of anxiety reduced for anyone, without a corresponding deficit to others in the system, then we can say a measurable "benefit" has taken place.

Having cast the net wide, the evaluator will then be left with the question for every "benefit" so identified: "Can this benefit be fairly attributed to a training program that took place for one man X number of months/years ago?"

7. Alternative Procedures for Evaluating

No specific evaluation design is proposed in these guidelines, but a number of points about evaluation procedures should be kept in mind. First of all, the program automatically should generate a number of "products" which serve as training and as testing. For example, the individual's written exercises should show the extent to which a unit is learned as "knowledge" at the time it is presented. Similarly, the logs which trainees make of their progress in the home setting should provide valuable self-report data which should reveal the extent to which learnings are being put into effect at home. Of even greater value should be the case reports which the trainee generates in the last months of the program. These cases should show the extent to which all the learnings have been incorporated and meaningfully integrated in the working life of the trainee.

Secondly, the three types of outcome, (attitudes, knowledge, skills) deserve distinct types of evaluation. Attitudes and attitude change can be determined by a straightforward self-reporting procedure (e.g., using Likert-type attitude items). There is no reason to disguise the intent of such questions or to devise elaborate scoring procedures. "Knowledge" outcomes can be measured no differently than they would be in college course exams. In fact, the trainees should become accustomed to being tested and to self-testing if individual exercises are included in every unit. Getting evidence of "skill" outcomes may present more difficulties but several alternatives are open. First of all, self-report by the trainee on his skills and behavior will have *some* validity and is certainly better than nothing; when trainees are asked to report on specifics of what they did for whom, when, and how, they will probably come close to giving the straight story. In addition to self-report are the reports of other individuals who are supposed to be affected by the trainee, e.g., role set members and clients. Some of the simulated activities included in the program can also be repeated at future dates serving the dual purpose of skill review and evaluation. Finally, it may be possible to observe on-the-job performance on some sort of time sample basis. Perhaps the best situation in which to observe the trainee's skills is when he, himself, is conducting training for others in the agency.

A third point to keep in mind is the need for the evaluator to work closely with trainer and trainee. There are a number of reasons for this. First, he should be as familiar as possible with the content and intent of the program. Second, the trainee as the prime data source must have a desire to cooperate fully in the evaluation. He must be willing to keep a log in a certain format on a day-to-day basis and to submit himself repeatedly to tests and observations of various sorts. This requires a good deal of patience and fortitude; hence, if the trainee does not think the evaluation is meaningful or worthwhile, he can easily scuttle it. Thirdly, the trainee and the trainer may have a number of insights on when, where, and how measures could be taken that would not have occurred to an outside evaluator working in isolation.

A fourth important point concerns the time frame of the evaluation. Even if the program worked perfectly it might not generate many measurable benefits for one or two years. Hence a short-term evaluation has to be content with a Level #1 analysis (training transfer) with some information on Level #2 (installation) and only a glimmer of Level #3 (benefit). Unfortunately however, most evaluation projects are restricted to a one or two year period. If forced to draw conclusions before the training has truly had its impact, the evaluator might be in danger of committing the Type II error, concluding "no effect" when a real effect was still emerging.

8. Feedback and Utilization of Evaluative Data

The evaluative process should not be conceived as the final step in program development but rather the prerequisite to reformulation of the program. Hence, utilization sessions should be arranged for feedback and dialogue between evaluators and trainees, other key SEA staff, trainers, funding agency staff, and program designers. Such feedback should be addressed to all three levels of analysis and should explore implications of the results in depth so that participants in such discussions can make specific plans and commitments to changing the program and developing a second generation program which is more powerful.

APPENDIX

In the following pages Dr. Sidney Dorros of the National Education Association has provided information designed to acquaint change agents with the ways in which the power and dissemination activities of educational professional associations may be utilized to effect change. Doros' discussion is highly relevant to the entire process of change agent training because the success of any model of training presupposes a network of relationships and a means of establishing contacts with educational practitioners and consumers. The educational establishment is not a tightly organized structure but a loose confederation of sub-structures for which the professional associations are the primary linkage mechanism. Change programs which ignore or by-pass the associations may achieve initial success in a limited geographic or functional area, but long-term survival of such innovative programs will depend on linkage and acceptance by the professions.

What Change Agents Should Know About Professional Associations*

Introduction

Teacher organizations are playing an increasingly important role in the lives of their membership; they affect not only the welfare of the teachers but also the attitudes and behavior of teachers in the classroom. Because of this, they are a force to be reckoned with whenever educational changes are planned. They may be a force either for or against change, but, in either case, the change agent can not afford to ignore them. In the former case, a change effort may come to naught if the backing of the teacher organizations are not sought; in the latter case, the organizations might be the key to persuading teachers to accept innovations.

It is our feeling that in the future there will be little significant change in education without the collaboration or at least the acquiescence of teacher organizations. Any change agent who is working in the field of education should therefore know the structure and functions of each of the major teacher organizations to make appropriate use of the powers which it possesses.

The major categories of professional organizations can be divided into

---

*Drafted by Sidney Dorros; edited by Mary C. Havelock.

three general groups and these may be briefly described as follows:

1. *General Purpose Teacher Organizations.* At the national level, these are represented by the National Education Association (1.1 million members) and the American Federation of Teachers (over 100,000 members). As they currently function, these groups use power to advance the welfare of their members and exercise their power primarily at the state and local levels.

The NEA does include some administrators and other educators in its membership, but it is now teacher-dominated and oriented. It carries on significant activities to improve education, in addition to advancing the welfare of its members.

The AFT works almost exlusively for teacher welfare, but it has made some efforts to disseminate research findings and to set up action programs to improve instruction.

2. *Administrative and Other Educational Specialty Organizations.* Examples of associations in this category are the American Association of School Administrators (AASA), Association for Supervision and Curriculum Development (ASCD), National Association of Secondary School Principals (NASSP), National Association of Elementary School Principals (NAESP), Department of Audiovisual Instruction (DAVI), and American Educational Research Association (AERA). These groups do exercise some collective power, but they operate primarily through dissemination and exchange of information. Most are loosely affiliated with the National Education Association (NEA), and the Association of Classroom Teachers is more like an integral part of the NEA than a separate organization.

3. *Subject Area Teacher Organizations.* Examples of organizations in this category are the National Council of Teachers of English and the National Council of Teachers of Mathematics. These organizations disseminate and develop some collective thinking, but they exercise little direct power. Most are loosely affiliated with the NEA.

1. *Implications for Change Agents*

Two general functions of teacher organizations are of particular significance for the change agent. The first of these is their function as *power blocks,* either for or against change. Their second general function is the *dissemination* of information to members. We will consider these functions as they are carried out by each of the three categories of teacher organizations.

a. General Purpose Teacher Organizations

Teacher organizations have recently begun to exercise great power, primarily through negotiated group contracts. Currently about one million public school teachers work under written agreements between their organizations and their school boards. Provisions of many of these agreements make it possible for teacher organizations to inhibit or to facilitate change.

i. *Examples of Power as a Block to Change.* In many instances, contract limits on staffing patterns have had the effect of thwarting change plans, and the situation which occurred in Montgomery County, Maryland, illustrates this point. The administration of the Montgomery County schools spent several years putting differentiated staffing plans into effect. However, the county education association (an NEA affiliate) was not significantly involved in the planning. After the association won exclusive bargaining rights, differentiated staffing was hampered and reversed by provisions of a negotiated contract. Some observers of the situation claim that had the administration worked more closely with the Montgomery County Education Association, more permanent progress could have been made in changing staff patterns.

Contract limits on faculty meetings can also serve to inhibit change. For example, the contract between the United Federation of Teachers and the schools of the city of New York severely limits the number and length of faculty meetings that may be called by the school principal. This kind of contract provision leaves the union or teacher association with more power to call meetings to consider and implement change than is enjoyed by the school administration. One implication of this for change agents is that it may be necessary for them to work through meetings of the teacher organization in order to communicate directly with teachers.

Resolutions passed by national, state, and local teacher organizations may also tend to limit innovations. At a recent annual convention, the AFT passed a motion which in effect condemned experimentation and innovation in education. The NEA Representative Assembly has passed resolutions tending to block innovations, particularly those involving differential pay for teachers or deviations from advocated maximum class size. Change agents should know that such policy decisions are made as a result of a very broadly based democratic process. The NEA Representative Assembly, for example, consists of about 7,000 delegates chosen by their local and state associations. Therefore, changing any policy requires a change in the thinking of a large number of the "rank and file" and not just the key leadership.

ii. *Examples of Power as a Facilitator of Change.* Teacher organizations have generally provided leadership in racial integration. Not only have they moved faster than many school systems in this area but, in addition, they have exerted pressure on the school systems to effect racial integration. The experiences of teachers working together in their associations and in human relations workshops sponsored by teacher organizations have helped prepare teachers for integration in many communities where the public power structures have resisted moves toward integration.

Teacher organizations may also facilitate change by endorsing proposed innovations. Policy statements such as NEA resolutions can have widely beneficial effects. For example, a recent resolution encouraging educators to experiment with patterns of organization such as team teaching has greatly stimulated such efforts.

Educational research and development have been greatly aided by demands from teacher organizations for increased funds for these areas. Massive lobbying by the NEA is partly responsible for financing research and development in education. Alienation and lack of communication between NEA and the U.S. Office of Education, educational researchers, and other agents of change endangers this support.

iii. *General Purpose Organizations as Dissemination Agencies.* Publications of teacher organizations are a very significant source of information on innovations for teachers. The NEA is by far the largest publisher of professional literature in education. *Today's Education: the NEA Journal* has a circulation of about 1.2 million and, because it is the official journal of the NEA, it probably influences its readers more than any nonorganizational periodicals.

There are also many important journals of the various state education associations. These have generally been neglected by change agents in favor of the higher prestige specialized national professional journals, but they are a significant means of communication with classroom teachers.

Among the non-periodical publications of the NEA, change agents will find the series of pamphlets "What Research Says to the Teacher" especially useful. This series is published by the NEA Association of Classroom Teachers. It currently consists of 34 titles; these are continually revised and new titles are frequently added. Another important series recently initiated by ACT is called "New Developments in Teaching."

Conferences and workshops sponsored by the professional associations also have great impact on their membership. These events are held at national, state and local levels, and they could provide change agents with important opportunities for interaction with teachers as well as offering a forum for dissemination.

b. Administrative and Other Educational Specialty Organizations

Although the administrative and other specialty organizations of educators do not have as much political power as the larger teacher organizations do, they are extremely important for the change agent because individual members each have more influence than the classroom teacher. The policy statements of most of these organizations are considered seriously by their members. Conferences and conventions are a more significant means of communication for these groups than they are for teacher organizations. Many members of these groups depend upon their association conferences as a major source of new ideas.

One convention which should be specifically mentioned is the annual convention of the American Association of School Administrators. School superintendents and many other educational leaders are among the 40,000 attendees at the annual Atlantic City convention. Exhibits as well as the numerous meetings are important means of communication.

c. Subject Area Teacher Organizations

Change agents should be aware of the communications media of the subject area teacher organizations and the separate positions taken by these associations. Their membership and activities have grown at a relatively greater rate than those of general purpose teacher organizations in recent years, and those affiliated with the NEA are becoming increasingly independent. Teachers are looking more and more to the periodicals, books and conferences of their subject area organizations for new ideas in their fields.

2. *Some Tips for Change Agents in Working with Professional Associations*

First, the change agent should be careful to select the appropriate professional organization with which to work. If he is trying to institute an innovation which deals with a specific subject area, such as mathematics, he should work primarily with the special interest organization in that field. If the proposed innovation affects general conditions of work, status or organization, the change agent should deal primarily with the general purpose teacher organizations and the administrative associations. The change agent should make use of the *NEA Handbook for Local, State and National Associations*, which is the best guide to the 8,000 organizations in the NEA "family."

Second, in local situations the change agent should study the relationship of negotiated contract provisions to proposed major changes. How effectively change agents work with the local associations may well determine whether such organizations become "featherbedders" or facilitators of change.

Finally, the change agent should involve the professional association early in the change process and he should allow enough time for group processes to take effect. The timing of organizational decision-making processes may delay implementation of change, but going through such processes may make the change more acceptable and lasting.

BIBLIOGRAPHY

Argyris, Chris
  "Explorations in Consulting-Client Relationships," in Bennis, W.G.; Benne, K.D.; and Chin, R. (eds.), *THE PLANNING OF CHANGE*, (Second Edition), New York: Holt, Rinehart and Winston, 1969.

Benne, K.D.; Bennis, W.G.; and Chin, R.
  "Planned Change in America," in Bennis, W.G.; Benne, K.D.; and Chin, R., *THE PLANNING OF CHANGE*, (Second Edition), New York: Holt, Rinehart and Winston, 1969.

Bennis, W.G.; Benne, K.D.; and Chin, R. (eds.)
  THE PLANNING OF CHANGE, (Second Edition), New York: Holt, Rinehart and Winston, 1969.

Boyan, Norman J.
  "Problems and Issues of Knowledge Production and Utilization," in Eidell, T.L. and Kitchel, J.M. (eds.), *KNOWLEDGE PRODUCTION AND UTILIZATION*, Columbus, Ohio: University Council for Educational Administration and Eugene, Oregon: Center for the Advanced Study of Educational Administration, University of Oregon, 1968.

Brickell, Henry M.
  ORGANIZING NEW YORK STATE FOR EDUCATIONAL CHANGE, Albany, New York: Commissioner of Education, State Education Department, 1961.

Caplan, Gerald
  "Types of Mental Health Consultation," in Bennis, W.G.; Benne, K.D.; and Chin, R. (eds.), *THE PLANNING OF CHANGE*, (Second Edition), New York: Holt, Rinehart and Winston, 1969.

Carlson, Richard O.
  ADOPTION OF EDUCATIONAL INNOVATIONS, Eugene, Oregon, University of Oregon, 1965.

Chelser, Mark and Franklin, Jan
  "Interracial and Intergenerational Conflict in Secondary Schools," Presentation made to the Meetings of the American Sociological Association, Boston, Massachusetts, August, 1968.

Chin, R., and Benne, K.D.
  "General Strategies for Effecting Changes in Human Systems," in Bennis, W.G.; Benne, K.D.; and Chin, R. (eds.), *THE PLANNING OF CHANGE*, (Second Edition), New York: Holt, Rinehart and Winston, 1969.

Clark, David L. and Guba, Egon G.
  INNOVATION IN SCHOOL CURRICULA, Washington, D.C.: The Center for the Study of Instruction, National Education Association, 1965.

Clark, James V.
  "A Healthy Organization," in Bennis, W.G.; Benne, K.D.; and Chin, R. (eds.), *THE PLANNING OF CHANGE*, (Second Edition), New York: Holt, Rinehart and Winston, 1969.

Cumming, E. and Cumming J.
  CLOSED RANKS: AN EXPERIMENT IN MENTAL HEALTH EDUCATION, Cambridge, Mass.: Harvard University Press for the Commonwealth Fund, 1957.

Eidell, T.L. and Kitchel, J.M.
  KNOWLEDGE PRODUCTION AND UTILIZATION, Columbus Ohio: University
  Council for Educational Administration and Eugene, Oregon: Center for the Advanced
  Study of Educational Administration, University of Oregon, 1968.
Far West Laboratory for Educational Research and Development
  *THE EDUCATIONAL INFORMATION CONSULTANT: SKILLS IN
  DISSEMINATING EDUCATIONAL INFORMATION*, A Project Report, Berkeley,
  California, July, 1971.
Far West Laboratory for Educational Research and Development
  EDUCATIONAL R&D INFORMATION SYSTEM REQUIREMENTS, A Task Force
  Report, Berkeley, California, 1968.
Ferguson, Charles
  "Concerning the Nature of Human Systems and the Consultant's Role," in Bennis,
  W.G.; Benne, K.D.; and Chin, R. (eds.), *THE PLANNING OF CHANGE*, (Second
  Edition), New York: Holt, Rinehart and Winston, 1969.
Glaser, Edward M.
  "Research Frontier: Utilization of Applicable Research and Development Results,"
  JOURNAL OF COUNSELING PSYCHOLOGY, 1965, Vol. 12, pp. 201-205.
Griffiths, Daniel E.
  "Administrative Theory and Change in Organizations," in Miles, M.B., *INNOVATION
  IN EDUCATION*, New York: Bureau of Publications, Teachers College, Columbia
  University, 1964.
Havelock, Ronald G.
  BIBLIOGRAPHY ON KNOWLEDGE UTILIZATION AND DISSEMINATION, Ann
  Arbor, Michigan: Center for Research on Utilization of Scientific Knowledge, Institute
  for Social Research, 1968.
Havelock, Ronald G.
  THE CHANGE AGENT'S GUIDE TO INNOVATION IN EDUCATION, Englewood
  Cliffs, New Jersey: Educational Technology Publications, Inc., 1973.
Havelock, Ronald G. (in collaboration with Alan Guskin) and others
  PLANNING FOR INNOVATION, Ann Arbor, Michigan: Center for Research on Utili-
  zation of Scientific Knowledge, Institute for Social Research, 1969.
Havelock, Ronald; Huber, Janet; and Zimmerman, Shaindel
  MAJOR WORKS ON CHANGE IN EDUCATION, Ann Arbor, Michigan, Center for
  Research on Utilization of Scientific Knowledge, Institute for Social Research, 1969.
Jung, Charles C.
  "Generalizations About Training," Portland, Oregon: Northwest Regional Educational
  Laboratory, 1970.
Jung, Charles C.
  "Two Kinds of Linkage for Research Utilization in Education," Paper presented at the
  American Educational Research Association 1967 Annual Meeting, New York, February
  16, 1967.
Jung, Charles and Lippitt, Ronald
  "The Study of Change as a Concept," *THEORY INTO PRACTICE* Vol. V. No. 1, Feb.
  1966.
Jung, Charles; Pino, Rene; and Emory, Ruth
  RUPS: RESEARCH UTILIZATION AND PROBLEM SOLVING, Classroom Version,
  Leader's Manual, Portland, Oregon: Northwest Regional Educational Laboratory, 1970.
Kimbrough, Ralph B.
  "Power Structures and Educational Change," in Morphet, E.L. and Ryan, C.O., *PLAN-
  NING AND EFFECTING NEEDED CHANGES IN EDUCATION*, Englewood Cliffs,
  New Jersey: Citation Press, 1967.

Kurland, Norman and Miller, Richard
  SELECTED AND ANNOTATED BIBLIOGRAPHY ON THE PROCESSES OF CHANGE, New York State Education Department and the University of Kentucky, 1966.
Lippitt, Ronald; Fox, Robert; and Schindler-Rainman, Eva
  HUMANIZING SCHOOL AND COMMUNITY: IMAGES OF POTENTIALITY; National Training Laboratories-Learning Resources Corporation, in press, 1972.
Lippitt, R.; Watson, J.; and Westley, B.
  THE DYNAMICS OF PLANNED CHANGE, New York: Harcourt, Brace and Company, Inc., 1958.
Lorsch, Jay W. and Lawrence, Paul
  "The Diagnosis of Organizational Problems," in Bennis, W.G.; Benne, K.D.; and Chin, R. (eds.), *THE PLANNING OF CHANGE*, (Second Edition), New York: Holt, Rinehart and Winston, 1969.
Merton, Robert K.
  SOCIAL THEORY AND SOCIAL STRUCTURE, New York: Free Press, 1957.
Miles, Matthew B.
  "Educational Innovation: the Nature of the Problem," in Miles, Matthew B., *INNOVATION IN EDUCATION*, New York: Bureau of Publications, Teachers College, Columbia University, 1964.
Miles, Matthew B.
  INNOVATION IN EDUCATION, New York: Bureau of Publications, Teachers College, Columbia University, 1964.
Mort, Paul R.
  "Studies in Educational Innovation from the Institute of Administrative Research," in Miles, Matthew B. (ed.), *INNOVATION IN EDUCATION*, New York: Bureau of Publications, Teachers College, Columbia University, 1964.
Richland, Malcolm
  FINAL REPORT: TRAVELING SEMINAR AND CONFERENCE FOR THE IMPLEMENTATION OF EDUCATIONAL INNOVATION, Santa Monica, California: Systems Development Corp., Technical Memorandum Series 2691, 1965.
Rogers, Carl
  "The Characteristics of a Helping Relationship," in Bennis, W.G.; Benne, K.D.; and Chin, R. (eds.), *THE PLANNING OF CHANGE* (Second Edition), New York: Holt, Rinehart and Winston, 1969.
Rogers, Carl R.
  CLIENT CENTERED THERAPY, Boston: Houghton Mifflin, 1951.
Rogers, Everett M.
  BIBLIOGRAPHY ON THE DIFFUSION OF INNOVATIONS, East Lansing, Michigan: Department of Communication, Michigan State University, July, 1967 (Supplement to the Bibliography, September, 1968).
Rogers, Everett M.
  DIFFUSION OF INNOVATIONS, New York: The Free Press of Glencoe, Inc., 1962.

Rogers, Everett M. with Shoemaker, F. Floyd
  COMMUNICATION OF INNOVATIONS, (Second Edition), New York: The Free Press, 1971.
Rogers, Everett M. and Svenning, Lynne
  MANAGING CHANGE, San Mateo, California: Operation PEP, 1969.

Ross, Donald H.

ADMINISTRATION FOR ADAPTABILITY: A SOURCE BOOK DRAWING TOGETHER THE RESULTS OF MORE THAN 150 INDIVIDUAL STUDIES RELATED TO THE QUESTION OF WHY AND HOW SCHOOLS IMPROVE, New York: Metropolitan School Study Council, 1958.

Sanders, H.C. (ed.)

THE COOPERATIVE EXTENSION SERVICE, Englewood Cliffs, New Jersey: Prentice Hall, 1966.

Sieber, Sam

"Organizational Influences on Innovative Roles," in Eidell, T.L. and Kitchel, J.M., KNOWLEDGE PRODUCTION AND UTILIZATION, Columbus, Ohio; University Council for Educational Administration and Eugene, Oregon: Center for the Advanced Study of Educational Administration, University of Oregon, 1968.

Skelton, Gail J. and Hensel, J.W.

A SELECTED AND ANNOTATED BIBLIOGRAPHY: THE CHANGE PROCESS IN EDUCATION, Columbus, Ohio; ERIC Clearinghouse on Vocational and Technical Education, Center for Vocational and Technical Education, The Ohio State University, 1970.

Spitzer, William K.

A BIBLIOGRAPHY ON THE PROCESS OF CHANGE, Melbourne, Florida: Institute for Development of Educational Activities, Inc., 1968.

Stuart, Michael and Dudley, Charles (eds.)

BIBLIOGRAPHY ON ORGANIZATION AND INNOVATION, Eugene, Oregon: Center for Advanced Study of Educational Administration, University of Oregon, 1967.

Thelen, Herbert A.

"Concepts for Collaborative Action-Inquiry," in Watson, G. (ed.), CONCEPTS FOR SOCIAL CHANGE, Washington, D.C.: NTL Institute for Applied Behavioral Science, 1967.

Watson, Goodwin (ed.)

CHANGE IN SCHOOL SYSTEMS, Cooperative Project for Educational Development, Washington, D.C.: NTL Institute for Applied Behavioral Science, 1967.

Watson, Goodwin

USING RESEARCH FOR CHANGE, Project under NIMH Contract No. HSM-42-69-1 entitled "Review of Literature on Research Implementation," Los Angeles, California: Human Interaction Research Institute, 1969.

Watson, Goodwin and Glaser, Edward M.

"What We Have Learned About Planning for Change," MANAGEMENT REVIEW, November, 1965, p. 36.

Woods, Thomas E.

THE ADMINISTRATION OF EDUCATIONAL INNOVATION, Eugene, Oregon: Bureau of Educational Research, University of Oregon, 1967.

INDEX